Paul Tillich, Carl Jung, and the Recovery of Religion

This book compares the theology of Tillich with the psychology of Jung, arguing that they were both concerned with the recovery of a valid religious sense for contemporary culture. *Paul Tillich, Carl Jung, and the Recovery of Religion* explores in detail the diminution of the human spirit through the loss of its contact with its native religious depths, a problem on which both spent much of their working lives and energies.

Both Tillich and Jung work with a naturalism that grounds all religion on processes native to the human being. Tillich does this in his efforts to recover that point at which divinity and humanity coincide and from which they differentiate. Jung does this by identifying the archetypal unconscious as the source of all religions now working toward a religious sentiment of more universal sympathy. This book identifies the dependence of both on German mysticism as a common ancestry and concludes with a reflection on how their joint perspective might affect religious education and the relation of religion to science and technology.

Throughout the book, John Dourley looks back to the roots of both men's ideas about mediaeval theology and Christian mysticism, making it ideal reading for analysts and academics in the fields of Jungian and religious studies.

John P. Dourley is Professor Emeritus, Department of Religion, at Carleton University, Ottawa, Canada. He graduated as a Jungian analyst from the Zurich/Kusnacht Institute and has published widely on Jung and religion.

D1496505

Paul Tillich, Carl Jung, and the Recovery of Religion

John P. Dourley

Routledge
Taylor & Francis Group

LONDON AND NEW YORK

First published 2008
by Routledge
27 Church Road, Hove, East Sussex BN3 2FA

Simultaneously published in the USA and Canada
by Routledge
270 Madison Ave, New York, NY 10016

*Routledge is an imprint of the Taylor & Francis Group,
an Informa business*

Typeset in Times by
RefineCatch Limited, Bungay, Suffolk
Printed and bound in Great Britain by
TJ International Ltd, Padstow, Cornwall
Paperback cover design by Anú Design

This publication has been produced with paper manufactured to
strict environmental standards and with pulp derived from
sustainable forests.

British Library Cataloguing in Publication Data
A catalogue record for this book is available from the British Library

Library of Congress Cataloging-in-Publication Data

Dourley, John P.
Paul Tillich, Carl Jung, and the recovery of religion / John P. Dourley.
  p. cm
Includes bibliographical references and index.
ISBN978-0-415-46023-1 (hardback)–ISBN978-0-415-46024-8(pbk.)
1. Tillich, Paul 1886-1965. 2. Jung, C. G. (Carl Gustav), 1875-1961. 3. Religion. I. Title
BX4827 T53D68 2008
230.092–dc22

                            2007042007

ISBN: 978-0-415-46023-1 (hbk)
ISBN: 978-0-415-46024-8 (pbk)

Contents

    science and technology   178

    Afterword   192
    References   194
    Index   201

Preface

What follows is the substance of my sustained reflection on the work of Paul Tillich and Carl Jung. The thought of the former led me to write a doctoral thesis on his work (defended in 1971). The power of the latter led me to train as an analyst in Zurich and to practice since 1980. What is most intriguing in the thought of both individuals is their identification of the origins of religious experience and so of the religions in the depth of the human being. Both hoped that their delineation of the origin of religion within the human would lead to the restoration of religious credibility both within and beyond the religious institutions of their society. Both embraced a radical immanence as the basis of a now emerging religious universalism which would appreciate the particularity of each religion while making each a relative concretion of an underlying generative power undermining all claims to a cumulative and final possession of an absolute truth. In appreciating while making relative the specific concretions of the religious instinct in the world's current religions, Tillich and Jung may well provide a sketch of a now emerging religiosity which will in fact make the future possible. This implies that the greatest current threat to the species is religious conviction, faith, in religious or political form. The reader is invited to at least consider the following presentation of their views and their importance to an inescapably religious humanity if religion is to enhance the present and enable the future.

Chapter 1

Toward a salvageable Tillich

The implications of his late confession of provincialism*

The texts and the context

Late in Paul Tillich's life a series of events conspired to effect a perceptible broadening of his theological perspective. This expanded consciousness was most evident in late confessions of an earlier and, by implication, somewhat sustained provincialism running throughout much of his theological endeavor to that point. Such confessions of provincialism led him, in his more occasional late statements, to positions in considerable tension if not contradiction with his earlier *Systematic Theology*. Some of these provincialisms are to be found even in the third volume of his *Systematic Theology* written at the same time, in the early 1960s, when he was deploring such provincialism in statements made elsewhere.

Tillich's battle against his and others' provincialism had a history. In an address as early as 1952 Tillich (1886–1965) identifies a number of provincialisms in the mindset he brought with him from Germany in 1933. (Tillich 1959a) The provincialisms indicted here are basically an amalgam of German theological, philosophical and cultural provincialisms, provincialisms he claims to have shed prior to 1952 in the face of various forms of American pragmatism and pluralism. (Thomas 1995: 19) In a reminiscent mood, in this address, Tillich is generous in praising the American theological and cultural environment he entered from Germany for its role in making him aware of his continental German provincialisms while, in turn, making no demand that he accept a new American provincialism, sensitive though he remained to the possibility that such a set-back could occur on American soil. (Tillich 1959a: 176) However, this earlier admission of provincialism pales in comparison to his later confessions of a further series of provincialisms only then to be fully exorcised. These later confessions force the question whether or not the defeat

---

* This chapter derives from a presentation to the North American Paul Tillich Society, meeting in Toronto, November 2002. A preliminary version of the chapter appeared in *The North American Paul Tillich Society Newsletter*, 29, 2, 2003, 10–14, amplified as "Toward a Salvageable Tillich: The Implications of his Late Confession of Provincialism", *Studies in Religion*, 33, 1, 2004, 3–26.

of these remaining provincialisms might well constitute a definitive growth beyond substantial portions of his earlier theology.

In his Harvard years, 1955–1962, his distinguished colleague, Wilfrid Cantwell Smith, had already challenged Tillich on the narrowing of his theological concerns to Christianity at the cost of a serious consideration and knowledge of non-Christian religions. Writes Smith on the matter, "probably Tillich belongs to the last generation of theologians who can formulate their conceptual system as religiously isolationist." Smith goes on to describe the note of finality that attaches to Tillich's claims for Christianity as "separatist" and belonging to an ecclesial "ghetto" mentality hostile to a now blooming global religious sense "which will make the work of even a Tillich appear parochial". (Smith 1976: 8)

Events in Tillich's later life no doubt contributed to the broadening of his mind. In 1957, while still at Harvard, Tillich may have taken a significant step beyond such parochialism in his dialogue with Dr. Hisamatsu Shin'ichi, a Buddhist monk and scholar. (Tillich and Shin'ichi 1990) Tillich was deeply impressed not only by the content of the dialogue but also by the personal sanctity of his conversant. (Tillich 1990a: 28) In 1960 his immersion in Eastern culture was deepened through a trip to Japan. The trip drove him to reflect more deeply on the differences, religious and political, between Eastern, especially Buddhist, and Christian perspectives. (Tillich 1964: 53–75) In 1961 in a talk on the occasion of Carl Jung's death he closely associated Jung's understanding of the archetypal with his own conception of the *Logos* as the ground of "the essences of all things". (Tillich 1962a: 32) From 1962 to 1965 he was the Nuveen Professor of Theology, at the University of Chicago. In his last year in Chicago he cooperated with Mircea Eliade in teaching a seminar on the history of religion. (Pauck and Pauck 1976: 272, 273) Eliade's position as a religionist, appreciative of a wide range of symbolic expression, no doubt deepened and extended Tillich's reflection on his own position as a Christian theologian. These events point to significant influences in the biographical and intellectual background to Tillich's late confessions of the provincial nature of his earlier theology and to his renewed warning that such provincialism remained an ongoing threat in the then current theological situation.

Let us turn now to the texts in which the late statements of provincialism are found. In 1988 Terence Thomas of the Open University, UK, a leading Tillich scholar, edited a work made up of two late lectures given by Tillich at smaller schools on the relation of Christianity to non-Christian religions plus a transcript of the 1957 dialogue between Tillich and the aforementioned Buddhist monk and scholar, Dr. Hisamatsu Shin'ichi. (Thomas 1990a) This last section of the collection is not as directly pertinent to the issue of provincialism as are the first two addresses. In them Tillich openly admits his continued shame at the provincialism that informed his theology when he "came to this country" (Tillich 1990a: 36), warns against the possibility of its contemporary recurrence, and precisely identifies the substance of a theological provincialism he still struggled totally to overcome both in his person and in the wider theological milieu in which he deemed it still prevalent.

The first set of lectures, the Matchette lectures, is made up of three lectures collectively entitled *The Protestant Principle and the Encounter of World Religions*. They were delivered at Wesleyan University, Middletown, Connecticut on April 9, 10 and 11, 1958. (Tillich 1990a) In the first of these lectures Tillich typically describes religion in its most universal sense as the experience of the holy and extends this experience to what he calls the quasi-religions; communism, nationalism and humanism. Tillich views the holy as operative in generating a sense of ultimacy around the values bonding these three communities. He then introduces his understanding of the Protestant principle to affirm that, though the holy can appear universally through any thing, person, or community, the holy can never be identified with that through which it appears including Protestant Christianity which ideally incorporates and champions the principle but, as a specific religion, stands under its critique. (Tillich 1990a: 3–17) None of these positions is without precedent in Tillich's previous work.

In the second Matchette lecture Tillich continues with his religious typology. Here he develops his conception of the sacramental as a universal substrate, the basis of humanity's universal religious impulse giving rise to the specific religions, then to be critiqued by the mystical or prophetic response to the idolatrous possibility ever latent in the historical concretions of the universal religious impulse. The mystic overcomes the idolatrous inevitability in the concretion of the sacramental by going beyond form to its source; the prophet by dissolving the idolatrous possibility as a spokesperson for the wholly transcendental frequently speaking in the name of justice. (Tillich 1990a: 19–36) Using these categories Tillich goes on in the third lecture to relate them to the interface of Christianity with other religions and the quasi-religions. He concludes that the key to the current dialogue between religions is not the exclusive affirmation of one's own religion but the joint standing of all religions under the Protestant principle which can be identified with none and relatively appreciative of all. (Tillich 1990a: 55, 56) Again none of the foregoing is without ample basis in Tillich's earlier work.

What is of startling novelty in this set of lectures is Tillich's frank and unforced indictment of his earlier theology as provincial. He states toward the end of the second lecture, "I am still ashamed of the extent of my provincialism when I came to this country." (Tillich 1990a: 36) The reference to his early provincialism occurs in the context of his discussion of humanism as a quasi or "world religion" best able to flourish "in Protestant countries today". (Tillich 1990a: 35) In context it is clear that Tillich judges the spirit of humanism to be compatible with his understanding of the Protestant principle in the defeat of a "natural provincialism" more prevalent in Europe and yet a current ongoing threat "even here". (Tillich 1990a: 36) In 1961 Tillich was again to reaffirm that he had in the course of his career in America "purged my mind of many conscious and unconscious European provincialisms without, I hope, having replaced them with American versions of the same evil". (Tillich 1964: 1) These sparse references to his and a wider cultural provincialism raise questions about its specific content and what effect the identification of this content would have on his late understanding of Christianity, Christian faith and the role of the Christian theologian. In contrast to his 1952 confession of provincialism, Tillich, in 1958, is now much more sensitive to the possibility of a religious provincialism taking root in American soil at the cost of the humanism he here closely associates with the spirit of Protestantism. In passing it can be noted that in the light of the current religious situation in the United States, Tillich's words and fears now appear prophetic a half century later.

The second lecture in Thomas' collection is entitled "Christian and Non-Christian Revelation" and does give explicit content to a lingering religious provincialism in both Tillich's personal perspective and in the wider theological and religious environment of that time. It was delivered at Lycoming College, Williamsport, Pennsylvania, October 27, 1961. (Tillich 1990b: 59–74) In this lecture Tillich wastes little time in moving to the issue of theological provincialism and to its content. Tillich spells out three forms of Christian theological provincialism which in the context he obviously thinks are still extant in the contemporary theological climate and in need of being brought to an end in the interests of religious dialogue. The first is the most all encompassing. It is simply designated "Christian provincialism" and in context means the denial of the redemptive efficacy of non-Christian religions. (Tillich 1990b: 60) The defeat of this provincialism would recognize the salvific validity of other religions and deny to Christianity its traditional claim to a culminating ultimacy and salvific capacity to which all other religions were ordered and to which they would submit. The defeat of this provincialism would obviously negate the claim of any religion to possess an exclusive or even superior means of redemption than that to be found in another. In effect, at this late date, 1961, Tillich is still fighting the doctrine of "*extra ecclesia, nulla salus*", or "Outside of the church no salvation". In amplifying this point Tillich argues that meeting members of other faith positions corrodes the narrow-mindedness of both Christian layman and theologian, a remark probably inspired, at least in part, by his dialogue with Hisamatsu Shin'ichi and by his travels in the East. (Tillich 1990b: 60, 61) In this address the "narrow-minded Christians" are given no further identification. (Tillich 1990b: 60)

The second provincialism is the "provincialism of theistic religions". (Tillich 1990b: 60) This provincialism would reduce religion to a relation to a transcendent and, usually personal, divine entity. Here Tillich is combating that form of Christian theological provincialism which would deny the status of religion to communities bonded without such a God. The obvious target is any form of literal biblical theism based exclusively on a relation to a wholly transcendent and personal God. In amplifying this point Tillich endorses as "great religions" the Buddhist, Confucian and Taoist traditions who thrive without the kind of God described by biblical personalism. (Tillich 1990b: 61) It could here be argued that Tillich's attack on biblical theism is not without ample precedent in his work. It is operative in his repeated contention that the most adequate theological response to a divinity immersed in the subject–object structuring of reality is atheism. (Tillich 1951: 172–173, 205, 245) Biblical portrayals of the divine–human relation are obviously thus immersed. God is a subject who objectifies the human. The human is a subject who objectifies God. Unfortunately Tillich is less specific in describing the consciousness operative in a relation to the divine which escapes the confinement of a subject–object relation. To do this he would have to move into an experience like that of apophatic mysticism which penetrates the formless or the nothingness beyond the subject–object split and loses the individual in moments of identity with the divine. Tillich was cautious with such moves. (Dourley 2005) Nevertheless his late authentication of Godless religions as truly salvific lies in direct continuity with his earlier and ongoing rejection of the biblical reduction of the divine–human relation to the wholly personal and marks an advance in his making explicit what previously had been at most a tantalizing implication in his thought.

The third provincialism is that "provincialism of religion proper over against the powerful quasi-religions of our time". (Tillich 1990b: 60, 61–63) In the light of his identification of the quasi-religions in these lectures, Tillich is here conferring on communism, nationalism and humanism a certain religious status as expressions of the underlying holy and, in so doing, implicitly affirming their values to be religious and at least potentially redemptive of their members. In amplifying this form of provincialism Tillich argues that such secular quasi-religions have "points of identity with religions proper". (Tillich 1990b: 61) Behind each of them there is always "a background of a religious character in the proper sense of religion". (Tillich 1990b: 62, 63) One cannot escape Tillich's implication that certain forces and the communities they create often identified and dismissed as "secular" by a provincial religious perspective can be themselves the bearers of salvation.

In this lecture Tillich also amplifies the meaning of the sacramental as that religious power endemic to humanity which gives rise to religion universally and to the mystical and iconoclastic responses to the specific religions this sacramental power inevitably generates. Here Tillich describes this power as "a universal revelation . . . which becomes the presupposition of every concrete and particular revelation". (Tillich 1990b: 64) In effectively equating the sacramental principle with a universal revelation as the generative power underlying all religions Tillich is making more explicit what remains more or less implicit in his previous theology. In the third volume of his *Systematic Theology* a universal revelation as the generative source of specific revelations grounds the distinction he draws between "formal faith", a universal ultimate concern, and "material faith", the inevitable and diverse expression of formal faith in finitude. Material faith then becomes the content of the specific religions such universal concern, formal faith, breeds by the necessity of its own dynamic toward expression in history. (Tillich 1963: 130–131) In an obviously lingering provincialism Tillich goes on to describe Christianity as the identity of formal and material faith and so as the culmination of religious history, "the fulfillment toward which all forms of faith are driven." (Tillich 1963: 131) To identify formal and material faith, thus understood, as coalescing in Christianity was an unfortunate and constraining position. Tillich had, in the distinction between formal and material faith, the possibility to show formal faith as fostering a multiplicity of material faiths of which Christianity would be one but not the exhaustive culmination of the others. Such an enlightened relativism and pluralism lay within his grasp and Tillich refused to take advantage of them at least in the very late third volume of his *Systematics*.

Such reluctance was not the case in his more private lectures. In what effectively constitutes a sustained attack on his own provincialism, still evident even in the third volume of his *Systematics*, Tillich, in the Matchette and Lycoming lectures, seeks to lay the groundwork for the dialogue between Christian and non-Christian religions. This groundwork would entail the defeat of a provincialism which would deny the salvific efficacy of other religions. It would undermine the supremacy of Christianity. It would corrode a Christian understanding of a relation to a transcendent and personal God as alone legitimizing a religion as a religion. Finally it would remove all religious blindness to elements of the holy at work in the secular in the form of quasi-religions.

The problematic

These positions raise, at least, two obvious and related questions. What relation do these occasional late lectures have to Tillich's earlier theology? And what are the implications of his denying in his lesser late addresses the provincial positions he continued to uphold as he was composing the third volume of his system? The first question divides into two points both addressing the effect Tillich's admission of provincialism would have on foundational elements in his early theology. The first point focuses on his understanding of the relation of Christianity to other religions in the first volume of the system. Here he describes Christianity as the "final revelation". (Tillich 1951: 132–137, 147–155) The second point relates to Tillich's earlier understanding of the nature of Christian theology itself and to the demand that Tillich then placed on the Christian theologian to be a member of the "theological circle", that is, to hold the Christ event as the object of the theologian's ultimate concern or faith. (Tillich 1951: 8–11)

But the second and equally important question, also raised by Thomas in his Introduction to his collection, is the perplexing fact that as Tillich was developing his attack on theological provincialism in his late lectures he was at the same time finishing parts of the third volume of his *Systematic*

Theology key sections of which revert to the earlier provincialism he was then deploring in his occasional lectures. (Thomas 1990b: xvi, xvii, xx, xxi) As will be seen, this regression is painfully evident in the third volume of the *Systematics* in Tillich's ecclesiology and missiology. They depict Christianity, and especially its iconoclastic community, as ideally the culmination of historical religion to which all religion, latent and manifest, is ordered. These questions deserve to be addressed singly and systematically.

The criticism of provincialism and Christianity as the final revelation

Tillich's late rejection of provincialism would call into question if not corrode the claim that he makes in the first volume of the system on behalf of Christianity as the "final revelation". There Tillich writes "Christianity claims to be based on the revelation in Jesus as the Christ as the final revelation." (Tillich 1951: 132) He goes on to define what he means by "final" in this context. "Final" means not "last" but "genuine" and genuine means "the decisive, fulfilling unsurpassable revelation, that which is the criterion of all others". (Tillich 1951: 132–133) The revelation in Jesus as the Christ is universally valid because it includes this criterion and as such is the "*finis* or *telos* (intrinsic aim)" of all revelation and so "the criterion of every revelation which precedes or follows". (Tillich 1951: 137)

On behalf of Tillich and to avoid a too easy triumphalist interpretation of these passages what Tillich means by the Christ event as the "criterion" of all revelation deserves amplification because Tillich closely relates this criterion to the Protestant principle itself. The revelation of Jesus as the Christ is final revelation and the criterion of all others because "it has the power of negating itself without losing itself". (Tillich 1951: 133) For Tillich this is the substance of the Protestant principle and the basis of his understanding of the nature of final revelation. In the context of the Christ event it means that everything finite in the revelation in Jesus as the Christ was sacrificed to his unbroken continuity with and transparency to God as the ground of being. (Tillich 1951: 133) This radical iconoclasm, culminating in the event and symbol of the Cross negates even "a Jesus centered religion and theology". (Tillich 1951: 134) In an even more radical statement, "It is the end of Jesusology." (Tillich 1951: 136)

Thus the claim to final revelation rests on the contention that in the Christ event, especially as carried by the symbol of the Cross, every dimension of the finite and the particular through which the holy appeared was sacrificed to the manifestation of the holy. The content of the holy, purified of all idolatrous potential, then becomes humanity, or in this case, a human life, wholly transparent to God or more simply put, "essential manhood". (Tillich 1957a: 94) In his more formal Christology Tillich can thus argue that the "paradox" of the final revelation is that of the revelation of essential humanity to existential humanity and mean by this formulation that the content of the revelation remains the image of a human life fully in existence and yet in unbroken unity with its essential truth, that is, its groundedness in God. (Tillich 1951: 133)

The question to be posited at this point in the inquiry is whether or not Tillich, repentant of his early provincialism, would be open to seeing the sacrifice of the finite to the holy happening in other religious variants and secular manifestations. The evidence is that the later Tillich would and in so doing radically alter themes in his early theology. Important among such themes would be the distinction between final and preparatory revelation and so the movement of all revelation to some kind of culmination in a Christianity informed by the Protestant principle understood to be fully realized only there.

In his earlier work Tillich plays off what he calls "preparatory revelation" in relation to the final revelation and identifies Judaism and especially the Jewish prophetic tradition as preparatory to the event on which Christianity is based. In these passages Tillich is explicit that the preparatory phase of the final revelation moves to the final revelation, "as the center, aim and origin" of preparatory revelation. (Tillich 1951: 138) The Christian claim is that in the Christ event a personal life surrendered totally to an unbroken unity with the divine and that this surrender is "the center of the history of revelation and indirectly the center of all history". (Tillich 1951: 143)

To soften the triumphalist notes in these passages, it cannot be denied that Tillich is explicit in clearly differentiating institutional Christianity, or Christianity as a religion, from the final revelation. He will write, "Christianity, without being final itself, witnesses to the final revelation." (Tillich 1951: 134) Thus Tillich is at times clear that Christianity, and especially institutional Christianity, cannot be equated with that to which it witnesses, although clearly that to which it witnesses should be most manifest through it. Nevertheless, it cannot be doubted that the tendency to equate or closely relate institutional Christianity, at least ideally, with the final revelation, in spite of the profound iconoclasm carried by the symbol of the Cross, is always there in Tillich and reappears even in his late systematizing. In the light of his late rejection of provincialism and dawning appreciation of both the legitimacy of the holy and the critical response to the holy in the world religions and in the secular sphere, it is not surprising that Tillich did not use the phrase "final revelation" in the last years of his writing.

The nature of Christian theology and the theologian's place in the theological circle

In his early treatment of the nature of Christian theology and the criterion determining the Christian theologian as a Christian theologian Tillich determines two circles. The first is based on what he calls a "mystical a priori" which rests on that point beyond the subject–object split where the subjectivity of the individual attains a "point of identity" with the ultimate. (Tillich 1951: 9) This circle, subject to cultural variation, describes the loop between the subjective consciousness of the religious philosopher and the reality of the ultimate present to the philosopher's humanity from the outset of the philosopher's experiential relation to and exposition of it. But the religious nature of this circle is not sufficiently definitive for the early Tillich. While the point of identity between human subjectivity and the ultimate is foundational to Tillich's own doctrine of God and of humanity's experience of God, it is not the criterion of standing within the Christian theological circle.

The Christian theological circle is much more circumscribed. It "adds to the 'mystical a priori' the criterion of the Christian message". (Tillich 1951: 9) This means that the Christian theologian must affirm "the universal validity of the Christian message", a point Tillich twice repeats in these passages. (Tillich 1951: 10) Tillich adds to the universal validity of the Christian message the note of its "unrepeatable uniqueness". (Tillich 1951: 10) Although the theologian may entertain personal doubts about the regenerative quality of one's individual faith, and so combine doubt in this precise sense with faith, nevertheless one can be a Christian theologian only on the condition "of the acceptance of the Christian message as his ultimate concern". (Tillich 1951: 11) In short the Christian theologian must affirm the universal validity, and unrepeatable uniqueness of Christianity as the substance of one's ultimate concern to qualify as a Christian theologian. Tillich confirms this understanding of the theological circle and of the Christian theologian's confinement within it elsewhere when he denies the possibility of the theologian's openness to other revelations. He writes, "If he [the Christian theologian] is open for other original revelations, he already has left the revelatory situation and looks at it in a detached way." (Tillich 1951: 132) Such detachment would forbid membership in the theological circle to all but those who have as their ultimate concern that final revelation, "the decisive, fulfilling, unsurpassable revelation, that which is the criterion of all the others". (Tillich 1951: 133)

Tillich's senior denunciation of theological provincialism and his identification of one of its major components to be the denial of salvific efficacy to other world religions and their revelations certainly imply that he was by then himself in his own terms "open to other original revelations". (Tillich 1951: 132) No doubt such openness would not extend to full participation in such revelation, though Tillich frequently affirmed that only that religious experience is intelligible in which one participates with one's total humanity. However understood, Tillich's late openness would certainly extend to an appreciation of the salvific validity of non-Christian revelation, call into question the universal validity and unrepeatable uniqueness of Christianity, and so exclude him from the Christian theological circle as described in his earlier work. No doubt one could still cling to the Christ event and its institutionalization as one's "ultimate concern" on whose behalf one did theology but the quality of such ultimate concern as expressed in Tillich's early works would be compromised if not corroded by the late recognition of the salvific validity of other religions and forms of secularity.

One commentator refers, with great acuity, to Tillich's late growing sense of "the implicit impeachment of the universality and finality of Christianity by competing world faiths" as a prominent concern in his later years. (Foster 1996: xviii) Thomas writes in agreement that when Tillich's late attack on his own theological provincialism is compared with his earlier understanding of the theological circle then one must conclude, "It would appear to mean that the boundary of the theological circle had in some sense been breached." (Thomas 1990b: xxii) In his later work Thomas was to advance a "codicil" theory about Tillich's late denunciation of his own provincialism which would extend to the relativity Tillich introduces into his late Christology. According to Thomas' conjecture Tillich attached his late substantial qualifications to his earlier systematic thought, written in large part before 1960, much as one would attach a codicil to a will which would then determine the meaning of all that preceded the codicil in the will. (Thomas 1995: 33–42) With this analogy Thomas argues that Tillich's late occasional work would modify and control the meaning of all his preceding theology including the three volumes of the system. Thomas' position would seem to be compelling given the textual evidence but is not uncontested. (James 1997, 2003)

In his late occasional addresses the theological circle may have been more than breached. Rather it was shattered toward a relativism that would frankly acknowledge that what had happened in the historical reality of the Christian revelation had happened in other cultures under different but equally valid expressions of the holy which Tillich early and late grounded in the depths of human being itself. In fact the late Tillich is explicit in extending what had happened in the Christ event, transmitted through the central imagery of the cross as the basis of the Protestant principle, to trans-cultural realization with no connection whatsoever to Christianity.

> That which has happened there [in the event of the cross] in a symbolic way, which gives the criterion, also happens fragmentarily in other places, in other moments, has happened and will happen even though they are not historically or empirically connected with the cross.
>
> (Tillich 1966: 89)

It is difficult to see how this passage can be read in a manner other than to affirm that what has happened for the Christian community in the Christ event can and has happened elsewhere. Unless one reads the qualifier "fragmentarily" to mean what happens in Christianity in a certain fullness happens elsewhere in fragment – and contextually this is not Tillich's intent – it is difficult to evade the relativity that Tillich here attaches to the Christian event and to evade his conclusion that Christianity is not a universal and unique revelation. Certainly the uniqueness as a revelatory event is denied and its universal validity would be compromised unless understood in some manner that had little or nothing to do with empirical institutional Christianity and membership therein.

This extension of the theological circle means that the Tillich who read the paper from which the above citation is taken on October 12, 1965, the day of the first of a series of heart attacks that were to take his life, was not a Christian theologian as he defined that role in the first volume of his system in the 1950s. In taking these positions Tillich has enriched the world of theology with the realization that a theologian in any of the major traditions, and especially the monotheisms, is not divested of the status of theologian by frankly acknowledging the salvific reality of other traditions and the relativity of one's own.

It is further obvious that the late Tillich, in dialogue with other religions and with religious secularity, came to experience his earlier description of the theological circle as a theological prison and sought in the end to break out of it. His escape turned to the appreciation of the religious symbolism of religious humanity itself in mutual reciprocity with specifically Christian symbolism. This process would expand the awareness of individual religions by casting their specifics against a wider knowledge of the symbols that have emerged in human history in the religious enlightenment of humanity. The relativity of this position frees Tillich and theologians of a variety of religions in self-reflection or in dialogue from the continuation of the provincialism he deplored. It encourages a receptivity to symbol systems other than one's own which could enhance one's understanding of one's own in fostering a deepening of the understanding of the religious nature of humanity itself.

Yet Tillich's victory over his own provincialism was not easily won and remained somewhat ambiguous to the end. Thomas is particularly acute in documenting the tension in Tillich's very late writing between the remnants of an early provincialism and his late efforts to broaden the boundaries of his own theology beyond it. On Tillich's critique of provincialism in his late lectures and his maintaining some blatantly provincial positions in the third volume of the system then being written Thomas writes, "The only question mark in this context relates to the apparent contradiction between what he writes within the system and what he says outside it." (Thomas 1990a: xx) Thomas goes on to make a point which would bear substantial textual support. "Outside the system Tillich appears to abandon much of what he would hold fast to within the system." (Thomas 1990a: xxi) Thomas could hardly be more explicit about Tillich's waffling when he concludes, "Theological provincialism has certainly not been overcome in the third volume of *Systematic Theology*." (Thomas 1990a: xxiii) This remark is particularly true in that section of the third volume where Tillich delineates the relation of the Christian Church to other manifestations of the holy, religious and secular, in a manner which would see the fulfillment of the latter to be accomplished in the former. This problem is of a significance which merits its own attention.

Lingering provincialisms

The contradiction between Tillich's denunciation of his provincialism and its remnant in the third volume of his system is most evident in the Christian imperialism informing his ecclesiology, specifically in the manner he relates what he termed the "latent" to the "manifest" Spiritual Community. (Tillich 1963: 152–155) Should the triumphalism evident in these passages be dissolved by his own critique of provincialism, its dissolution would resonate, in domino fashion, throughout the rest of his system due to the organic connectedness that Tillich, as a thorough systematic thinker, builds into the system.

Tillich's ecclesiology rests on his symbol/concept of the Spiritual Community which in turn rests on his Platonic understanding of the divinity of the essential and its recovery in existence as the basis of religion universally. Since, for Tillich, the essential grounds all existential life, this understanding of the relation of the existential to the essential enables Tillich to include humanity potentially and universally in what he will call the latent Spiritual Community. In itself this is not a triumphalist position but simply a logical consequence of Tillich's foundational position that the essential undergirds the existential and that the existential seeks universally to recover the essential. This dynamic is the base meaning and energy at work in history, its cultures and its religions. More, with these categories Tillich can argue correctly and incisively that not everyone in the Christian Church, as the ideal manifestation of the Spiritual Community, is actually in the Spiritual Community at all and that many who are beyond the manifest Spiritual Community, and even reject it in its ecclesial form are. Those in the institutional church who are not in the Spiritual Community would be those whose membership is divested of the experience and so participation in the New Being, that is, in the essential humanity manifest in the Christ event.

Those outside the manifest Spiritual Community in the latent Spiritual Community could potentially be extended to humanity itself. But, in the context where Tillich seeks to differentiate the latent from the manifest Spiritual Community more precisely, the members of the latent Spiritual Community are distinguished by their visible participation, communal or individual, in the essential humanity worked by the New Being though they may belong to a variety of religious or secular communities not affiliated with or even rejective of the manifest Spiritual Community. (Tillich 1963: 153) Effectively being in the Spiritual Community means living out of one's essential being whether within or beyond ecclesial boundaries.

So far so good, but the residual provincialism of such a distinction becomes clear when the manifest Spiritual Community is identified with the Christian Church and the latent Spiritual Community is incredibly described as "teleologically related to the Spiritual Community in its manifestation", and even more incredibly identified as being "unconsciously driven toward the Christ" even when such communities and individuals reject the Christian Church in its presentation of the Christ. (Tillich 1963: 154) Shades of the anonymous Christian! In taking this position Tillich divides humanity into two basic groups: those who consciously participate in essential humanity in its culminating manifestation in the Christ and ideally in the Church and those who are unconsciously driven by the deepest religious impulse active in humanity and its history to do so.

Who then are the members of the latent Spiritual Community who are unconsciously driven to their fulfillment in Christ and the Christian Church? In order of appearance they are first

> youth alliances, friendship groups, educational, artistic and political movements, and, even more obviously, individuals without any visible relation to each other in whom the Spiritual Presence's impact is felt although they are indifferent or hostile to all overt expressions of religion.
>
> (Tillich 1963: 153)

But then the idea of latency is greatly extended to the specifically religious sphere. Thus extended, those unconsciously driven to their religious fulfillment in the ideal Christian Church would include the Jewish community, the Islamic community, the communities based on the mythological Gods, the Greek philosophical schools, as well as the mystical traditions of Asia and the monasticism to which they gave rise. (Tillich 1963: 154) In short all non-Christian religions as well as every individual and group participating in the essential prior to or currently beyond the Christ event and its fullest concretion in the Church are driven to the reality of Christ and membership in the manifest Spiritual Community, the Church, for their completion. It would be hard to formulate a more provincial and triumphant ecclesiology.

The Protestant principle and the defeat of ecclesial and missiological provincialism

The profound paradox at the heart of Tillich's lingering provincialism is its basis in Tillich's understanding of the Protestant principle itself. This principle functions throughout his system, in interplay with the sacramental principle, as the ultimate resource against idolatry. It is ironic, then, that it becomes itself the basis of an idolatrous ecclesiology in the heralding of the Christ event and its institutionalization as the completion of the historical development of religion. How an iconoclastic principle becomes itself the basis for an idolatrous ecclesiology requires more precise examination. Tillich rests his case for the effective equation of Christianity and the Church with the manifest Spiritual Community by first contending that the faith and the love of the Christ is lacking in the latent Spiritual Community, itself a rather provincial position. (Tillich 1963: 153, 154) But the deeper reason then follows.

The members of the latent Spiritual Community documented above lack in themselves the "principle of resistance" against profanization and demonization. Such a spirit of resistance is to be found in the "Spiritual Community organized as a church". Spelling out this position Tillich continues, "As a consequence of their [the latent Spiritual Community's] lack of this criterion, such groups are unable to actualize a radical self-negation and self-transformation as it is present as reality and symbol in the cross of Christ." (Tillich 1963: 154) The "principle of resistance" and the "radical self-negation and self-transformation", which the Spiritual Community manifest in the Church possesses and the latent Spiritual Community does not, is, as the reference to the Cross makes clear, the Protestant principle itself. (Tillich 1963: 1554) The use of this principle to herald the supremacy of the Christ event as ideally incorporated in the manifest Christian Church, to which humanity itself is allegedly unconsciously ordered, turns iconoclasm into idolatry and triumphalism and demands a closer look at the Protestant principle itself.

In the wider framework of his thought there are at least two bases for Tillich's understanding of the Protestant principle whose foundational operational insight is that the holy can never be identified with that through which it appears. One is the Platonic philosophy Tillich uses to support his conception of religion as universally human. Tillich would argue with Plato that, though humanity can never attain absolute truth, the existential mind participates in it, and so cannot cease its search for it nor fail to appreciate its fragmentary and ambiguous realizations when they occur in history. In fact Tillich pays tribute to the Platonic myth of the fall and so of the fallen mind as a precedent to the specifically Christian understanding of the fall in his most sustained systematic treatment of the fall and original sin. (Tillich 1957a: 29–44) He concludes that the mind in existence can never exhaust the truth to which it experientially belongs, from which it is alienated and toward which it is driven. This dialectic enables Tillich logically to ground the universality of religion and faith on the universality of existential humanity's experienced remove from its essential ground in God. This remove then becomes the dynamic at work in a fuller recovery of the essential in existence, a recovery which can never be more than fragmentary. This dialectic enables Tillich to establish the universality of religious experience and to make doubt an intrinsic element of it, to be definitively removed only in the post-temporal, unambiguous recovery of the essential. In the meantime claims to the absolute remain fragmentary and ambiguous.

The other and more significant basis for the Protestant principle is Tillich's theology of the Cross. In his hands the symbol of the Cross would remove all possibility that the Christ event could be identified with anything finite, passing or particular to it, so that the meaning of the reality of Christ would shine through such potentially idolatrous detail. As discussed above the meaning of the biblical picture of Christ lies in the picture of essential humanity realized in an individual life in its unexpected, hence paradoxical, unbroken unity with its ground in existence. (Tillich 1957a: 93, 94) With this Christology Tillich can present Christ as essential humanity, a humanity at once the object of a universal human longing and yet unexpected or paradoxical in its coming because human experience, to that point, had been thoroughly disappointed in its hope for the appearance of the unqualifiedly essential in existence.

To this point the Protestant principle is indeed a valuable and sophisticated statement of that iconoclasm protective of humanity in its ineradicable and self-destructive tendency to identify the appearance of the holy with the medium through which it appears. (Tillich 1990b: 70, 71) The Protestant principle is especially valuable when Tillich brings it into full dialectical interplay with what he occasionally terms "Catholic substance". Catholic substance is effectively the essential underlay of existence and the existential mind. It implicates a dimension of all reality inhering in the divine and is therefore the basis of humanity's sense of the sacred and of the sacramental. The dynamic unity of the Protestant principle and Catholic substance thus constitutes a brilliant synthesis of the sacramental basis of all religion with the need of every concretion of such universal sacramentalism, the onto-logical source of religion itself, to submit to the rigors of iconoclastic critique. (Tillich 1963: 245)

The Protestant principle loses its validity, however, when it takes on the provincial affirmation that only Christianity through its symbol of the Cross, particularly as appropriated by Protestant and prophetic Christianity, is in possession of such a principle and as such is superior to and the culmina-tion of all other religions through such possession. Admittedly Tillich will explicitly modify this position at times in very clear statements that the Protestant principle cannot be restricted to the Protestant or any church or religion. (Tillich 1963: 245) Yet, the temptation to do so is always there and, at least in the context of his late ecclesiology, it obviously breaks through to seriously question the outcome of his own battle with provincialism. The affirmation that other religions, and their secular equivalents, are relatively dispossessed of such self-criticism becomes itself an unconquered provin-cialism. This provincialism would imply that the history of religion culminates not only in Christianity but also in Protestant Christianity. Surely the Pro-testant principle needs to be applied to itself when it concludes that the fullness of its realization abides in the iconoclastic community within the Christian tradition.

The extension of the Protestant principle in the defeat of provincialism

The question then becomes how the Protestant principle can be applied to its own idolatrous potential. The obvious move is simply to deny that Christianity is in a surpassing possession of such self-critical iconoclasm and admit that such iconoclasm and its sacramental substrate would function in other religions and segments of the secular in discernible affinities with the Christian variant. The Christian or any theologian, religionist or missionary would then be freed from claims of a privileged superiority and become interested in the interplay of sacramental and iconoclastic elements in other communities, religious or secular. One would assume that these elements would be there and would indeed enhance and extend the self-understanding of the representative of any religion through conscious contact with and appreciation of symbols systems other than one's own.

Indeed, Tillich does move this way even in the passages in which he uses the Protestant principle so provincially. He argues that the universality of a latent Spiritual Community would enable the missionary to assume that other religions or quasi-religions (pagans, humanists and Jews are named) would be appreciated as members of the latent Spiritual Community and so relieve the missionary of "ecclesiastical and hierarchical arrogance" in approaching them. (Tillich 1963: 155) Tillich makes this assertion in the conclusion of the same passages in which his own arrogance enables him to describe all other religions as teleologically and unconsciously ordered to Christianity. Yet the tortured ambivalence of Tillich's late mind on the issue is evidenced in the fact that "Christian ministry" is to be exercised toward these groups. All that really changes is a lessening or removal of "ecclesiastical and hierarchical arrogance" in their regard. (Tillich 1963: 155) The evangelical and aggressive imperative to "convert" others remains in the third volume even if "in the relative sense of transferring them from a latent to a manifest participation in the Spiritual community". (Tillich 1963: 220)

The same contradiction and waffling between the demise of provincialism and the priority of Christianity is seen in Tillich's very late suggestion that at least an element of a theology of "offense" in the style of Kierkegaard and Barth be combined with his mediational approach in the current *"uphill battle"* to make Christianity once more relevant to the wider culture. (Tillich 1996: 7–10, 63) Here Tillich seems willing to compromise on his lifelong struggle against Barth whose theology he rejects one more and final time in his last formal address. (Tillich 1966: 80) The tension is again visible in the expression of a certain sadness that the Christian missions in India are effectively dismissed through a too easy but corrosive acceptance (Tillich 1990a: 38) and in his fear that democracy might not survive in Japan without the Christian presuppositions that gave rise to its modern form. (Tillich 1990b: 72; see also Tillich 1964: 73–75) Just what the nature of his concern over the Indian missions was and just why Christianity should support the implementation of Western democracy in Japan are questions left unexamined in these remarks but remain questions with the profoundly provincial implications that religions in India and democracy in Japan would be improved were they to be more closely related to Christianity and its cultural values.

On the other hand Tillich at the same period in time could swing to a position that would either dismiss or greatly reduce evangelization of any kind. In a less aggressive mood and speaking about his "Jewish friends", he suggests that only those exceptions who ask to enter the Christian communion should be received into it. (Tillich 1990a: 29, 30) In these passages he simply eliminates entirely the need of active evangelizing with the intention of conversion. At most missiology and evangelization would describe cultural missions fostering discussion between members of different religious communities. In the face of these expressed tensions Tillich apparently waffled to the end on the issue of the Christian mission in the context of his ongoing battle with his own and with wider ecclesial provincialism. The agony behind the waffling might well have been resolved and, in the context of the movement of Tillich's mind, could have been resolved through resources latent in his own theology. These resources would extend the dialectic between sacramental and iconoclastic principles to human religion universally and locate the Christian variant within the context of this extension. In short universalizing the dynamic between the sacramental and the iconoclastic would make relative each and all of their historical appearances.

The defeat of Christological provincialism

If Tillich's own version of the Protestant principle were thus used to liberate his late ecclesiology and missiology from theological provincialism, such liberation would move to his Christology as the critical area where the extended sense of the Protestant principle would work most dramatically. The stakes here are high. The question is whether the Christ event can be divested of potential idolatry through a relativity that would honor it even as it was made relative. There is substantial evidence that Tillich did move beyond provincialism in this crucial area. As already documented, the early Tillich describes the Christian theologian as "an interpreter of his church and its claim to uniqueness and universal validity". (Tillich 1951: 10) A legitimate Christian theologian must be a theologian in the "theological circle" and is so only if he accepts the Christian message as his ultimate concern. (Tillich 1951: 11) Acceptance of this message demands the affirmation of "the universal validity of the Christian message" and its "unrepeatable uniqueness". (Tillich 1951: 10)

In his last major public address Tillich effectively denied such universality and uniqueness to the Christ event when he listed the "systematic presuppositions" then guiding his thought toward the theology of the future. The fourth reads, "A fourth assumption is that there may be – and I stress this – there *may* be – a central event in the history of religions . . . an event which, therefore, makes possible a concrete theology that has universal significance." (Tillich 1966: 80) The use of the subjunctive to describe what Tillich previously describes, in so forceful a use of the indicative, as unique, unrepeatable and as history's defining *kairos*, or fullness of time, implies a considerable shift in the quality of the ultimate concern attaching to the Christian theologian and to Christian faith. The indicative mood used in the first volume of the *Systematics* to champion the unrepeatable uniqueness of a message with universal validity switches to the subjunctive and to the qualification that such a message may or may not have been received historically. In this one sentence Tillich removes any vestige of provincialism attaching to his Christology, locates it as one of many significant revelatory experiences, and frees the Christian theologian to accept this relativity and to remain a Christian theologian.

This breakthrough is consistent with the first of the named provincialisms in his late writing, namely, Christianity's contention that it possesses a salvific capacity not to be found or found so fully in other religions. In the introduction to the 1961 talk where Christianity as itself a form of provincialism is given priority of place, Tillich identifies himself as a Christian and Protestant theologian (Tillich 1990b: 59) but obviously not with the same job description as given to the role in the first volume of the *Systematics*. Tillich confirms this shift of position on the nature of the Christian theologian in his last published talk when he describes what previously was described as a "final revelation" as an event that may or may not have happened and could happen in variation elsewhere. A Protestant and Christian theologian can now apparently still have the Christian message as one's ultimate concern but in a consciously held relativization of the object of that concern which would not only allow but presuppose that what had happened in the Christ event could happen with equal efficacy in other cultures and times in the history of religions. Moreover, in this extension and relativizing of ultimacy and so of faith, the Christian theologian would stand under the moral imperative to be sensitive to all symbolic expression of ultimacy in the interests of an enhanced religious pluralism informed by an extended religious sensitivity now able to gain from the symbols of the other a fuller appreciation of one's own.

Indeed in his understanding of what he symbolizes as the "Religion of the Concrete Spirit" (Tillich 1966: 87), Tillich is working toward a conception of revelation as compensation to whatever the dominant religious needs may be of that community into which such compensating revelation comes. Religion thus conceived would be based on what he identifies as "a universal revelation", functionally identical with the sacramental principle as the generative ground of all particular religions including Christianity. (Tillich 1990b: 64) As this universal power generates the specific revelations and religions the idolatrous possibility and inevitability occur, then to be overcome on the one hand by mysticism and on the other by the prophetic and sometimes secular critique. (Tillich 1990b: 70, 71) Ideally, and Tillich does suggest that the ideal occurs in Pauline Christianity, the sacramental and its moderating expressions in the mystical, the prophetic and the secular would coalesce into that totality of the religious resource which he calls the "Religion of the Concrete Spirit". (Tillich 1966: 87–88)

But such a religion could draw on any one of its total resources in any given situation to produce the religious compensation the individual and cultural moment required. In this manner does Tillich explicitly refute any remnant of Hegelian provincialism in this theology, namely, that the history of religions culminates in Christianity and that religious configurations prior to Christianity are negated in the Christian sublation or appropriation of whatever truth they may have held. (Tillich 1966: 86) Rather the sacramental impulse as the basis of all religions, and the needed critique of its concretions in mystical or prophetic response, would address the existential situation out of whatever specific resources of the Religion of the Concrete Spirit were needed to compensate the existential situation it would address. Ongoing revelation would be tailor-made to redress the vagaries of the cultural situation it compensated. On occasion this compensation could be prophetic, on occasion mystical. On every occasion religion, thus conceived, could never rest with its current concrete situation but would be driven constantly to its supersession toward ever more adequate reciprocity between its sacramental matrix and whatever mystical and prophetic response to the particular historical manifestation of that matrix was currently demanded.

An example of such compensation is to be found in Tillich's late attitude to Reformed Christianity in then contemporary North America and serves to illustrate the compensation the Religion of the Concrete Spirit would provide. The senior Tillich feared that current institutional Protestantism had lost touch with the sacramental basis of all religion. Such severance led Tillich frequently to appeal for the recovery of the sacramental sense within Protestantism itself. In this context he would write on the permanent significance of Catholicism for the Protestant tradition. (Tillich 1962b) Were Catholic substance, in his specific understanding of it, not recovered he feared that institutional Protestantism would lose touch with the religious basis of religion and reduce itself to a sterile moralism or moral club with activist tendencies devoid of religious depth. (Tillich 1990b: 68, 69) The prophetic had become severed from the sacramental, and, by extension, from the priestly and mystical. By implication the compensation of the Religion of the Concrete Spirit would mean in this situation a recovery of the sacramental, and even of the mystical sense, within the Protestant community itself.

This issue touches on one of the areas of theology that Tillich identifies as provincial, namely, the degeneration of biblical theism into a deism based on a distant personal God, the author of creation and of humanity but not discernible in the former nor immediately experienced by the latter. The defeat of this provincialism would mean the transformation of the then presiding Protestant biblical deistic divinity into one that was much closer to humanity and to human experience. (Tillich 1990a: 49) But Tillich would express serious doubt about this compensation ever taking place. Such frustration was nowhere more evident than in his remarks about the Protestant "neurotic anxiety" about "pantheistic elements" that would bring God "too near to us". (Tillich 1990a: 49, 50) What Tillich is arguing here as an unlikely prophet on behalf of the recovery of the sacramental was that institutional Protestantism would have to recover a much deeper sense of the presence of God if it was to be informed by the full resources of the total human religious experience. His concern and critique was that a one-sided prophetic and moral sense had obscured or annihilated the sacramental and mystical sense and reduced Protestantism and its spirituality to a superficial dogmatism and moralism. The flexibility of redress inherent in the Religion of the Concrete Spirit would, in this instance, use the Protestant Principle to corrode the prophetic and the moralistic as themselves the demonic face of idolatry then most in need of dissolution in the service of the enhancement of the sacramental and mystical.

Tillich's late concern about the then current loss of a deeper religious interiority infecting both the Protestant world and the wider culture, though fully justified, might not have become so urgent in his later years had he more forcefully and candidly exploited the relevant foundational themes in his early theology. He waited till the third last page of the third volume of his *Systematics*, before he made explicit the pantheistic or, in a more timid formulation, *pan-en-theistic* ontology and epistemology foundational to his conception of the mind's native and conscious participation or inhesion in the movements of divine life. (Tillich 1963: 421) This inhesion is there from the outset and prominent in his theology from the first volume of the system. For instance such pan-en-theism was there in the panlogism of his first volume evident when he writes about God as the source of structure within and beyond the mind. "He *is* the structure; that is, he has the power of determining the structure of everything that is." (Tillich 1951: 239) The italics in the citation are Tillich's. Making it more explicit that the mind *is* in the *Logos* and the *Logos* in it and, more, that consciousness is possessed of and by an inchoate and primordial sense of the total movement of Trinitarian life itself (Tillich 1951: 250) would have given greater definition to the experienced intimacy Tillich posited between the divine and the human from the outset of his system. Such emphasis could have worked earlier on and more consistently throughout Tillich's theology to heal the crippling spiritual effects of the neurotic fear of pantheism in the interests of a more compelling, immediate and inclusive Christian spirituality. One is forced to wonder if Tillich himself suffered from the effects of a neurotic anxiety about pantheism and the response to it of the wider theological community in delaying so long the frank admission of the panentheistic foundations of his own theology.

Making such ontological and epistemological panentheism even more obvious from the outset would have earlier on drawn a clearer distinction between his own theology and what it had to offer as compensation to the then reigning Protestant deism and moralism, and its equivalent Catholic supernaturalism equally divested of an immediate sense of the divine. Giving earlier prominence to his panentheism would lend further justification to Tillich's sardonic self-depiction as *"Christianis paganus"* or "to the Christians, a pagan". The phrase confirms his suspicion that current deistic theology with its neurotic anxiety about panentheism would indict his theology as pagan. It clearly points to the ever expanding freedom and wider embrace of his religious and theological spirit, deeply imbued with a natural sense of God's universal presence to mind and nature. It is not surprising, then, that the development of Tillich's spirit, possessed of so great a sense of the divine depths of humanity supporting a more universal embrace, would culminate in his late effort to conquer a residual Christian provincialism in himself and society in the interests of reviving a societal and functional sense of the divine as a prelude to the restoration of the credibility of religion itself.

The defeat of eschatological provincialism

Tillich grounds much of his late revisioning of religion and revelation on the compensatory agency of the universal basis of religion manifesting across time and cultures addressing the specific existential needs of the cultures in which it incarnates. Revisioning religion in this way implies a fecundity in the universal basis of religion that with difficulty could achieve an exhaustive expression in one revelation or set of symbols. This position points to yet another provincialism in his early eschatology, one which was only to be overcome in his very late writing. Tillich's late defeat of eschatological provincialism also brings with it sweeping implications for wider portions of the system.

Throughout his earlier theology and much of his life Tillich fought a running battle with process theology. He denied that a God "conditioned" by the outcome of history was truly a God. "A conditioned God is no God." (Tillich 1951: 248) Tillich would seem to modify, if not abandon, this position in the third volume. In its final pages Tillich describes the dynamics of the intersection of the essential with the existential in history with a new term, "essentialization". (Tillich 1963: 400) Tillich's late introduction of this term and its affinities with process thought has not escaped notice in Tillich scholarship. (Foster 1996: xiv; 2000) The term was borrowed from Schelling and Tillich used it to mean that the essential, grounded in the dynamics of divine life, was itself completed through processes of its realization beyond divine life in existential human history. More, the completion of the essential in human history contributed to the ontological well-being of both the divine and human in eternity. This position would have profound affinities with the foundational insight of process thought, namely, that divinity and historical humanity are engaged in processes of mutual enhancement in time and is at the core of Jung's late "Answer to Job". (Jung 1969a)

The position would place a certain necessity in the divine creative act. Divinity would be forced to create to seek a fuller completion in its expression in the human. The human itself would be completed as a necessary expression of the divine to the extent it cooperated with the realization of the essential in personal and collective existence. Further, essentialization would imply that creation, though necessary, could not be without evil in existence. This evil is the evil Tillich so thoroughly documents in the process of the movement of the essential into universal estrangement in existence mediated by human freedom in its drive to stand alone. (Tillich 1957a: 33–36) Finally essentialization means that the actualization of the essential in finitude becomes the ontological content of divine and human blessedness in eternity. "It [the process of essentialization] is the content of divine blessedness." (Tillich 1963: 422)

In these pages Tillich argues that unless divinity had a stake in the world and its own completion through creation in processes of essentialization, divinity's self-sufficiency would reduce human history and its religious and cultural development to something "of a divine play of no essential concern for God" (Tillich 1963: 422) and so of no ultimate worth for the human. The very late Tillich is thus clearly arguing that the divine is, in fact, diminished or enhanced by the success of the process of essentialization in time, that is, by the degree to which individual and collective humanity recover and realize in existence, finitude, and time their essential nature as grounded in the dynamics of Trinitarian life in eternity. This radically altered eschatology not only is a major concession to process theology, but also calls up a vision of divinity creating human consciousness to become fully self-conscious and so completed in it, a point that Jacob Boehme makes explicitly and which Tillich, even in his dependence on Boehme, evades till the concluding passages of his third volume. (Dourley 1995a)

In the context of religious pluralism and relativity, the idea that so fecund a source of human consciousness driven to express its fullness in human consciousness could find final satisfaction for such divine passion in one symbol system or revelation seems premature if not arrogant and but another form of Christian provincialism. Tillich's late suggestion that the Christian theologian seek in the history of religions the symbols which amplify one's own defeats any provincial eschatology whose symbols are taken as absolute and so terminal because they would effectively deny the possibility of further future revelation as processes of essentialization move forward in time.

Indeed Tillich's reopening the canon through the study of the history of religions, when combined with his late understanding of essentialization as contributing to the final fullness of being of the divine and human wrought through temporal processes, opens up the possibility of a revelatory consciousness superseding Christianity and other revelations to date. Such a development of the religious impulse would be a further contribution to the wealth of divine being seeking self-expression and realization as it became increasingly conscious in human consciousness. The conception of a divinity enriched by the human reception and enactment of its expression in finitude breaks a provincial eschatology which would deny such divine aggrandizement to historical processes. The late Tillich opens up to vistas of divinity and humanity as two poles in an eternal play destined to confer redemption on each other through the resolution in history of the divine creative urgency underlying and creating history for its ever fuller expression. These themes are prominent in Jacob Boehme, one of Tillich's admitted theological ancestors, and are central to Carl Jung's understanding of the psyche.

Conclusion

Given the power of Tillich's mind as the ranking philosophical theologian of the twentieth century, it is not surprising that he moved to a universalism, pluralism and relativity whose major victim was Christian provincialism in all its forms. His efforts to save Christianity from itself are most evident in his location of the absolute only in that universal sacramental substrate from which all historical religion including Christianity derive. All religions are valuable expressions of this common matrix. The mature Tillich exposes the claims of any of them to an exhaustive finality as a now dangerous idolatry.

In the end Tillich's theological anthropology outstrips his Christology. His universalism undermines the contention that the religious process did or could culminate in an individual person, event, or religion. In fact his anthropology in relativizing his Christology makes the latter safe in a world on the brink of self-destruction in the conflict between civilizations based on religions in either their easily identifiable institutional or more disguised secular forms. Only recently have the social sciences, at least in their geopolitical form, come clearly to see that the major future wars will be battles of religiously based civilizations wherever their "fault lines" meet or where they share common territory. (Huntington 1996) Tillich's mature theology works to undermine such destruction through the humanizing relativization of each of the religious participants involved in such present and future carnage. His mature theology makes it more difficult to kill in the name of any of the divine variants all of whom share a common origin in the depths of humanity and emerge to consciousness from the ground of humanity's common being. The words of Terence Thomas in his introduction to the essays in which Tillich identified and deplored his provincialism are truer today than when they were written in 1990:

> Finally in a world where fundamentalisms of all kinds, political, national, cultural as well as religious seem to be on the ascendancy and intolerance, bigotry and fatal conflict seem to attract so many supporters, it is essential that we remind ourselves of the thought of a great soul for whom such tendencies were regarded as distortions of the human spirit.
> (Thomas 1990b: xxviii)

Tillich's lifelong alignment with "the fight of God within religion against religion" is no longer an abstruse theological fight. (Tillich 1966: 88) It is currently a fight to save the species by saving it from its religion and God-creating propensity. The late Tillich's contribution to this fight remains immense. It is a contribution which should be continued into the present and future in the direction that his mind was taking in his final days, a direction toward the heightened appreciation of the religious dimension of humanity manifest in the variety of its expressions beyond the provincial claims of any to a final realization and formulation of the religious possibility. In a late tribute to Tillich immediately following his own imprecation to historian, philosopher and theologian to transcend the provincial, Eliade writes:

> Faithful to his vocation and his destiny, Paul Tillich did not die at the end of his career, when he had supposedly said everything important that he could say. On the contrary, he died at the beginning of another renewal of his thought.
>
> (Eliade 1966: 35, 36)

The spirit of the renewal is worth the fostering.

Chapter 2

The problem of essentialism

Tillich's anthropology versus his Christology*

The problematic: the universal and the particular

The opening chapter concluded that the mature Tillich continued to affirm that humanity was religious by nature even as he sought to substantially qualify, if not abandon, earlier positions that humanity's historical religious development culminated in some definitive sense in the Christ event. Tillich's late move toward relativism and pluralism can easily be understood as a natural, if not necessary, development of his essentialism and of his under-standing of the relation of the essential to the existential. His essentialism provided Tillich throughout his corpus with a platform to argue that human-ity cannot escape its religious propensity. A religionless humanity remained for Tillich impossible and so unthinkable. On the other hand the senior Tillich came increasingly to realize that such essentialism could with great difficulty identify one or other of its historical expressions in existence as definitive or exhaustive of its potential. For Tillich the essential always is grounded in God and remains alive in existential consciousness imbuing it with a profound sense of removal from and drive back to its essential or divine origin. This dialectical play between essence and its existential distor-tion establishes the universality of religion as a human phenomenon even as it would question or undermine the claim that any specific religion as an expression of the essential could exhaust its possibilities in the form of a "final revelation".

Thus understood, Tillich's essentialism endowed posterity with a valuable and still credible picture of individual and cultural humanity as universally, necessarily and incorrigibly religious. And yet the notes of necessity and universality Tillich attributes to humanity's religious experience carry with them a spirit of relativism and a more encompassing religious empathy which defied confinement in one concrete religion. It was inevitable that in his later

* A version of this chapter was originally presented at the International Paul Tillich Conference, New Harmony, Indiana, June 17–20, 1993, and was published in F. Parrella (ed.) (1995) *Paul Tillich's Theological Legacy: Spirit and Community – International Paul Tillich Conference, New Harmony, 17–20 June 1993*, Berlin: Walter de Gruyter, 125–141.

period this relativism and universalism came to prevail. At the same time it cannot be denied that this stream in Tillich's late thought came to the fore in still discernible tension with his earlier contention that the essential has appeared in existence in unsurpassable manifestation in one singular histor-ical life and its institutional extension deemed somehow to be the "final revelation" to which all others are somehow ordered. As seen in Chapter 1, evi-dence of both sides of Tillich remain in his late writings provoking the question of the movement his thought naturally sought at the end of his life. Textual indications are that his thought was moving to a universalism that could appreciate the particularity of Christianity while also acknowledging its rela-tivity as one significant expression of essential humanity in a mythical idiom.

Tillich's movement toward a universalism supporting a pluralism and rela-tivity becomes more intelligible when it is focused through a closer examin-ation of his conception of the essential as the universal basis of religion taking existential form or concretion in specific religions in history. His theological thrust at the end gave a precedence to a focus on the ground of all religion in the essential as the foundation for the appreciation of each historical religion as a relative expression of the essential. Each religion would then be under-stood as derivative of a common source, as potentially mutually complemen-tary with other expressions of the essential, and so as shedding light on other religions as expressions of and existential contributions to the wealth of their common origin.

The priority of the essential as the basis of the universality and relativity of religion

To frame the problem of religious universalism and its attendant relativity in tension with the claims to finality of Christianity or any religion within the context of Tillich's total work, one must first expose the basis of Tillich's consistent contention that humanity is in and of itself religious. Responsible exposition of this claim leads immediately to an examination of certain foun-dational elements in Tillich's rich and lively conception of the essential on which he grounds humanity's universal religious propensity. On the last page of his work on nineteenth century Protestant thought, Tillich is cited as saying, "Often I have been asked if I am an existentialist theologian, and my answer is always short. I say fifty-fifty." (Tillich 1967: 245) By this remark Tillich meant that without an essentialist basis existentialism, religious or otherwise, is incomprehensible, even though many modern existentialists might remain unaware of their surreptitious essentialist presuppositions. Existentialism served Tillich well to identify in existence the distortion of the essential but distortion always depends on the reality of the distorted. In fact the distortion of the essential in existence becomes, for Tillich, the basis of various forms of human suffering which provoke the quest for an alleviation only the manifestation of the essential can provide.

After the passage cited above he goes on to make typical affirmations that pure essentialism and pure existentialism are equally impossible. An unqualified essentialism is impossible unless one identifies with the viewpoint of the absolute, or divine. In Tillich's view an unqualified essentialism remains an eschatological category fully attained in what he calls "divine blessedness" when the essential, to the extent realized in time and preserved in eternity, will be totally transparent to its origin. (Tillich 1963: 422) In these remarks Tillich is simply restating his and others' traditional reserve to Hegel's alleged hubris. For Tillich the actualization of the essential in existence can never be more than fragmentary. On the other hand, continues Tillich, existentialism presupposes essentialism. In an argument he uses throughout his work, Tillich first contends that without the essential human discourse would be impossible since discourse presupposes the universals and so the essential structure of mind and reality. Pure existentialism in this sense would demand the total silence of the existentialist, mute testimony to the fact that human discourse presupposes the essentialist structure of speech and of ideas spoken. When language and the ideas it communicates break silence, they express, with varying degrees of depth, the essential structures of mind, divine and human, and of nature beyond the mind. Few existentialists, and, for that matter, few contemporary deconstructionists follow the logic of pure existentialism or deconstructionism into the silence such purity would demand. Only Beckett has taken existentialism to its conclusion in the total silence of a world without essence and so meaning. On the contrary, not only do existentialists talk and write fluently and incisively, but also they do so about numerous aspects of the human plight, usually unaware that their discourse implies contact with a situation beyond the plight.

At this point Tillich introduces a second critique of a pure existentialism. To speak of the human plight, argues Tillich, here and throughout his work, presupposes some acute awareness of the contradiction between the goodness of humanity's essential nature and its distortion in existence. The very description of the plight implicates some consciousness of a state beyond it. More, the essential as the basis of what ought to be and is not is also the basis of the moral imperative. Anyone with an ought and a program based on it is an essentialist and much existentialist writing is imbued with an imperative however subtle it may be. The only real question is the degree of the essentialist's and the moralist's consciousness of the essentialism supporting their "ought". Tillich's vision of the ontological and epistemic intimacy of essence and existence leads to the conclusion, "This means that for me essentialism and existentialism belong together." (Tillich 1967: 245) In an even more succinct formulation Tillich writes, "So mere existentialism does not exist." (Tillich 1967: 143)

The same point is made more precisely and formally in the *Systematics*. Tillich concludes an early treatment of essential and existential being by putting the problem at the center of all significant philosophical and theological discourse. He contends that the "experience and vision" behind the distinction between essence and existence is in some sense laden with a primordial religiosity and precedes philosophy itself. (Tillich 1951: 204) This inchoate religiosity is based on humanity's capacity for numinous experience of the essential in early mythological formulation (and in contemporary experience of the deeper psyche) and on the early perception of the conflict between the is and the ought. Tillich points to the theological import of the distinction when he writes:

> The distinction between essence and existence, which religiously speaking is the distinction between the created and the actual world, is the backbone of the whole body of theological thought. It must be elaborated in every part of the theological system.
>
> (Tillich 1951: 204)

His use of the method of correlation remains unintelligible without its metaphysical foundation which relates existential question to the manifestation of the essential in Christian revelation, the culmination of all revelation at least for the early Tillich. Tillich's apologetic theology demands that honest Christian theology has to relate its revelation to the prominent questions its culture asks. Tillich's understanding of the power of the essential as the basis of the existential human demand for God as the ground of the essentially human gives the system whatever vitality and impact it exerts on the mind exposed to it.

It is thus impossible to read Tillich on the crucial point of the relation of the essential to the existential without coming to the position that in some very real sense the essential precedes the existential in power and in importance in the religious and Christian experience which the system seeks rationally to elaborate. The essential expresses Tillich's conviction that being in its depths is good because divine. The essential lies at the heart of Tillich's appropriation of Augustine's statement, "*esse qua esse est bonum*", or "being as being is good". Without the precedence of the essential the system does not work. For in Tillich's usage the essential functions to give to that which exists its native inherence or participation in the divine. In his vision this radical sense of the essential as the foundation of the existential seeking ever to permeate the existential more fully means that every existent participates in the being of the divine and is moved by the dynamic of the essential to ever fuller participation. At the human level this participation becomes the basis of the drive to intensify such participation and so as the basis of religion universally. His understanding of the essential would thus ground his famed principle of identity, that principle which affirms that at one point in the being of every existent that existent is identical, though never unqualifiedly so, with the being and life of its divine ground. Tillich would see such natural participation of the being of the human in the being of the divine as prominent in the thought of Spinoza, Eurigina, Schleiermacher, in many forms of mysticism, and in Schelling. (Tillich 1967: 74, 94, 95, 100, 143, 147)

At the level of self-conscious existence, then, humanity's participation in the essential is the basis of humanity's universal and native awareness of its natural continuity with divinity and of the underlying divinity of nature. This awareness carries with it the acute sense of humanity's separation from the essential as the basis of its drive to recover it. (Tillich 1951: 61, 62) Thus, in Tillich's logic, without the experience of the essential, humanity would be divested of its religious sense, that is, of both the sense of alienation and the joy of alienation overcome. There would and could be no religion, at least no religion endemic to the human urging its enhancement through the recovery of its origin. Without humanity's experienced participation in and removal from the divine, that is, without the experience of its essence, revelation as a divine intervention in human affairs would remain conceivable but only as a further form of dehumanization by a wholly alien God. (Tillich 1951: 116–118)

For Tillich the notion of revelation thus understood becomes demonic. For in Tillich's opinion any deity imagined to approach a humanity severed from a sense of its essential participation in divinity would approach it from beyond humanity's native sense of and search for its essential truth. The approach would be wholly from outside. Such alienating externalism is at the heart of Tillich's understanding of heteronomy. For Tillich heteronomy makes of such a deity a stranger to the humanity it addressed from beyond with an allegedly salvific intent. Tillich's distinction between a God from whom one is estranged and a God who is a stranger seeks to refute the imagination and horror of God as intrusive other. Rather the distinction favors a God with whom the human shares a prior identity now impaired but to be recovered in and through the divine approach revisioned as restoring to humanity a fuller connectedness with its native point of coincidence with the divine. (Tillich 1959b: 10)

In the light of this revisioning, revelation received from a distant God with whom humanity shared no common being means that the revealing God would destroy as revealer the structures of the mind it had authored as creator. In Tillich's words, "This would be the method of a demon and not of God." (Tillich 1951: 139) Such revelation if it were possible "dehumanizes man and demonizes God". (Tillich 1951: 139) By revealing answers to questions that humanity could not and had never asked revelation would remain a piece of indigestible information imposed on the autonomous mind from beyond, much as a wound introduces inassimilable toxics into an organically functioning bloodstream. In Tillich's imagery a notion of revelation divested of a sense of the essential as the basis of humanity's search for that which the experience of revelation provides reduces revelation to the heteronomous, a body of foreign content, that "must be thrown at those in the situation – thrown like a stone". (Tillich 1951: 7) The statement does not identify such a conception of revelation as Barthian or as having affinities with fundamental-ism, however sophisticated, but leaves little to the reader's imagination who and what Tillich is targeting in this typically strong statement.

Tillich's understanding of the essential is the only foundation of his con-tention that humanity is universally endowed with faith consciousness, that is, faith as ultimate concern. The universal basis of humanity's ultimate concern is its universal experience of the essential from which it feels its estrangement and to which it is driven as to the recovery of its truth as grounded in God. Through his essentialism Tillich can thus identify the uni-versality of guilt or estrangement as the sense of something radically amiss in existential humanity distanced, though never severed, from its essence and also identify the deepest and universal experience of human eros as the drive to recover that essence from which humanity is removed in existence. In the same essentialist logic, history becomes the search for the essential and so all of history becomes the history of religion culminating in the kairotic moment or moments when the meaning of history is revealed in the epiphanies of the essential. The essential–existential relationship thus allows Tillich to give pre-cise philosophical description to humanity's universal religious instinct and so to honor the variety of humanity's religions even if, as in his earlier Christian provincialism, these religions are somehow ordered to the Christ event.

In the third volume of the system Tillich more exactly defines and correl-ates the universal and particular, a universal ultimate concern as the basis of the particularity of its culminating expression in Christianity. Here he writes simply, "In this formal sense of faith as ultimate concern, every human being has faith." (Tillich 1963: 130) Then he goes on to describe specific religions as giving to formal faith, thus understood, material content. Against the back-ground of the universal dynamic of the essential as the basis of all religion, Christianity is then singled out as the "fulfillment toward which all forms of faith are driven". (Tillich 1963: 131) The problematic of Christianity as the fulfillment of all religion will be addressed later. Here the focus is on the way Tillich works to establish humanity's universal religiosity as the basis of a humanizing economy between the divine and the human based on an essentialism as the prior condition to whatever concrete form the essential might assume in existential incarnation. At this point in the discussion it becomes obvious that only against the background of a universal religiosity does Tillich understand any specific religion, including Christianity, to be truly humanizing.

This formal or universal understanding of humanity's faith based on its awareness of and response to the essential is evident again in Tillich's appreci-ation of the ontological argument. For Tillich the immediate, universal, but ambiguous experience of the lost essential in existence and the question of its recovery becomes both the ontological and psychological basis of the onto-logical argument. The ontological argument, for Tillich, proves nothing. One is not left with more knowledge upon its successful completion than one had before going through it. The ontological argument does nothing other than point to the unmediated human experience of the ultimate or unconditioned as the basis of the possibility and necessity of asking the question of God or asking after God. More precisely, the ontological argument simply documents the experiential basis of humanity's quest for God. In the experiential sense that Tillich attributes to it, the ontological argument weds ontology and psychology. The ontological argument becomes a psychological description of humanity's quest for God based on a compelling ontology and epistemology of estrangement and the ever present impulse for its defeat.

All of this dialectic is implicit when Tillich writes, "The question of God is possible because an awareness of God is present in the question of God." (Tillich 1951: 206) Thus humanity's experience of the essential makes possible the question of God as the universal basis of religion itself. But because the question is possible, it is also inevitable or necessary. Humanity cannot help but search for its felt but absent totality. Again, as previously argued, only the experience of the essential as the basis of humanity's asking after God makes possible a divine revelatory response which would not destroy humanity in its reception. Unless God asked the question through humanity, humanity could not graciously receive an answer whose reception would respect its search and the autonomous integrity of its mind. "Unless such an element [the infinite within finitude] were present, the question of God never could have been asked, nor could an answer, even the answer of revelation, have been received." (Tillich 1951: 206)

At this point in his discussion of the arguments for the existence of God, Tillich moves from a focus on the essential as grounding the possibility of humanity's asking the question of God to the essential as a salvific response to a question existential humanity must necessarily ask. In this move Tillich precisely identifies the dynamics of the possibility and necessity of humanity asking after God or posing the question of God. In the identification of these dynamics Tillich makes it clear that the quest for the essential is more than an intellectual question, more than a workout in argumentative logic or rhetoric as the quest so often becomes in debates about God's existence. In Tillich's hands the quest for the essential takes on a note of inescapable necessity because it extends to the search for the courage which would enable existential humanity to bear the burden of an existential anxiety universally attached to its finitude. For Tillich this is the valid function of the cosmological argument. (Tillich 1951: 209) It documents the terrors of existence and asks after their alleviation through participation in the essential as the ground of courage. In a similar manner the possibility of the disintegration of life's opposites and the resultant fragmentation and meaninglessness of a life in which this occurs necessitates the search for an integrating power or ground of meaning to offset existential disintegration. (Tillich 1951: 210) This need becomes for Tillich the legitimate basis of the teleological argument which documents the meaning brought to existential life through its integration in divine life captured in cultural expressions transparent to humanity's depths and so providing access to those depths. In both cases the existential necessity of asking the question need not be proven. It need only be pointed to in the threat to courage and meaning in every life. Effectively in this revisioning of the proofs for God's existence, Tillich transposes the ontological, cosmological and teleological arguments into a profound psychology describing humanity's quest for its essential truth, its need for the courage to withstand the negations and fragmentations of life, and its drive to express the deepest meaning of its spirit in the creation of its culture and its culture's expressions. In this endeavor he joins with Jung in birthing a modality of consciousness which synthesizes the ontological, epistemological, theological and psychological without demeaning the role of each in their contribution to a perspective which surpasses all of them.

In deference to his Christian bias regarding the priority of the divine in the gracing of the human, Tillich is adamant in his insistence that the quest after the essential as the basis of the possibility and necessity of religion can neither be avoided nor culminate in the quester's conquest of the essential through human effort or agency. The gracing of the human takes on the following paradox. Humanity can and must ask after the essential. Yet the human does not confer the essential upon itself. The answer comes not from the question but from "beyond it". (Tillich 1951: 64) But the location of Tillich's "beyond" is not to be found in the stranger God who addresses humanity as wholly other than the human. Rather the "beyond" is to be found in those theonomous depths of the human where divinity dwells as the ground of the human, depths for which humanity thirsts but which it cannot willfully access or exploit. (Tillich 1951: 61) What Tillich does so well is to show to humanity the inescapability of its quest and need for the God who rises unforced to meet it from within. Effectively Tillich's sense of an immanental divine life force native to the human and forever urging greater ingression in human consciousness is the basis of his understanding of the precedence and gratuity of grace, which is at the same time a grace for which humanity longs with a longing Tillich describes with metaphysical and psychological power, precision and coherence.

Because of the vital urgencies involved in the search for the essential it would be a profound misreading of Tillich to think that his understanding of the essential is static or confining as is the case in Aristotelian-Thomistic philosophy and theology. Tillich's essentialism escapes and refutes Heidegger's critique of static essences functioning as confining determinants to human freedom. On the contrary Tillich locates the *ousia*, the essential, in the divine depths of every existent's being. From these depths the essential gives to the existent "the power of being". (Tillich 1951: 101) From these same depths the essential "empowers *and* judges" the existential and so functions as both the ground of existential humanity's courage and meaning as well as the source of its goodness and so of its conscience. (Tillich 1951: 203) In this latter function the "essential self" (Tillich 1963: 235) never allows the existential human to evade or ignore the gap between one's essential goodness ever seeking greater realization in each life and the relative poverty of what has been and is realized. The individual in existence remains related always to this essential truth and so is imbued with an unremitting sense of a potential that can never be fulfilled nor denied. Its partial fulfillment urges ever greater fulfillment. Its denial is the ultimate form of self-betrayal and an option for nothingness. Guilt is not imposed from without but follows naturally from the denial or rejection of the essential self as a presiding power within.

When this kind of statement about the essential self is related to what Tillich means by the depths and power of being he is clearly identifying the essential self with the divine, and, in particular, with the ground of the essential self in the divine *Logos*, as the primordial expression of form and so of individual truth. In Tillich's Christian categories the *ousia*, or essence, of the individual is eternally expressed in the dynamics of Trinitarian life. "In the *Logos* God speaks his 'word', both in himself and beyond himself." (Tillich 1951: 251) The individual's identity takes on its first form there, a form which imbues existential human consciousness with the sense that it is primordially grounded in the divine life and is impelled to intensify its participation in that life in existence as an abiding contribution to the wealth of human and divine life in the eschaton. The *ousia* or essential self of the individual ingrained in the *Logos* is alive with the life of the Trinity. The Trinity itself is for Tillich an intensely living antinomy far removed from the static rest of that Aristotelian God who is pure act. "The God who is *actus purus* is not the living God." (Tillich 1951: 246) On the contrary, divine life, for Tillich, is a seething unity of opposites constantly enlivened by the battle and resolution of its polarities. Participation in the Spirit worked unity of opposites is the basis of whatever fragmentary integration occurs in existential human life and becomes the creature's contribution to the fullness of divine life in eternity. (Tillich 1963: 403–406)

It is in such a turbulent yet blessed matrix that the essences are forged and first expressed. Even when humanity's existential will breaks the dreaming innocence of this primal process within the Trinity and willful self-creation comes to coincide with fall, the impress or impact of the essential can never be forgotten and lives on in the memory of existential reason and humanity. (Tillich 1957: 22, 33–36, 43, 44) Some memory of a pristine and eternal expression in the *Logos* dogs existential humanity throughout its days and makes the recovery of the essential both the basis of religion and the foundation of both human fortitude in the face of finitude and of whatever divinely grounded meaning and integration humanity attains in existence.

What Tillich is doing here is brilliantly connecting existential consciousness with its essential rootedness in the dynamics of Trinitarian life. In doing this he works with a single paradigm of God which organically unites in itself so many sides of the divine character. For Tillich this God can be identified without confusion or forcing connections through the synonyms "living", "Spirit" and "Trinity". Life for Tillich is made up of the unity of opposites worked by the Spirit eternally in the Trinity as the precedent and power behind the working of the union of opposites in existential human life. (Tillich 1951: 249–252) Thus the adumbration of the essential in natural existential consciousness carries with it an intuition of God as a unity of opposites and so as Trinitarian. Tillich puts this powerfully and poetically when he writes, "As Spirit he [God] is as near to the creative darkness of the unconscious as he is to the critical light of cognitive reason." (Tillich 1951: 250) When the same insight is put in terms of human awareness of this situation it reads, "Human intuition of the divine always has distinguished between the abyss of the divine (the element of power) and the fullness of its content (the element of meaning), between the divine depth and the divine *Logos*." (Tillich 1951: 250) In humanity's natural and unmediated experience of its essential connectedness with the divine life as the basis of its own, Tillich would therefore imply some natural and so universal intimation of the Trinitarian God. In terms of a more traditional theology this means that Tillich can make no distinction between the treatment of the unity of God and the treatment of the Trinity.

It is to an ever deeper inhesion in such a vital yet balanced life that the essential in existence lures and drives the human. This inhesion may be imagined in many ways but two major modes of imagining it come to mind from Tillich's pages. One is personal and entails the ever greater assimilation in existential consciousness of what Tillich calls the "essential self" originally spoken in the *Logos* and so implicated in God's internal self-expression and definition. (Tillich 1963: 235; 1952: 158) The essential self in this context is the basis of the courage to be. The other is more vital and entails an ever more intense entrance into the flow of Trinitarian life itself as the Spirit moves to unite the conflictual opposites of the individual's life in existence by leading it into greater participation in divinity's intensely active rest, the blessedness that attends the Spirit's uniting of the opposites in the Trinity. In the end these approaches are but two sides of one dynamic reality.

Both these functions of the essential self would imply that the deeper self of each individual is eternally expressed in the *Logos* and seeks to realize itself in existence over the course of the individual's life in a process the late Tillich calls "essentialization". (Tillich 1963: 421, 422) In one of his more beautiful passages Tillich compares the essential self to a portrait somehow preceding each life yet seeking ever greater realization in it over the course of its unfolding in time. Such a portrait would express the essential truth of that life and pervade its every moment but could be fully caught in none nor exhausted in its totality. (Tillich 1963: 413) By implication the successful portraitist captures in whatever material and at whatever moment the essential self and so eternal truth of the subject.

In a similar vein Tillich will describe the truth of the individual's essential self as grounded in the divine perspective. Such a perspective captures the individual's essential truth in its totality as the basis of what one most truly is and must become in the journey through time. Tillich writes, "In the creative vision of God the individual is present as a whole in his essential being and inner *telos* and, at the same time, in the infinity of the special moments of his life-process." (Tillich 1951: 255) The essential self thus understood is the ultimate foundation of the individual's identity. The recovery of the essential self becomes then at once the recovery of one's truest identity and the substance of personal sanctification. Again in poetic expression Tillich describes the fragmentary but real experience of the sanctity of one's true identity in time as the essential self shining through "the contingencies of the existing self". (Tillich 1963: 235)

With these categories Tillich can equate without residue the experience of the essential self with the experience both of the holy and of the individual's truest identity because the essential self is grounded in the eternal *Logos* as the ground of existential life unfolding in time. Psychological maturation and sanctification become one process. As the experience of the ingression of the essential self in existential consciousness would build over a lifetime, Tillich implies that it would give not only psychological maturation but also providential and moral direction to the consciousness in which it became increasingly incarnate. For Tillich the role of the Spirit in leading the individual into "essential being" creates the saint and provides the saint with a moral instinct that is at once mature, sure and yet always one's own. Of this process he writes with disarming simplicity, "The saint (he who is determined by the Spiritual Presence) knows *where* to go and where *not* to go." (Tillich 1963: 270)

The contemporary critique of essentialism might be tempted to depict Tillich's understanding of the essential self as a somewhat constrictive, reified conception impeding personal development through a tight determinism, or slavish submission to an ideal grounded in a distant God. The critique is misplaced. It does not appreciate the vitalistic or energizing power Tillich attributes to the essential self. For Tillich the recovery of the essential self assimilates the initiate into the integration and balance of opposites constituting the life of the Trinity. As such the marks of this recovery are always a more integrated individuality in harmony with an ever extending compassion for what is. Tillich understands the integration of different sets of opposites to constitute morality, culture and religion respectively. Recovery of the essential self thus works an integration of these crucial dimensions of Spirit in the life thus blessed. Tillich works this side of his theology through his metaphysics of what he terms "the ontological elements". (Tillich 1951: 174–186) Summarily put, he is arguing that all of life consists of the successful unification or syntheses of the many conflictual polarities that make life up. The tension between individual and the other he identifies as the basis of morality. The tension between potential or dynamic and form he identifies as the basis of culture. The tension between freedom and destiny he identifies as the basis of religion. Essential life, the life of God, unites these polarities through the Spirit from eternity. These potentially disruptive opposites, individuality–participation, dynamics–form, freedom–destiny, are rooted in the divine life as the basis of their working and hoped for synthesis in human life. These opposites are in divine life as overcome in the Spirit as the basis of their being overcome in the human. (Tillich 1951: 243) In a particularly compelling passage Tillich describes the divine *parousia* in Platonic terms as the ever present power of divine life within human life working there to lead human life into the integration of divine life through the same Spirit at work in life universal, human and divine. (Tillich 1951: 245) On the basis of Tillich's sharpened sense of the possibility of the disintegration of human life through the dissociation of the opposites that make it up, he joins Teilhard de Chardin in the assertion that wherever life is held together, to the extent it is held together, is held together by the Spirit.

In these Spirit worked syntheses morality, culture and religion also come into fragmentary unities in history as a pledge and always ambiguous anticipation of the final unities to be fully realized in a transtemporal reality. Recovery of the essential thus always unites the notes of an ever greater unity with the sacred self at the personal level as a contribution to a collective consciousness in which morality, culture and religion would move toward coincidence as diverse binary expressions of a common human depth. In resonance with this depth each of these dimensions of spirit would respect each others' autonomy and so contribute to a society rendered more profound through their diverse expression of the ground of society itself. The unifying Spirit working through these sets of opposites would alleviate and eventually eradicate all tension between the existentially conflicting worlds of morality, culture and religion.

Thus understood Tillich's essentialism is itself always eschatological because it affirms that essence in existence of its own dynamic constantly urges the final unambiguous unity with the essential in the mythical situation when God will be all in all. As stated in the opening chapter on the third last page of the third volume of his *Systematic Theology*, Tillich reveals finally and fully the intimacy of the divine with the human his understanding of the essential has implied from the outset. He does this when he introduces the word "pan-en-theism" then and now so suspicious to Christian ears. The panentheistic elements of his thought are evident from the first volume and throughout wherever his understanding of the participation of the existential in the essential is discussed. One may speculate that possible fear of the Christian response to so daring a word deprived him of its use till nearly the end. When he does use the term he relates it to his conception of essentialization which does little more than describe the dynamic life he attaches to the essential throughout his work. Here clearly he identifies the essential as being in God, potentially in the state of dreaming innocence (paradise), actually as

the supportive power on which all depends in existence, and eschatolog-
ically as transtemporal fulfillment in the essentialization of all creatures in
unambiguous unity with their essential truth in God. (Tillich 1963: 421)

The enduring tension: the essential as universal, the Christ as particular

At this turning point in the discussion, Tillich should be credited in terms of
the foregoing for a lasting achievement in painting so compelling a picture of
humanity as related, through its ineradicable essential being, to the divine
as the ground of its identity and support and source of its integration in
existence. Humanity thus understood remains incapable ever of divesting
itself, for better or for worse, of its religious instinct and nature. Atheism as a
human possibility is as impossible for the individual as secularism is for a
culture. Tillich could not be more explicit on this point when he writes,
"secular culture is essentially as impossible as atheism". (Tillich 1959b: 27)

For religionist, theologian and believer of every stripe these words can be
at once assuring and frightening. Tillich's essentialism assures those with a
positive attitude toward religion that religion is grounded in the fabric of
humanity. For those who look more critically at religion in the light of its
historical and current atrocities, Tillich's depiction of humanity as irredeem-
ably religious forbids too sanguine and superficial an approach to the alleviation of the suffering, death and divisiveness religious faith and its political
equivalents continue to work on the human scene. From Tillich's perspective
efforts to remove the shadow of religion should not naively entertain the
possibility of the removal from the human of religion itself. In the light of
Tillich's location of religion in the essential nature of humanity, projects to
end it in principle as envisioned by certain streams of Enlightenment rationalism and of twentieth century existentialism, atheism or secularism go beyond
the naive to the dangerous. They fail to see what Tillich saw so clearly, namely,
that when religion is negated as religion its shadow can return in non-
religious, often political/ideological dress, to wreak an equal or even greater
harm on the truncated humanity that turns unconsciously to deity in the
secular disguise of "quasi-religions" who then assume the oppressive and
"demonic elements" of the religions themselves. (Tillich 1966: 90) In this
respect Tillich's critique of the quasi-religions, which he does concede can
legitimately mediate the essential, has profound affinities with Jung's conviction that the archetypally based "isms" can breed unconscious communities
possessed by their bonding truth and hostile to all the differently bonded.
(Dourley 2003)

Switching perspectives and looking upon religion as human resource
rather than threat, Tillich gives to religion a dignity and necessity which many
of its institutional advocates cannot because they fail to locate primary
religious experience in the essential core of the human. Tillich can show to

often anxious or beleaguered promoters of one or other particular religious tradition that they might be reassured and rendered less frenetic through the realization that the universal experience of humanity's God grounded essence convinces it of the reality of the divine. Ecclesial leaders might then be freed to ask the more relaxed question of how their religious specificity might best serve humanity's universal religious life and nature.

For it cannot be denied that Tillich's argument on behalf of humanity as religious depends on a religious sensitivity often remarkably absent from both current religious leadership and its constituency. Yet it also remains difficult to deny that the cultivation of humanity's native and authentic religious sensitivity, as Tillich would understand it, is in humanity's favor and an ultimate resource for its enrichment. The question remains open that if the churches do not have the theology to cultivate these depths from what direction will this cultivation come and in what forms, personal and collective? Can it be that the secular realm will be the vehicle through which the development of deeper religious sensitivity is currently emerging, one that will conflict with and eventually surpass the more attenuated religious sensitivity now informing ecclesial circles? Indeed Tillich would argue that the cultivation of this sensitivity leads cultures themselves into their depths where religion can become their living substance in all the major functions of the spirit, namely, morality, creativity and religion diversely transparent to their generative source. Effectively no culture is without a relation to this core expressed in its values and held to be ultimate. Because of their religious core, manifest or surreptitious, and certainly open to degrees of legitimate ultimacy, no culture can be purely secular if the meaning of secularity is that of the absence of the absolute in the bonding of a society. These reflections lie behind Tillich's famous formulation "culture is the form of religion and religion the substance of culture". (Tillich 1963: 158) Thus the sense of God that pervades Tillich's theology might currently work to heighten the sense of the sacred manifest in the various religious traditions and the cultures that they support while persuading both that they serve a more universal reality than any one of them currently encompasses let alone exhausts. This consciousness would, in effect, be a cultural statement of Tillich's desired union of catholic substance and Protestant principle. All cultures could then be seen to manifest the divine as their bond even as all are denied identity with the divine manifest through them and their relatively valuable religious and ethnic expressions. But to make relative all cultural and religious expressions in relation to the surpassing wealth of a divinity common to humanity as their collective origin involves the emergence of a new societal myth. This myth would subject all religious and cultural expression to an origin which outstrips them all and renders them respectful and appreciative of each other out of growing sense of their common human origin.

Yet the very compelling power of Tillich's brief on behalf of humanity as religious and on behalf of the intimacy of the divine and the human on which his brief rests causes the problem to which we now turn. The problem lies in the tension between Tillich's essentialism and the universalism it supports and his contention at the heart of his Christology that "essential manhood" has appeared paradoxically yet fully and without impairment in existence in a concrete historical life. (Tillich 1957a: 94) Put succinctly the problem is this. Tillich's description of religious humanity can stand on its own. It can do much more than simply serve his Christology by showing humanity's search for the essential to have culminated in the Christ event. Tillich's essentialism could equally well be used in the service of the current imperative to imbue the absolute claims of competing religions and cultures with a redeeming relativity in the interests of the preservation of the species whom these competing religious claims allegedly serve.

To depict humanity in universal search for the essential and to show this search to be the meaning of personal and collective history has its own internal convincing power. So does the depiction of divinity as a supportive and integrating power working on behalf of life from life's depth. Since this universal ground of the totality is operative in the person as the ground of the individual's being, its entrance into the individual's consciousness always carries with it an extended sympathy for all that is, a sympathy that few religions in their particularity can evoke. An alchemist, experientially convinced that the surfacing to consciousness of one's native divinity was the gold and the goal of the transformational process, could identify as a purely natural process the realization of the personal integration, assurance and extended empathy that naturally accompany the recovery of one's divine essence. The alchemist's description would differ very little from Tillich's. In more modern dress, Tillich's essential self can with difficulty be distinguished from the concept of the self in Jung's analytic psychology, a self whose ushering into consciousness is a joint venture between the self and the response of the ego to the self's urgencies to become conscious in it. Nor could the description proffered by analytic psychology of the integrating and relational capacities of the self as it is born into consciousness be easily differentiated from Tillich's description of the religious experience of the essential self. This is especially true of Jung's perception of the self as working the integration in consciousness of the many conflicting energies whose harmony contributes to a fully functioning life as it moves toward an ever more encompassing sympathy for all that is.

But Tillich, at least till he approached the end of his life, seems driven by his membership in the Christian theological circle to affirm that the essential which empowers and underlies all of life and religious experience appears in its fullness in the figure of Christ. Even though he admits the circularity of this conclusion, it seems, from today's perspective, forced, somehow a limitation to the breadth and depth of the universal presence of divinity to humanity which his essentialism so convincingly establishes. Indeed one could be forced to wonder whether or not his essentialism is but an elaborate construct in the service of an imperial Christology. Should this be the case Tillich's thought, in the end, would be reduced to the erudite fundamentalism of Kierkegaard's leap of faith or Barth's arrogant distinction between one (true) revelation and many religions. Tillich would then be seen as a theologian whose elaboration of the essential enabled him to wait longer before he made the leap to the Christ event as the full realization in history of the long lost and awaited essential his metaphysics so ably depicts.

In a very real sense the problem precedes his Christology, or at least its formal treatment, and derives from the first sentence of the first volume of the *Systematics* where he depicts theology and, by implication, himself as a theologian as serving the needs of the Church. (Tillich 1951: 3) As such the theologian is bound by what Tillich calls "the criterion of the Christian message" as the normative object of the Christian theologian's ultimate concern. (Tillich 1951: 9) In this role the theologian serves as "an interpreter of his church and its claim to uniqueness and universal validity". (Tillich 1951: 10) This validity in turn rests on "the *Logos* of being, manifest in Jesus as the Christ". (Tillich 1951:64) This revelation is the "final revelation", and, as such, is "the decisive, fulfilling unsurpassable revelation, that which is the criterion of all others". (Tillich 1951: 133) Because of the finality of the Christian revelation, "Apologetic theology must show that trends which are immanent in all religions and cultures move toward the Christian answer." (Tillich 1951: 15) Even in the 1950s Tillich remained blind to the possible connection between the final revelation and the final solution.

In a point touched on in the first chapter, when Tillich takes up his ecclesiology in the third volume of the *Systematics* he repeats the above positions at least in their substance. (Tillich 1963: 152–155) He does extend the Church, here called the Spiritual Community, to those who are possessed of and by the New Being. The New Being is a symbol-concept for the individual's participation in the Christ event which in turn is understood as the Spirit conferred appropriation of one's essential being. In these passages, then, Tillich obviously makes the criterion of membership in the Spiritual Community, or, the vastly extended church universal, the working in the lives of its members of those processes later described as essentialization. With this norm of membership he can speak of a latent church referring to the actualization of the New Being, of the essential, in individuals and groups beyond the manifest or Christian Church and, in a spirit of prophetic criticism, deny the experience of New Being to some who are members of the manifest Church.

Yet even with this broadening and crossing of boundaries, he argues that the latent Church is ordered to the manifest Church and that the New Being is most fully present within the manifest Church. In this discussion, as we have seen, Judaism, Islam, the classical mysticism of Asia and other religious and secular communities are relegated to membership in the latent spiritual community. "The ultimate criterion, the faith and love of the Christ, has not yet appeared to these groups – whether they existed before or after the years 1 to 30." (Tillich 1963: 154) Tillich here argues that these groups lack the principle of self-negation at the heart of the Protestant principle. He concludes that "they are unconsciously driven toward the Christ" even when consciously rejective of the Christ of ecclesial evangelization. (Tillich 1963: 154) Though Tillich concludes the passage by arguing that recognition of other religious and secular communities as belonging to the latent Church would undermine Christian ecclesial arrogance in approaching them, his own position sounds to contemporary ears itself arrogant, imperial and hostile to the universalism and diversity of religious expression his own essentialism would support.

It is this forced tailoring of the universalism at work in his understanding of humanity as religious to the much narrower confines of his Christology that lies behind Wilfred Cantwell Smith's critique when he writes, "probably Tillich belongs to the last generation of theologians who can formulate their conceptual system as religiously isolationist". (Smith 1976: 8) Smith goes on to describe the note of finality which attaches to Tillich's claims for Christianity as "separatist" and belonging to a "ghetto" mentality hostile to a now blooming global religious sense "which will make the work of even a Tillich appear parochial". (Smith 1976: 8)

From the distance of over a quarter century one can bow to the validity of Smith's remarks and still remain indebted to Tillich for his lasting contribution to humanity's philosophical and psychological understanding of its religious propensity. Smith himself has much less, if anything, to offer in this regard other than a benign religious positivism. Such positivism does little more than point with near uncritical approval to the plethora of humanity's religious corporate traditions and to the "faith" – never critically analyzed – of the devotee always related to one or other of these religious traditions. No responsible effort is ever made to uncover the metaphysical roots of either the faith of the devotee or of the dynamics of the origin of the cumulative traditions in which faith flourishes. This would require an ontology and epistemology of revelation itself, an endeavour Smith never undertakes. Because he declines the task of responsibly locating the nature and dynamics of religion within the human, as Tillich does so well, Smith can never rule out the possibility that both faith and its traditions are epiphenomenal if not pathologizing though perennial aspects of the human spirit.

It is true that Smith's pre-critical positivism can take non-Christian religions more seriously in terms of providing sensitively treated data about their beliefs and practices than does Tillich at least in his early work. Nevertheless, it remains equally true that Tillich's essentialist understanding of humanity as religious would provide Smith with a much needed insight into what religion is as the basis of a deeper critique of religion able to address both the benign and destructive faces it continues to show to the humanity it possesses. Such a much needed critical resource would go well beyond a thinly disguised admiration informing the documentation of religion's diverse appearances in human history in the tenuous hope that dialogue among devotees would breed a global ethos of higher tolerance and consciousness between too often still warring religious traditions and their secular equivalents. Tillich's essentialism could provide the framework to appreciate the various religions as expressions of the common ground from which they arise to consciousness while clearly identifying the antisocial tendency involved in their unqualified claims to ultimacy especially lethal when such claims inform the bonding of ethnic, national or political communities in geographical or geopolitical interface.

At this point Tillich's last published address again becomes relevant to the discussion because it evidences a movement in his thought toward a gracious relativizing of Christianity by taking the history of religions and their symbols more seriously. In this piece he makes it clear that his understanding of the Christian theologian's appropriation of the history of religions is not progressivistic. (Tillich 1966: 90) By "progressivistic" he seems to mean some form of literal future fulfillment of the religious impulse in time, a position he dubiously attributes to Teilhard de Chardin. Rather than such progressivism Tillich proffers an alternative reminiscent of ground themes in his *Systematics* and his earlier writings.

He once more rehearses the major typological elements in humanity's religious experience namely, the sacramental, the mystical and prophetic-rational-critical. Their occasional balanced synthesis becomes an ideal religion which can never be realized in more than fragment in time. The ideal interplay of these ever present elements of religiosity he terms the "Religion of the Concrete Spirit". No specific religion is identical with it though he thinks it has reached its highest expression in Paul's doctrine of the Spirit combining *agape* and *gnosis*, a love informed by an experiential knowledge of God. In terms of the nature and dynamic of the religion of the concrete spirit, the clash of sacramental/mystical and iconoclastic/prophetic forces, "the fight of God within religion against religion" is both the ideal expression of religion and the key to the understanding of its most foundational energies. (Tillich 1966: 88) This is but a restatement of Tillich's understanding of the interplay of Protestant principle and Catholic substance operative throughout his thought. As such it is not new, though he does concede, and it is an immense concession, that the religious and salvific import of the Cross, the symbol of the interplay of the sacramental and iconoclastic, "happens fragmentarily in other places, in other moments" with no historical or empirical connection with the specifically Christian symbol of the Cross nor the historical event from which the symbol derives. (Tillich 1996: 89) In this formulation Tillich must be understood to mean that what is symbolized for the Christian in the central symbol of the Cross has happened in variation for other cultures and times no doubt captured in different symbols appropriate to them. Though these remarks may be fleeting, through them Tillich would distance himself definitively from his earlier affirmation of Christianity as the final revelation to which all others are ordered as the normative object of the Christian theologian's ultimate concern.

In another critical passage he makes his departure from the unqualified ultimacy he had attributed to Christianity in the telling use of the subjunctive in reference to what previously he had termed the "final revelation" in a much more indicative, if not imperative, mood. He writes:

> there may be – and I stress this there *may* be – a central event in the history of religions which unites the positive results of those critical developments in the history of religion in and under which revelatory experiences are going on – an event which, therefore, makes possible a concrete theology that has universalistic significance.
>
> (Tillich 1966: 81)

The "central event" referred to in this passage is obviously a description of the Christ event of the *Systematics* where there was no question that such an event was and remains, and not may have been, the final revelation. There it was the final revelation in whose service the Christian theologian worked as the object of the theologian's ultimate concern. More, if the Christian message was not the theologian's ultimate concern that theologian could no longer be described as a Christian theologian whose theology was done on behalf of the Church. When this statement from his last address is compared to his earlier formulations one is forced to conclude that the Tillich who made them would no longer consider himself a Christian theologian according to the earlier Tillich's normative description of this role. The earlier theologian would be allowed no room whatsoever to waffle on whether or not there may have been a final revelation and whether or not it coincided with the Christ event.

It is difficult, therefore, to escape the conclusion that Tillich's late brush with the history of religions resulted in a liberating relativism which would now allow the theologian, even the Christian theologian, to relativize the ultimate concern expressed through one's tradition without that tradition losing its valid, though now limited, ultimacy, and that individual the valid status of theologian. One has the sense that though this position may have cost Tillich immensely in its securing and expression, it was nevertheless indicative of the direction his mind was taking in its maturity, an expansive and freeing development for himself and for those who would follow him.

He died before he could further develop his late expansiveness. The form it might have taken is suggested by two then contemporary thinkers of whom he thought highly. Once in the third volume of his *Systematics* (Tillich 1963: 5) and twice in his last address on the history of religions (Tillich 1966: 86, 91) Tillich speaks with critical admiration of the work of Teilhard de Chardin. Teilhard also spent his life working a correlation between human question and Christian response, in his case, the correlation of evolutionary science with Roman Catholic Christianity and its theology. Briefly put Teilhard came to identify the very energy that worked through evolution in the creation of the human brain and so of humanity, with the reality of God and of Christ taken in an extended or cosmic sense. More, this same energy, having produced the brain now worked through humanity toward a final completion of deity and humanity in the Pleroma or point Omega. That Teilhard had to identify this divine energy with his Christ and so with Christianity is evidence in Teilhard's case of the same provincialism the late Tillich came to deplore in his own. Even though the late Tillich drew back from the optimism and progressivism he saw in Teilhard, he nevertheless acknowledged an affinity of concern over the need to elaborate a theology depicting humanity's relation to divinity as natural and mutually completing. No doubt Teilhard's identifying the underlying energy empowering evolutionary creation as Christic is itself an imperial imposition on universal natural energies. But such an extended vision would breed a sense of God active in all cohesive or organic life and community, and make the various religions relative but valuable servants of a universal energy working toward a hopefully emerging theonomous human communion better able to sustain the one species which bears the many religions deriving from a commonly possessed energy.

Tillich also wrote knowingly and incisively of Carl Jung's psychology on the occasion of Jung's death. He is particularly insightful when discussing Jung's fear of metaphysics which to Tillich were blatantly present in Jung's archetypal theory. (Tillich 1962a: 31) In this piece Tillich deftly and accurately exposes the metaphysic latent in Jung's psychology so often denied by Jung himself. In Tillich's hands the primordial archetypes become the eternal or transtemporal structures belonging to being universally. Archetypal forces are those potentialities or powers seeking revelatory expression through the symbols which make conscious and incarnate the mystery of being in human life. Writes Tillich, "The archetypal forms behind all myths belong to the mystery of the creative ground of everything that is." (Tillich 1962a: 32) True to his essentialist perception he then identifies Jung's archetypes as "the essences of all things" grounded in the *Logos* structure of divine life and so of human life. (Tillich 1962a: 32) As if in unwitting compliance with Tillich's metaphysical analysis of archetypal reality and power, Jung himself in his extended conversations with the Dominican monk, Father Victor White, on more than one occasion related the *ousiae*, the essences, to the archetypal powers of the unconscious. (Jung 1973a: 540, 555; 1975a: 60)

Had Tillich pursued a Jungian perspective he might have been able to understand the history of religions as expressions of a possibly infinitely fecund unconscious which partially realized itself in all of the religions but could exhaustively express itself in none. In a similar vein he might have been able to see the Christ figure as a still reigning culture hero but one expression of the communal self among many. (Jung 1968a: 36, 67–68) Such a possibility might have forced Tillich to dwell on Jung's contention that the symbol of Christ, though historically valuable, is currently being corroded by the unconscious urgency toward a symbol of the self which would embrace a greater totality of opposites. (Jung 1968a: 42–45) Such an unconscious imperative would demand an image of the self more inclusive than that of the Christ image which has no apparent positive relation to the demonic, the feminine or the bodily instinctual. From this perspective Jung might confront a broader minded later Tillich with Tillich's own repeated proposition that symbols grow and die (Tillich 1957b: 43) and ask him if he could envision such a fate for the Christian symbol as it sought to supersede its current state and incorporate elements more inclusive of humanity's matrix in a humanity then enabled to give divine status to more of what is.

All of this hopefully creative speculation will be taken up again in later discussions. Such speculation and critical appreciation of Tillich is made in full acknowledgment of the debt owed him for what he has taught contemporary humanity about its being religious and about its essential and experiential connectedness with the divine. In the end the investigation suggests strongly that Tillich's essentialism provides a powerful understanding of religious experience ingrained in the fabric of the human spirit itself. It further suggests that Tillich's religious anthropology, his understanding of humanity as religious, can be extricated from his theology as the greatest contribution he has made to theology and religious studies. It is as if his anthropology freed from a constrictive Christology could still appreciate itself even more profoundly but now as one expression of the essential among many. Isolating his theological anthropology gives it precedence to his Christology. The precedence of his religious anthropology makes all religion relative in relation to its origin in the ground of humanity. This relativity extends to Christianity and to the figure of Christ and asks if Christianity can remain itself and accept the relativity and pluralism Tillich's late development demand. This question is more fully examined in the next chapter in relation to the place of Christ in history.

Chapter 3

Christ as the picture of essential humanity

One of many*

A theonomous Christ as "essential manhood" and the defeat of a heteronomous Christology

Chapter 2 concluded that Tillich's understanding of humanity as religious precedes, relativizes and humanizes his Christology by philosophically depicting the Christ event as the answer to humanity's search for the essential. It went on to present evidence that the late Tillich drew back from identifying the Christ event as the definitive moment of the realization of the essential in history. The same reticence prompts the question of whether the Christ event can any longer be simply described in terms of Tillich's understanding of *kairos* as "the center of history". (Tillich 1963: 147, 364) The question of history is closely related to Tillich's late qualifications of his earlier Christology because, for Tillich, human history is simply the history of humanity's search for its existentially impaired essence. History thus understood is itself religious. Historical moments of humanity's recovery of its essential truth are its crowning moments. Such moments constitute the fullness of historical time, the *kairoi*, that give to history its meaning and reward its innate religious quest. Because he identifies history with humanity's search for the essential, Tillich, at least in his earlier Christology, could make the substance of his Christology the unqualified and unique appearance of "essential manhood" in a personal life in existence. (Tillich 1957a: 94) There is no explicit religious language in this description nor is there a need for any. In Tillich's own words the use of religious language to describe the meaning of the Christ event would be "redundant". (Tillich 1957a: 94) Christ as essential manhood says it all. From this basis follows the question of whether or not the completion of history as the realization of the essential in existence can be confined to the Christ event as the earlier Tillich and most of Christian orthodoxy would still contend.

* A version of this chapter was read at the X International Paul-Tillich-Symposium, Frankfurt/Main, June 4–6, 2004, and published in P. Haigis, G. Hummel and D. Lax (eds) (2007) *Christ Jesus – the Center of History!? Proceedings of the X International Paul-Tillich-Symposium Frankfurt/Main 2004*, Berlin: Lit Verlag, 100–112.

The reason why explicit religious language is redundant in the depiction of Christ as the realization of essential manhood lies in the connection that Tillich establishes between his understanding of essence, existence and theonomy. As the meaning of Tillich's usage of these terms becomes clear the danger of understanding the figure of Christ as a heteronomous and so arbitrary imposition on history sponsored by a divinity beyond history is wholly defeated. When essential manhood becomes the foundation of a Christology, Christ, as other or heteronomous, cedes to a theonomous Christ symbolic of a fulfilled humanity toward which all humanity and its history naturally drive. This is not to address the wider question of whether or not Christ is the only and exhaustive realization of the essential in history. It is to affirm that Tillich's Christology is able to show the Christ event as in organic continuity with and an answer to humanity's search for its essence.

At this point a tension in Tillich's underlying universal religious naturalism and his specific Christianity becomes initially apparent. This tension, if not contradiction, rests on an ambiguity or subtlety in his philosophical theology which Tillich himself may never have fully resolved. At its root, this tension pits nature against grace, a dualism Tillich's methodology of correlation sought to overcome in principle. His methodology of correlation rests on his rejection of supernaturalism as dualistic and of a naturalism divested of the divine as superficial and truncating. (Tillich 1951: 64–66) Rather the honest theologian works to correlate the human quest for the essential evident in the questions of each cultural situation with the response found in the Christian revelation. Against the heteronomy of a Christ imposed on history from beyond and the autonomy of a Christ reduced to the confines of reason, Tillich introduces the conception of a theonomous Christ who would meet humanity's deepest internal drive, that to the recovery of its essential humanity, from within the dynamics of this drive itself.

Tillich's notion of a theonomous Christ would demand that, on the one hand, the Christ event met existential humanity's native and natural demand for the recovery of its essence and, on the other, remained a paradox. (Tillich 1957a: 90–94) Tillich's understanding of the Christ event as a paradox elevates it to the level of grace because the event contradicted humanity's prior collective experience, namely, that the recovery of its sought for essence had escaped historical realization and indeed, as Tillich, the Christian, would have it, lay beyond humanity's ability to confer upon itself. (Tillich 1957a: 92) Tillich's picture of Christ is thus painted against the background of a residually hopeful yet despairing humanity; hopeful, because it could never erase the memory of its essential nature from its consciousness, despairing because it could never attain it. (Tillich 1957a: 92) Thus the actualization in existence of essential humanity, remains itself a tortured concept. On the one hand it is historically "expected", even demanded by existential human nature itself. (Tillich 1957a: 93) Yet in its happening it is unforced, an act of grace which at the same time responds to humanity's deepest longing. In effect, essential humanity appears in history as both wholly demanded and as a graceful surprise.

The resolution of this tension in Tillich's understanding of the Christ event would rest on the validation of the universality of Tillich's religious naturalism as supportive of all manifestations of the essential in history. Such validation would simultaneously confer a humanizing relativity on each such manifestation. From this perspective Tillich's valuable contribution to the understanding of religion as humanity's universal search for its essential nature would confirm religion itself as inescapably human. Humanity would come to be seen as unable to divest itself of its religious nature and aspiration. As seen in Chapter 2, this position would give a certain priority to Tillich's theological anthropology over his Christology. His theological anthropology is universal; his Christology remains singular. The basic claim his Christology makes is that the universal, humanity's eros for the essential, is realized in a particular historical event. Tillich's theological anthropology thus lays a humanizing basis for his Christology by showing the Christ event as meeting humanity's demand for the essential in history. Yet his Christology cannot disguise the fact that it claims a universal human concern finds final and exhaustive realization in one historical instance or definitive *kairos*. In his Christology, then, Tillich's universalism cedes to the particular and, as he was to admit in his very late work, to the provincialism that would equate the biblical picture of Christ with the picture of essential manhood understood to complete all other pictures and to which other pictures point.

Yet even Tillich's early Christology did not need to go this way. His broader theology has within it the resources to identify the universal dynamics of the human religious impulse, the recovery of the essential in existence, and to frame the Christ event within this context as one significant, but not final, realization of this impulse. If the singularity of his Christology were to submit to his universalism both would be enhanced. His universalism would identify in humanity both the possibility of and need for the Christ event and so provide a humane basis for its reception. The Christ event itself would remain an epoch making, but hardly exhaustive, actualization of essential humanity in history for those who were grasped by its symbolism. Such a Christology could then candidly acknowledge that other actualizations were equally efficacious and transformative for those grasped by them in different cultural contexts. Tillich's early commitment to Christianity as a "final revelation" (Tillich 1951: 137) would cede to the appreciation of the diversity of symbolic and mythical portraits of essential humanity throughout "the history of the human race". (Tillich 1966: 93) The reality of humanity's religious nature would be firmly secured and the Christian version of "essential humanity" respected, even cherished, as its claim to universal validity was corroded by the very universality of the aspiration it allegedly uniquely satisfied.

Tillich's panentheism as the key to a theonomous Christology

Tillich grounds the universal possibility and necessity of humanity's religious experience on its purely natural consciousness that in existence it is removed from, though experientially continuous with, its essence. (Tillich 1957a: 31) Tillich, the Christian, locates this essence, as the basis of both the universal ideas and the individual's "essential self", in the *Logos*, the eternal expression of the abyss dimension of Trinity. (Tillich 1951: 158; 1963: 235) The notion of the divine *Logos* is itself hardly confined to Christianity. Yet whether the *Logos* is understood in its Christian variant or not, Tillich can argue, on the basis of the Christian version, that existential humanity is aware of its plight and seeks to recover in existence its unity with its pristine essence primordially expressed in the *Logos*. For Tillich the essential always carries the inference of participation or ontological inhesion in the divine in varying degrees of intensity ranging from prehistory, through history to post-history. (Tillich 1951: 245; 1963: 421) Without humanity's consciousness of its ontological inhesion in and removal from the divine, Tillich's notion not only of religion itself, but also of creation, fall, redemption and history are rendered unintelligible in the context of their precise meaning in his *Systematics*. But such inhesion of the existent in the essential is also the basis of his late admission of pan-en-theism. (Tillich 1963: 421) To tie these strands together, then, Tillich's notions of panentheism, theonomy and the essential are but three faces of the underlying and unifying notion of the inhesion of the created totality in the divine, an inhesion made self-conscious in humanity.

Consequently, establishing the link between the essential, the theonomous and panentheism is of great importance in the construction of a theonomous and relativistic Christology able to honor humanity's universal religious nature and the picture of Christ as significant to it but not a cumulatively exhaustive expression of it. Why is this so? It is so because the dynamic of Tillich's relation of the essential to the existential would prompt the suspicion that humanity's universal aspiration toward the essential would with difficulty be fully met in a single historical instance. And why is this so? It is so because the infinite fecundity of the ground of the essential would outstrip, in its very fecundity, its historical concretions in a process that could neither be denied nor completed in finitude.

Let us examine this claim more closely through Tillich's epistemology and ontology of theonomy. Theonomy identifies a consciousness that is distinguished from both autonomy and heteronomy. In his most succinct formulation Tillich states, theonomy "means autonomous reason united with its own depth". (Tillich 1951: 85) Theonomy is first distinguished from heteronomy. Theonomy places access to divinity within humanity at that point at which the two coincide beyond their estrangement in existence, a point Tillich terms "the depth of reason". (Tillich 1951: 79–81) Heteronomy places divinity wholly beyond the human so that the only possible relation between them is external and takes the form of the imposition of the divine on the human and human reason from without. Because heteronomy denies the panentheistic point of coincidence between the divine and the human it can have nothing in common with theonomy. Theonomy and heteronomy thus remain mutually exclusive and incompatible.

This is not the case with autonomy. Autonomy describes the legitimate structure and dynamics of the human mind working out of its natural conscious resources. Autonomous reason and consciousness came to the fore in the Enlightenment. There and since it has waged a largely victorious battle against heteronomous conceptions of divinity rightfully perceived as hostile to the dignity of the human mind and occasionally to human rights when religious heteronomy served or serves as the warrant for political repression. (Tillich 1951: 148) Tillich's conception of theonomy is an effort to overcome the hostility that must exist between heteronomy and autonomy and to heal the wounds to the Western collective psyche left by their historical battle. His basic strategy here is to show to autonomous consciousness that it is naturally and organically continuous with its divine depths, the depths of reason, that common ground from which both divine and human reason derive and the sole basis of a non-demonic approach of the divine to the human. This natural continuity of autonomous reason with the depth of reason enables Tillich to contend that humanity's religious consciousness derives from its own depths and so is not an extraneous imposition on the mind. Rather religious experience and expression greatly enhance the mind through myth and cult, the only language and activity, through which the depths of reason can be expressed and enacted by autonomous reason when actualized in existence. Tillich will concede to the Enlightenment that "There should be neither myth nor cult." (Tillich 1951: 80) There should be neither because in existence reason is estranged from its depths whose impact it can never wholly evade nor express with the acuity of a relatively superficial rational autonomy so ambiguously related to its depths. And yet the emergence of these depths into consciousness in the religious and revelatory experience could greatly enhance autonomous reason without violating its autonomy if the expression of this experience were realized to be always symbolic, never literal, and to be mediated to consciousness from its own depths.

Just as he contends that, in its depths, reason is at one with the divine, Tillich will bluntly state that "human nature is essentially theonomous" (Tillich 1963: 250) and mean by this statement much the same thing. In this latter formulation he means that in its essential nature humanity in existence consciously and immediately participates in the being of the divine and is consciously driven by this participation to become ever more deeply transfused by the divine in which it natively inheres. In fact in passages where he structures his Christology on theonomy, Tillich adds to his basic description of Christ as essential humanity the note that such humanity remained wholly transparent to the ground of being in every existential moment of its life. (Tillich 1951: 147) Thus Tillich's ontology of essential humanity and his epistemology of the depth of reason intersect with his conception of theonomy and make humanity naturally and universally religious because endowed with a point of identity with the divine as the basis of religious experience and the source of humanity's universal ultimate concern. Without this native concern for the recovery of its essential and theonomous nature writes Tillich, "The question of a final revelation could not have been asked; therefore, the answer could not have been given." (Tillich 1951: 139)

All of these categories and the experience they describe are naturally human. As a result when Tillich describes a theonomous Christology as the total actualization of humanity's transparency to its depths, he is describing a potential that is imbedded in human nature itself and so seeks its realization in the human with the same kind of necessity that drives all human potential. Consequently Tillich's Christ stands as a symbol of the fulfillment of humanity's deepest natural concern fully satisfying its most powerful eros or drive. But here again the conflict between the uniqueness of Christ and universal human aspiration becomes sorely obvious. The conflict is even intensified by the compelling picture Tillich paints of the religious concern and drive so deeply imbedded in existential human nature itself. Tillich's very success in his description of human nature universally seeking its essential truth, admittedly diminished or maimed though never absent in existence, prompts again a well-founded expectation of and search for the essential equally manifest in individuals, times and cultures beyond the Christian realm.

This expectation strongly suggesting the necessity of variant pictures of essential humanity throughout the history of humanity's experience of its depths rests, no doubt, on Tillich's well-argued religious naturalism as it lays the basis for his conception of the theonomous Christ. The immense benefits of such naturalism would enable the specific biblical picture of Christian theonomy to be revered for its contribution to the formation of Western culture even as the particularity of the Christ event would be open to and expect, if not demand, variant manifestations beyond the culture for which it has and continues to serve as one image of essential humanity. In the end Tillich's picture of the theonomous Christ could afford to forgo claims to finality and exclusivity in an attitude of respect for various historical theonomies whose symbols could then serve to amplify, critique, and so deepen the appreciation of the specifically Christian variant. Such relativism or pluralism could serve to enhance rather than corrode the power of the picture of Christ as essentially human even as it would imbue that picture with a liberating relativity.

The psychological circularity of faith in the figure of Christ

In the nineteenth century religion came to understand itself through sociology and in the twentieth century through psychology. Tillich's understanding of faith and faith in Christ are profoundly psychological. His conception of faith as ultimate concern stands in admitted continuity with Schleiermacher's "feeling of unconditional dependence". (Tillich 1957b: 38, 39) Both Tillich's and Schleiermacher's approaches to faith ground the search for the essential on a compelling psychological analysis of human finitude and, with Tillich, of the anxiety such finitude universally generates. A psychological analysis of Tillich's correlation of Christ with the ultimate concern of those who stand within the theological circle reveals that the biblical picture of Christ so grasps those grasped by it that their concern for the essential is realized in the transformation the picture works on those it grasps. (Tillich 1951: 10, 11) Tillich does not step back from the circularity of this argument even though it risks the comparison of the biblical picture of Christ to a religious version of the Rorschach Experiment because the biblical picture of Christ bears the essential only for those who see the essential in it. Yet Tillich is correct in the inescapability he attributes to this circularity in matters of theological and philosophical commitment. Whatever other agencies may be involved, philosophical and theological commitments are always linked to an "a priori of experience and valuation". (Tillich 1951: 8) Such experience and valuation can be linked to the deeper psychological power of humanity's ultimate concern which urges commitment through their native instinct for the essential whenever and wherever it appears in history. At this point Tillich's understanding of the allure the essential carries with it corresponds to Jung's understanding of the archetypal power of the self when it manifests through the numinous impact it exerts on consciousness not infrequently through the power of the dream individually and of revelation collectively.

However, when Tillich goes on to attribute "uniqueness and universal validity" (Tillich 1951: 10) to the object of the specifically Christian ultimate concern, namely, to the Christ event as the Christian theologian's sole legitimate ultimate concern, he effectively negates or reduces to the status of the preliminary other expressions of ultimacy which, as it turns out, are to find their completion in the Christian variant toward which "they are unconsciously driven". (Tillich 1963: 154) He does this in spite of the fact that there is no need within the context of his own theology and Christology for such triumphalism, today increasingly viewed as religiously repulsive and socially dangerous. For his own ontology, epistemology and their attendant but largely unacknowledged depth psychology are well equipped to undermine all forms of religious and theological imperialism while honoring Christianity as one among many valid pictures of the essential expressed in existence. Tillich's theology can perform this task because of the universal sentiment endemic to the ontology and epistemology on which his Christology rests. This universal sentiment prompts the question: if Tillich's depiction of humanity's deepest plight and dynamic as its conscious removal from and drive toward the essential is valid, would one not expect a plethora of appearances of the essential in existence, all with their peculiar salvific efficacy for those grasped by them? The answer to this question is clearly in the affirmative and prompts the further question: what is there about the human religious mind that prompts it to defeat a true universalism by attributing universal meaning to the singular thus endowing the latter with its inhuman imperialism?

If this question is addressed philosophically it asks: is there something about the allure of the essential, the absolute, or the unconditioned that so possesses the mind that the mind so possessed cannot tolerate variant, even contradictory, expressions of it? If the question is addressed religiously it asks: is there something in the religious impulse that leads to the assertion that divinity's commerce with humanity has reached a revelatory culmination in one's own tradition to which all others are ordered? Is this element in religion most evident, for instance, in the Joannine Christ's proclamation that he is the way the truth and the life taken by the Christian tradition to mean the only access to the divine? (John 14: 5–7) And are such exhaustive claims a peculiarly specific pathology of the competing monotheisms where they are most in evidence? Again if the question is addressed psychologically it asks: is there anything in the human psyche, which Tillich links so closely to his conception of ultimate concern, that demands the fulfillment of such concern in a consciousness that completes all other consciousness and toward which all consciousness strives? Where a psychology such as Jung's might indeed suggest that there is an inborn movement to such completeness, in individual and society, such a psychology would usually have the grace to concede that such states of completion can only be approximated never residually attained in actual life and, furthermore, lend themselves to multiple expressions. (Dourley 2003)

These questions and their implied reservations make of the contention that any depiction of an exhaustively realized essential humanity toward which all other such manifestations tend an overstatement and bring into question its underlying motivation. An examination of their motivation leads to the suspicion that such claims are prompted by a pathological fear of doubt and a lust for an inhuman certitude which should be countered by Tillich's contention that doubt is not only compatible with faith but also a living dimension of it. (Tillich 1951: 10) The pathology of the lust for an inhuman certitude is intensified only when such revelation serves as the bonding power for national, political and economic communities. Given the now recognizable danger of competing religions grounding conflicting civilizations, a much chastened and enlightened contemporary consciousness seems prepared to move from the position that such religious truth shall set us free to the current conviction that the doubt will set us freer and certainly make us safer.

It cannot be questioned that Tillich makes a stirring appeal for the supremacy of the Christian revelation through his synthesis of the sacramental with the iconoclastic, a synthesis difficult to surpass. His understanding of the Protestant principle would rightly forbid the equation of the sacramental appearance of the essential with that through which it appears and so would demand the ability of the truly ultimate to survive the annihilation of its finite medium. For Tillich this interplay of the universally holy with the negation of its particular medium becomes the meaning of the Cross and the basis of Christian claims for supremacy in its radical iconoclasm. (Tillich 1963: 154) Yet in the final analysis cannot and has not every valid appearance of the essential spirit of humanity survived the elimination of its particularity, most obviously in the religious, philosophical and political domains? Judaism has survived two millennia of biblically based Christian opposition culminating in the Holocaust. Islam and the Eastern religions have survived the contempt of the West, that reality Said describes as "Orientalism". Both Plato and Aristotle have survived their mutual opposition reenacted throughout history. Democracy appears capable of surviving its current marriage to capitalism and militarism. Socialism has already outlived Marx and Stalin. Tillich would better serve the genius of his own spirit were he to forgo the contention that Christianity has some peculiar purchase on the ability to survive the destruction of its originating and pristine medium and show, instead, how this capacity attaches to all truly archetypal manifestation in whatever dimension of the human spirit such manifestation occurs. To do so would be the first step toward peace in the interface of such manifestations.

The religions as never final nor forgettable

The religious bonding of disparate communities around the symbols of the ultimate that inform and differentiate each one is currently the greatest single threat to the survival of the species. The threat these communities pose derives its power from the lethal synergy of religious, national and ethnic bonding united with military power as in contemporary forms of theocracy and democracy. This deadly combination can occasionally parade as a purely secular even scientific position but the more evasive absolutes informing such commitments are as constrictive and dangerous as the more easily identifiable bonds of visible institutional religion, always much more at home with traditional theocratic power. When these religiously grounded cultures meet in geographical contiguity or share common geography they produce the "fault lines" Huntington identifies in his work, *The Clash of Civilizations*. (Huntington 1996; Dourley 2004a, 2006) The most distinct characteristic of the "fault lines" is the elevating body counts they inspire historically and currently. As it becomes increasingly apparent that so called secular realities such as democracy, capitalism and globalization are not concepts but symbols imposed by military missionaries, who not infrequently unite a specifically religious with a political commitment, the conclusion that all current wars are religious can no longer be avoided.

Foundational themes in Tillich point to the basis of the problem and could contribute to its alleviation. He clearly realized that cultures ultimately rested on their religious ultimates whether expressed in religious or non-religious form. This is the insight informing Tillich's terse but penetrating statement, "religion is the substance of culture: culture the form of religion". (Tillich 1963: 248) However, Tillich did not see the shadow side of this position revealed in current geopolitical reflections such as Huntington's. Tillich did not see that the same religious bonding that unites individual cultures can serve to lower the individual consciousness and so moral responsibility of its members and lead them to demonize the differently bonded. (Dourley 2003: 135–139) Then the only religious and political options left toward the differently bonded are to convert or to kill the other, that is, to turn the other into oneself or to malign their bonding absolute and the community it bonds as evil because they stand as a living contradiction to one's own. This scenario is currently most evident in the war in Iraq where religiously bonded powers face each other. There is little to choose between the fundamentalism informing the Taliban and that informing the religiosity of its opponent. The war is effectively between the Islamic and Christian democratic Taliban. Neither can transcend their faith induced unconsciousness even as the carnage mounts.

To deal with the threat to humanity posed by the religious substance of diverse cultures in conflict with each other, one must go beyond Tillich's helpful insight that all cultures are, under whatever guise, religiously bonded. To prevent the absolute at the heart of each culture from acting out its natural enmity for all other absolute cultural expressions other foundational themes in Tillich's thought must be brought into play. The first is the identification of the origin and dynamic of humanity's universal and ineradicable religious nature within human nature itself. The second is the closely related idea of theonomy as the basis of the marriage of the mind or reason with its natural religious depths. These two foundational themes in Tillich's theology working in tandem could serve to ground the understanding of all expressions of ultimacy including that of the Christ figure as expressions of the autonomous mind wedded to its depth, a depth common to all of humanity. Once this common ground and origin of the religions was to be identified in the human it would be harder to kill in the name of specific religions or political persuasions and easier to appreciate, even embrace their differences. Such understanding would enable a universal appreciation of all symbolic expression while denying finality to any. Tillich was himself to endorse this position or one similar to it in his last public lecture. (Tillich 1966)

In that lecture the spirit of Tillich's religious naturalism and universalism, implicit in his conception of theonomy throughout his corpus, comes finally to the fore and settles the tension between the universal religious impulse and its singular concretions in favour of a relativizing universality. For the dynamics of theonomy demand that the religious depths of the human drive toward conscious expression through religious experience and the symbols and myths to which such experience gives rise and from which the historical religions derive. Tillich will indeed concede that the inner theonomous power which births the Gods and so the religions in human consciousness stands ever vulnerable to the threat of existential degeneration into heteronomy and that a fully theonomous humanity remains ever an eschatological notion susceptible to only fragmentary realization within history. (Tillich 1951: 148) Nevertheless, it is only humanity's universal theonomous substrate that enables and demands humanity's experience of divinity at all. This universal ground and its drive to consciousness frustrates the possibility of humanity's extirpation of the memory of the divine from its depths even as it functions to forbid the attribution of finality to any and every divinity and revelation.

If, then, the theonomous truly rests on that point in humanity where the divine and the human coincide then the theonomous would partake of the inexhaustible fecundity of the divine. As suggested above, this fecundity itself would forbid its exhaustion in any single historical concretion. Such fecundity as the basis of finitude itself would be inexhaustible in finitude. Each one of its expressions would be treasured. None would claim finality. Both the hope and the claim for such exhaustive finality would come to be seen as at least premature, a serious threat to the human future. The moral status of such claims would be seriously questioned in a religiously maturing humanity. The connection, which Tillich could never make, between the final revelation and the final solution, could be extended to all such absolute claims in whatever area of the human spirit they are likely to arise. Such corrosiveness would be a major contribution to guaranteeing the future of humanity though Tillich was to put this corrosiveness much more positively in his last major paper. There he seems finally to have capitulated to the universalism operative from the outset and throughout in his understanding of the divine–human relation. The late triumph of the universal was at the cost of attributing an exclusive or cumulative universality to the singular or particular in history. In the end his theological anthropology overrode without negating his Christology. It did this when he conceded that the future study of religion, by theologian or religionist, need not rest on a definitive historical *kairos*, the defining appearance of the essential in existence, and that the future study of religion would turn to the study of other like events and their symbols. (Tillich 1966: 81, 89)

In effect the late Tillich is here contributing to a surpassing myth that could conceive of religious differentiation among cultures contributing to mutual appreciation rather than conflict. Such a myth would undermine Huntington's grim but realistic analysis that religion as the substance of culture can only serve the self-interests of the culture for whom it provides the substance. Tillich's universalism would prevent religion as it informs culture from taking on diverse forms of Huntington's disease. The key to the new myth offering humanity its future rests on the recognition of the universal divine ground of humanity as the source of all its diverse religious expressions. As this universal sense develops, often in the face of fundamentalist intransigence in specific religions, each religious manifestation of the essential would be treasured even as it was made relative. Such a saving relativity would extend to the image of Christ. The road to such universal compassion may well be the current cross that would demand the death of humanity's adolescent religiosity, especially that of the monotheistic theisms, to a resurrected consciousness able and willing to deepen the appropriation of its own cherished religious symbols through the appreciation of others in a process without a completion or even the hope for one in human history. This new mythic consciousness is the substance of Tillich's final appeal to "an openness to spiritual freedom both from one's own foundation and for one's own foundation". (Tillich 1966: 94)

Chapter 4

Tillich on Boehme
A restrained embrace*

Introduction and problematic

Tillich's late revisioning of the future of theology and the study of religion around the symbol systems of the religions of the world strongly suggests that these symbols have a common generative source in the human. All of them become legitimate expressions of the essential, humanity's natural divine core seeking self-manifestation in human consciousness. In Tillich's own idiom, his metaphysics and anthropology identify this source as the "ground of being" and "depth of reason". The broadening of the scope of religious studies beyond the confines of specific religions would serve to illuminate the nature of this common source through the variety of its expressions in human history and religion. Each significant expression would be seen as an effort of the common source to attain a fuller entrance into human consciousness in the broadening of such consciousness and in the realization of its own potential made conscious in human consciousness. This sense of a common human origin of the diverse religions serves as an initial affinity with Jung's understanding of the archetypal dimension of the psyche. For Jung this dimension of the psyche generates religious experience and so the religions. This same sense of the depth dimension of human interiority drew both Tillich and Jung to certain representatives of the Western mystical tradition and to mystical experience itself as the most primordial form of religious experience. Specifically both Tillich and Jung were influenced by Jacob Boehme (1575–1624) as by a common spiritual ancestor and to differing degrees allowed Boehme major entry to their thought.

In his last major statement Tillich broadened his Christian vision by denying the necessity of assuming that a definitive manifestation of the ultimate had occurred in history. In doing so he freed Christian self-understanding to accept a relative position in a religiously pluralistic world. How does this freedom relate to mystical experience? It does so through a clear recognition of

---

* A version of this chapter appeared as "Jacob Boehme and Paul Tillich on Trinity and God: Similarities and Differences", *Religious Studies*, 31, 4, 1995, 429–445. *Religious Studies* is edited by Peter Byrne and published by Cambridge University Press.

Tillich's early understanding of the "mystical a priori" as the basis of religious experience itself. The earlier Tillich would identify "a mystical a priori" grounded in "the point of identity" between the "experiencing subject" and the religious ultimate. This is the point in the human which precedes the split into subject–object categories even in the relation of the divine to the human. (Tillich 1951: 9) Effectively this experienced point of identity between the divine and the human grounds Tillich's own philosophy of religion. For Tillich this point of identity is the substance of the ontological argument, humanity's natural sense of God. (Tillich 1951: 206) It is the basis of his own conviction that the quest for the divine is both possible and necessary because humanity's latent sense of the divine empowers and demands the further search for the divine. "God can never be reached if he is the *object* of a question and not its *basis*." (Tillich 1959b: 13) But in his earlier work Tillich will argue that the mystical a priori cedes to the "criterion of the Christian message" and so is constricted by the universal claims of Christian particularity. (Tillich 1951: 9, 10) However, Tillich's late relativizing of Christianity's universalistic claims would deny it the right to subsume the mystical a priori as somehow completed or given a surpassing definition in Christianity. Rather Christianity could come to see itself as one expression of the mystical a priori which generates all religious experience. This revisioning would achieve two effects. It would restore the mystical to a place of precedence as the primordial source of religious experience. It would also identify the psychological basis of this experience as an expression of that human depth in which not only the divine and the human but also the psychological and religious coincide.

For both Tillich and Jung this reading of the mystical a priori rests on variants of the contention that divinity and humanity are engaged in an inescapable mutuality whose dynamic is the basis of the movement and meaning of individual biography and collective history. Their affinity in this matter makes of Tillich's theology an in-depth psychology and of Jung's psychology a theology of the depths. The connecting link is the psychological immediacy of religious and mystical experience. Jacob Boehme anticipated them both in their implication that divinity and humanity confer a mutual completion on each other through the historical process itself. Tillich was drawn to Boehme's mystical thought because it throbbed with a sense not only of God but also of a Trinitarian God, a pulsating unity of opposites, deeply involved in the unfolding of history as history moved to both individual and collective integration of divinity's eternally unresolved opposites in the human. Jung also was deeply influenced by Boehme and did not hesitate to draw out the more far reaching conclusions of Boehme's mysticism forbidden to Tillich through the latter's commitment, at least earlier in his career, to a theology in the service of Christianity. Jung in his late writings, especially in his "Answer to Job", is closer to Boehme's more radical experience that divinity is forced to create humanity to resolve in historical human consciousness the conflict that remained eternally unperceived and unresolved in the divine life itself. (Jung

1969a) We will return later in the work to this tension between Tillich and Jung in their reception of Boehme after a prior examination of Tillich's relationship to Boehme's experience.

Paul Tillich frequently identified Jacob Boehme as a significant influence on his own theology as did those commenting on Tillich's theological antecedents. (Tillich 1951: 62 note 19, 141, 189, 232, 246; 1957c: 7, 8; Braaten 1967: xxi, xxix) The influence is most evident in Tillich's insistence on the experiential nature of theology built on humanity's immediate and natural experience of the deeper movements of divine life as the ground of human life. (Tillich 1951: 40–445) His insistence on the experiential basis of theology touches all of Tillich's work but, in affinity with Boehme, is particularly evident in his treatment of humanity's experience of Trinity. Tillich considers humanity's native experience of Trinity as latent in humanity's natural experience of God and so as the humanizing basis of the fuller revelation of the specifically Christian conception of Trinity. (Tillich 1951: 250; 1963: 283) The same experiential basis of his theology is evident in Tillich's understanding of human estrangement, emerging unforced from his understanding of creation and fall as two aspects of the same ontological and psychological event, namely, the universally sensed remove of existential humanity from its divinely grounded essence worked through the universal human will to independent existence. (Tillich 1957a: 44) In these theological motifs Tillich both appropriates and evades Boehme's suggestion that creation was necessary in divinity's attainment of self-consciousness in the human, and that there could be no creation without evil since the latter was present in God and so destined to be expressed in the divine emanation. The foundational role of the experiential is again to the fore in his theology of history and eschatology through his depiction of the culmination of the human longing for God in the mutual eternal bliss of divinity and humanity to whose content the essentially human contributes. (Tillich 1963: 442) This theme is continuous with Boehme's conviction that only human consciousness can perceive and serve the reconciliation of the eternally unresolved divine conflict. The late Tillich came to understand the eternal preservation of this reconciliation to be the substance of divine and human fulfillment.

At issue in these matters is nothing less than the foundational paradigm of the divine–human relation running throughout Tillich's entire system. The unmistakable affinity between Tillich and Boehme on the foregoing points brings up the question of how far Tillich in the twentieth century can embrace the totality of Boehme's experience in the fifteenth and sixteenth. When both are read closely it is difficult to escape the conclusion that Tillich's appropriation of Boehme is extensive and enriching, but, in the end, falls short of the central assertion Boehme makes in the expression of his mystical experience. That assertion is that a deity unable to unite its own conflictual opposites in eternity created humanity out of necessity in order to perceive and resolve in human historical consciousness the self-contradiction it could neither perceive nor resolve in its own. Boehme's core experience makes of human historical consciousness the sole theater in which the mutual redemption of divinity and humanity, now seen as two aspects of the same process, is played out. The question raised by this critical comparison is this. Can Tillich or any orthodox theologian, even with Tillich's genius for political theology and theology of culture, give to creation and history the same value and urgency as does Boehme through the intimacy he establishes between divine need and its satiation in the history of the unfolding of human consciousness? For, if the symbol of Trinity points to the definitive resolution of God's conflict in eternity, does not such eternal self-sufficiency reduce history to an afterthought, a footnote to a drama long since decided in principle in eternity? Does a divine life process characterized by the reconciliation of its opposites in Trinitarian completion simply offer to the human some participation in this unity eternally achieved as much of Tillich would have it? Or does divinity create to achieve in its creature the unification of life's opposites it could not find in its own? This discussion also raises the question as to whether or not certain moderns like Jung are closer to Boehme's intuition when they depict human consciousness as the locus in which divinity achieves the integration it lacks in isolation from the finite consciousness it authors.

Boehme and Eckhart in context

To grasp fully Boehme's specific contribution to the development of Western religion and culture it is helpful to relate his thought to that of Meister Eckhart, another major influence on Jung and to some extent on Tillich, in order to understand how Boehme shares, but goes beyond, the experience of his mystical predecessor. Eckhart, whom Tillich calls the "the most important representative of German mysticism", died during his trial for heresy in Avignon in 1328. (Tillich 1968: 201) Boehme died in 1624 and yet, to a point, both men shared similar experiences and expression of those experiences. What they hold in common prior to their differences is an experience of what contemporary scholarship calls a union of indistinction (*unio indistinctionis*) with the divine in which all difference between their human being and the being of the divine is annihilated. (McGinn 1998: 216–218) From this moment both imply a return to a more pedestrian presence in and to the world and yet a presence greatly enhanced by what they have undergone. Both share this cycle. Yet Boehme gives to the moment of return a valence beyond that of Eckhart but closer to modernity.

More recent Eckhart scholarship identifies two discrete and possibly sequential moments in his experience. (Schurmann 1978: 163) The initial birth of God in his soul (*Gottesgeburt*) is somehow related to an even deeper movement into divinity, the breakthrough (*durchbruch*) in which Eckhart identifies with the Godhead (*Gottheit*) beyond the compulsive impulse of the Trinitarian God (*Gottes*) to create. (Schurmann 1978: 114) The breakthrough is Eckhart's deepest ingression into divine life to the point of unqualified identity with it. (Caputo 1978: 106, 127–134; Schurmann 1978: 164, 165) This experience of unqualified identity with the divine lies behind Eckhart's strange prayer to God to rid him of God. Eckhart is here praying to the Godhead as the God beyond the Trinitarian God of creation (*Gottes*) to annihilate all difference between creator and creature in the interest of Eckhart's recovery of his total and natural identity with the Godhead (*Gottheit*). (Eckhart 1978: 216, 219) The enigma at the heart of Eckhart's mystical experience is this. The Godhead and identity with it recovered in the breakthrough carry no impulse to external expression or activity. (Eckhart 1947a: 148) This side of his experience grounds Eckhart's profound doctrine of resignation (*gelassenheit*) or of "letting be". On the other hand his experience of God as trinity and creator is of a God whose inner turbulence (*bullitio*) necessarily and of its own dynamic "boiled over" (*ebullitio*) into creation. (McGinn 2001: 72–74) In thus distinguishing these distinct moments and movements in the life of God, Eckhart can identify one dimension of divine life beyond any impulse to create and one which cannot resist the temptation to do so. In so doing he combines freedom from all urgency with a compulsive Hegelian necessity in his understanding of the full range of divine life. Consequently his depiction of divine life remains itself a contradiction, split between the dimension of divinity which rests in itself and creates nothing, and that subsequent dimension which creates with an urgency it cannot resist. In the end these aspects of his mystical experience defied resolution in Eckhart's own pages and at his trial. (Schurmann 1978: 159–164)

The double quaternity

In the end, one side of Eckhart's religious experience, the deepest, is of resting in a wholly undifferentiated identity with the Godhead. The other is of a consequent God driven to create a world in which every creature speaks of God but none is happy because the word of God they speak is of their otherness and so alienation from their source. (Eckhart 1978: 219) With Eckhart the fourth dimension of the divine is thus lodged in the furthest reach of divinity itself, the Godhead, which precedes and gives rise to Trinity. Only return to and identity with this dimension of the divine, however ephemeral the experience probably was in his life, alleviates the alienation involved in created consciousness itself.

Boehme lived almost three hundred years later. He too journeyed to the point of identity with God, but resolves what is never more than implicit in Eckhart by explicitly stating that this moment of identity with the primordial ground (*ungrund*) precedes but finds its completion in a movement back to "the very grossest and meanest matter of the earth", in Tillich's idiom the existential distortions and profound estrangement of this world. (Boehme 1911: v) In doing this Boehme not only makes Eckhart explicit, but also goes beyond him by arguing that the soul's return from the moment of identity with divinity contributes to the ongoing creation of divine self-consciousness in human consciousness in time. Moreover, Boehme is explicit in describing this contribution. It takes the form of an enhanced reconciliation of the eternally unresolved divine self-contradiction in the consequent consciousness of the soul thus blessed. With Boehme, in contrast to Eckhart, then, the fourth dimension of the divine becomes human historical consciousness itself where the Spirit works the unity of the warring sides of God defiant of resolution in eternity.

Thus both Eckhart and Boehme are dealing with a quaternity. For Eckhart identity with the divine lies in the Godhead as the fourth beyond the Trinity. For Boehme the fourth is human consciousness as the locus in which the divine opposites achieve whatever conscious synthesis they attain after the mind has gone beyond them to an identity with that unity from which the divine self-contradiction emerges in the inner life of both divinity and historical humanity. If the two mystics were combined they would present a double quaternity in which a moment of identity with the divine beyond Trinitarian opposites becomes the necessary prelude to the resolution of Trinitarian conflict in human consciousness as the fourth in time and history. From the perspective of a psychologically informed spirituality this double quaternity would describe a moment of the dissolution of consciousness in its divine matrix as a prelude to a heightening of divine consciousness manifest as a closer unity of opposites in the finite consciousness of the individual returning from it. The unification of divine consciousness worked through the unity of its opposites in the human would contribute to the progressive integration of humanity individually and collectively and so make the process at once both profoundly religious and psychological. In effect, in Boehme's paradigm, the difference between religious and psychological maturation in the realms of the personal and the societal would cede to a total fusion. (Dourley 2004b)

A humble and self-educated shoemaker and merchant chronically unable to give philosophical precision to the intensity of his immediate experience, Boehme's impact on the consequent development of Western religious and philosophical thought has been immense. Hegel, through Franz Von Baader, was familiar with and highly appreciative of Eckhart as Boehme's predecessor (Schurmann 1978: 245 note 111) Yet it was to Boehme that he paid the highest tribute when he wrote that in Boehme's "barbaric" mystical formulations, "philosophy of a distinctive character first emerged in Germany". (Hegel 1990: 119, 120) Indeed, some see the entire substance of Hegel's philosophy as an effort to give to Boehme's mystical perceptions, especially around the relation of eternity to time, a rational lucidity Boehme could not give to them himself. (Darby 1982: 123) If Hegel's philosophy relates the absolute or the divine to the human by showing their mutual redemption in history, then Tillich's discussion with Hegel has Boehme in the background as a common ancestor. Tillich constantly sought to show that his essentialism was not as all encompassing as Hegel's. In trying to distance himself from Hegel and the alleged hubris of his unqualified essentialism, Tillich is also stepping back from the full implications of Boehme's total experience, namely, that only in the human does the divine become self-conscious.

Tillich and Boehme on the experience of the Trinity and the function of the Spirit

Let us turn then to a comparison of Boehme and Tillich on specific points. Boehme and Tillich were both proponents of a humanity immediately aware of the divine however described. Indeed, Tillich made such native awareness the truth of the ontological argument. For Tillich, as seen above, the onto- logical argument was neither an argument nor a proof but a simple docu- mentation of a psychological fact. The psychological fact was that of the universal human quest in finitude for what Tillich will describe variously as "the absolute", or "the unconditioned", that is, for God as the universal depth of the individual's reason and as the ground of individual and totality. (Tillich 1951: 205, 206) However, Tillich insists that the referent of the onto- logical argument, the psychological experience on which it rests, is not static nor dead but alive and that life, divine and human, is always of opposites in tension. In this position the influence of Boehme is central. For when Tillich describes the divinity of which humanity is naturally aware, it is a divinity alive with potentially conflicted opposites. (Tillich 1951: 241–244) What Tillich is doing here is really recasting the ontological argument in psychological terms and affirming that humanity's experience of God is universal, immediate and points to a God whose opposites are united in and by Spirit eternally in the divine life as the ultimate resource for their integration in human life. Here Tillich joins Boehme in "the use of psychological categories for ontological purposes". (Tillich 1951: 62 note 19) In this position Tillich would share much common ground with the Jung of the "Answer to Job" who simply describes divinity as a living antinomy, though Tillich might well draw back from Jung's assertion, as he does from Boehme's, that this living antinomy can find its relief only in human consciousness. (Jung 1969a: 455, 461)

Thus in his treatments of Trinity in the first and third volumes of the *Systematic Theology* Tillich twice argues that the specifically Christian doc- trine of Trinity, elaborated over the centuries in the wake of the Christ event, has a natural basis in humanity's native "intuition" of God. (Tillich 1951: 250, 251; 1963: 283, 284) The ontological argument thus points not only to God but also to Trinity. Tillich can then go on to give near poetic descriptions of humanity's natural sense of the Trinitarian ground of human life. The first moment, highly reminiscent of Boehme's description of the Father as a living hell to which the fallen angels regressed, is a "chaos", "a burning fire", irra- tional or pre-rational, potentially demonic in isolation from the light of the

Logos, inaccessible in its magnificent seclusion, the "naked absolute" so threatening to Luther that he is alleged to have thrown his ink-well at it. (Tillich 1951: 250, 251) On the basis of his own immediate experience of this side of the divine reality Boehme would probably agree with Tillich in the latter's contention that the absence of the demonic dimension of divinity in the theology of the last centuries has produced an emasculated God robbed of its power and majesty. (Tillich 1951: 251)

The second moment of divine life is the *Logos*, the principle of divine communication and reason operative in all forms of life, divine and human. As such the *Logos* gives the preceding abyss its light just as the abyss gives to the light of *Logos* its power. (Tillich 1951: 251) At this point Tillich introduces his concept of Spirit as the third moment in divine life and the agency which unites the conflicted opposites, power and meaning, in eternity. This enables Tillich to describe Spirit as the all-encompassing and so the most adequate, because the most embracing, description of God as living. Effectively, for Tillich, to say that God is Spirit and that God is life is to say the same thing. The Spirit thus functions to work the coincidence of opposites constitutive of life divine and human. All of this is implied when Tillich writes so simply, "God *is* Spirit." (Tillich 1951: 249)

This synthesizing function of Spirit uniting all of life's opposites enables Tillich to be quite contemporary and to describe the work of the Spirit in the language of modern depth psychology. Tillich's Spirit "is as near to the creative darkness of the unconscious as he is to the critical light of cognitive reason." (Tillich 1951: 250) Similar affinities with psychologies of the unconscious have not gone unnoticed in Boehme's experience of the dark and light sides of God. (Weeks 1991: 179, 181) Indeed if Tillich's understanding of divine Trinitarian life were compared to Jung's model of the psyche, the resemblance between the relation of the dark first principle to the light of the *Logos* would bear striking affinity with Jung's conception of the relation of the unconscious to consciousness. In his own essay on the Trinity, Jung understands the symbolic relation of the Father to Son to have as its referent the relation of the unconscious to consciousness. (Jung 1969b: 148–163)

From Tillich's imagery one must conclude, then, that the war within divinity has been eternally resolved in the blessedness of the Spirit's victorious unification of eternal opposites. In the Spirit the opposites in God are beyond the "threat of dissolution". (Tillich 1951: 243) Hence divine life, intensely alive in the interplay of its polarities, rests always in their Spirit worked resolution beyond disintegration. (Tillich 1951: 247) Tensions in the divine life are there as overcome. The triumph of the Spirit in eternity becomes the basis of the saving integration of opposites in the temporal life of the individual and of humanity itself to the extent, never more than fragmentary and ambiguous, that the Spirit introduces created life into the union of opposites it has established in divine life from the outset.

In Boehme's experience the victory of the Spirit within divine life was far from so complete. As stated Boehme does describe a moment of identity with the preceding and deepest dimension of divinity, which he terms the *ungrund* and equates with the "eternal unity of God". (Boehme 1911: v) The only place in Tillich's corpus where such radical apophatic experience is approached is in his reference to "the God above the God of theism" in *The Courage To Be*. (Tillich 1952: 187) The theme of the "God beyond the God of theism" is not further elaborated in his work or in his *Systematic Theology* possibly because Tillich's logocentrism turned him away from more radical apophatic thought which would precede all form and relativize its concretions. For Boehme the divine unity or *ungrund* into which he momentarily dissolves contains all opposites as creative potential. Yet it is only in their manifestation through the Trinity and into creation beyond Trinity that they attain full differentiation and so reality. Writes Boehme on this remote but crucial difference with Tillich:

> If there were not such a desiring perceptibility, and outgoing operation of the Trinity in the eternal Unity, the Unity were but an eternal stillness, a nothing . . . there would be nothing in this world . . . there would be no world at all.
>
> (Boehme 1911: 5)

Here Boehme makes two points. First, the opposites in divine life are not united in eternity as traditional Trinitarian theology would have it. Second, divinity necessarily creates to unite in finite consciousness the opposites it could neither perceive nor unite in itself. In the dialectic Boehme then establishes on the basis of this side of his experience the *ungrund* craves for manifestation and self-realization through the Trinity and into the creature just as the creature craves for immersion in the healing nothingness of the *ungrund*. (Weeks 1991: 193)

Beyond the note of necessity he here introduces into creation, Boehme further identifies the *ungrund* as the "cause and ground of the eternal Trinity". (Boehme 1911: 2) In this passage Boehme resolves the enigma that Eckhart could posit but not resolve. Indeed the *ungrund*, Eckhart's Godhead, does precede and "cause" the Trinity and as such constitutes a deeper or deepest dimension of the divine or the psyche. Might Boehme not still argue, then, like Tillich that the opposites within divinity symbolized in Trinity come into integration in eternity as the possibility and promise of human integration in time? Boehme's experience does not allow such an option. Like Tillich he clearly identifies the opposites within divine life. Here Tillich's indebtedness to Boehme becomes obvious from Boehme's side. For Boehme the first principle of the Trinity is a dark, burning fire, masculine, astringent, and angry. This principle is equated with the hell into which the angels were cast in their opposition to the light and love of the second principle and in their implied reluctance to follow the *logos* into manifest creation. (Boheme 1909: 15, 48–50)

Boehme attributes to this principle the characteristic of unrelated affirmation in conflict with the relational nature, the lucidity and warmth, of the second principle, the androgynous Christ figure (Stoudt 1957: 284), whom Boehme will relate to the feminine in the person of "Sophia, as the bride of Christ". (Boehme 1978: 154; Stoudt 1957: 212–217) The Christ figure so closely related to Sophia are thus imbued with a warming light in relation to the dark fire of the Father. All these powers go forth into all forms of manifest creation and most importantly the human mind. In alchemical terms, then, the Spirit is challenged to work a tincture of dark fire and warming light in uniting Father and Son in human consciousness itself. Where worked this union is effected in both divine and human life. What is worked below is also worked above.

It should be clear that Boehme's experience quite clearly does not locate the Spirit worked resolution of the divine self-contradiction within divine life understood as somehow preceding human life. Rather all of nature and human consciousness are stamped or signed with the unresolved conflict in their creative ground, a conflict only to be resolved in the creature. Only in the "*blick*" of human intuition in which God and the human jointly experience the union of their opposites does the Spirit work their syntheses, a synthesis that Tillich locates in divinity from eternity. (Stoudt 1957: 259) That this resolution is truly a victory purchased at the cost of immense human and divine suffering, now experienced as two sides of the same agony, is evident in the imagery in which Boehme wraps it. Boehme depicts the suffering undergone as the Spirit works the unity of divine opposites concurrently in human and divine consciousness as a "crack", a "shriek" and as a "flash of lightning". (Weeks 1991: 124–125) This imagery shifts the achievement of the Spirit uniting the divine opposites from eternity to time and into a very human anguish. God and humanity suffer a mutual redemption in a history and consciousness born for that purpose. In so shifting the divine–human economy, Boehme's vision compromises, if it does not undermine, the substance of Tillich's conception of Trinity, and its central affirmation of the eternal resolution of divine conflict within intra-Trinitarian life as the basis for the resolution of a conflicted humanity beyond the divine. Now the resolution takes place in human and divine consciousness concurrently.

Tillich and Boehme on freedom and necessity in creation, and the role of the human in history

Their differences in Trinitarian thought continue into more important differences in their understanding of creation, fall, and the religious dynamics of history. Boehme experiences creation as a necessity demanded by a divinity incapable of perceiving or uniting its own opposites and so needing to perceive and resolve them through their reflection in human historical consciousness. As an orthodox Christian Trinitarian, Tillich could not accept the full import of this side of Boehme's experience. The brief Tillich brings against twentieth century process theologians would extend to Boehme. Beyond the question of necessity in creation, Boehme's experience of God would be of a God in the process of real becoming and so, in Tillich's view, fated by a reliance on the human to work or fail to work an integration of divine opposites in human life that divinity could not work in its own. At any moment in the process God would never be more conscious than the highest level of consciousness attained in the evolution of religious consciousness. The early Tillich's terse rejoinder to such a conception of divinity is simple: "A conditioned God is no God." (Tillich 1951: 248)

Furthermore, Tillich's theology of creation rests on the movement of the essential into existence, a movement that confers a reality previously lacking to the essential even as the same movement universally distorts the essential in its very stepping out of its divine matrix. This enigma prompts Tillich to identify, in this egression, a point at which creation and fall coincide. (Tillich 1951: 255, 256; 1957a: 44) The fact that the essential, which Tillich grounds in the dynamics of Trinitarian life and especially in the *Logos* (Tillich 1963: 421, 422) went forth at all cloaks a latent necessity disguised as love in Tillich's theology of creation and eschatology. One is left with the impression that somehow the essential is more real in its existential expression than it was prior to its expression, much as an artist's painting is more real on the canvas than in the artist's vision even if the canvas fails to embody the artist's full inspiration. The divine and human dilemma as Tillich paints it is this; the essential is more real in existence than in its divine precedent even though the cost of its actualization through human will is its distortion. (Tillich 1957a: 44)

If Tillich were capable of the candor of either Boehme or Jung on this issue, he could simply affirm that the essential had to proceed from its source even if necessarily distorted in doing so in order to complete both creator and creature who confer joint and mutual completion on each other in the process. In fact, as we have seen, the very late Tillich did approach this position through his understanding of essentialization as contributing to the being of the divine in the post-temporal situation. Tillich uses a number of ploys to address this enigma in deference to his Christian need to affirm the unforced gratuity of creation and to avoid the obvious implication that there could be no creation without evil understood as the creative distancing of the creature from its essential self in the divine.

The first ploy is his conception of "dreaming innocence". In Tillich's usage the import of the phrase "dreaming innocence" is that the individual in willing to exist steps out from and so beyond an unqualified, though innocent and unreal, identity with one's essential truth in God. (Tillich 1957a: 33–36) In this manner does Tillich hope to show how the truth of so called "original sin" is both universal and yet always mediated through individual acts of free will understood as self-affirmation in the self-conferral of existence and so removal from the essential. (Tillich 1957a: 36) The gain of such lost innocence is real existence in embodied finitude. The loss is an unreal or premature identity with the divine. Yet memory of this moment of identity empowers the longing for the recovery of the essential, which then becomes the basis of religion universally. In this paradigm dreaming innocence has as its subject the human prior to its willing itself into existence. Boehme would reverse Tillich on this issue and make God the subject of such dreaming innocence. Creation would then describe a process in which God loses his dreaming innocence to discriminating human consciousness and in so doing discovers his conflicted nature, including the opposites of good and evil, now seeking and demanding resolution in the very human consciousness through which alone God knows himself. (Weeks 1991: 105; Walsh 1983: 84–88; Berdyaev 1958: xxv, xxix, xxx) Boehme's experience might also serve as a corrective to a second dimension of Tillich's evasive position in defense of an unforced creation potentially free of evil. This corrective would address Tillich's ploy which established the dialectical coincidence of creation and fall. Tillich reflecting on the sad fact that the movement from the essential to the existential always involves a fall away from the essential confesses that this truth is inexplicable. He describes it as a "leap" without structure (Tillich 1957a: 44), "a fact, a story to be told" (Tillich 1957a: 29), the sole instance of the specifically "irrational" in his system. (Tillich 1963: 284)

Boehme might well provide the missing rationale to the coincidence of creation and fall, one more compelling than Tillich's singular concession to the irrational throughout his entire system. Boehme's rationale for the coincidence of creation and fall would probably be as unacceptable to Tillich's orthodoxy as the implication that it is God, not the human, who loses his dreaming innocence in creation. For Boehme, true to the logic peculiar to his experience, can consistently argue that the *ungrund*, out of its eternally undifferentiated state, creates human consciousness to differentiate its own opposites in that consciousness. The coincidence of creation and fall then is given a compelling rationale though one unacceptable to Christian orthodoxy. The creation of consciousness coincides with its fallen nature because created consciousness is first to perceive and identify the reality of evil in the first principle of divine life, that is, in the unconscious, dark, and powerful but unrelated affirmation of what orthodoxy calls the "Father". In the wake of this perception humanity universally suffers the impact of the divine urgency to unite its dark or unconscious potential with the light of consciousness symbolized by Boehme as an androgynous Christ figure, a vocation that humanity can neither evade nor ever exhaustively acquit. In the logic of Boehme's experience, God would come to know itself for the first time in the human and the human would complete itself and divinity in the mutually redemptive unification of divine opposites within human historical consciousness. History thus understood could increasingly approximate but never exhaust the dynamic that drives it on, namely the unification of the inexhaustible divine antinomy in a human consciousness ever more expressive of the resolution of the conflict responsible for its birth.

The task as potential would always outstrip its realization and so be a permanent negation of religious, ethnic or political claims to have worked the completion of the process in any of the forms such claims might take. Both God and the human would be destined ever to remain works in progress. Such a God understood to be maturing in human maturation would make for a safer world. Such a God would forever negate the now lethal pretension that the mutual redemption of the divine and the human had been completed in any epoch by any community. In the story thus told, from Boehme's experience and its affinity with Jung's understanding of the psyche, God's dreaming innocence necessitates created consciousness as the single resource for the perception and resolution of divinity's latent polarities. Because of the fecundity that empowers the necessity of the creation of consciousness the process in history can neither be evaded nor completed but only approximated. This story is not "irrational" but quite reasonable in the logic of Boehme's experience that it expresses.

Tillich and Boehme on eschatology: the location and nature of blessedness

Theologies of creation and its divine motivation connect as naturally with eschatology as do origins with ends and goals. Here again the difficulties of Tillich's Trinitarian position emerge, now in the form of the question: how possibly can history and its completion in the eschaton bring anything truly new to a self-sufficient divinity whose perfect integration is worked from eternity? The most adequate element of Tillich's answer to this question is his late appropriation of Schelling's conception of essentialization, though the resources for this appropriation are present from the outset in Tillich's understanding of the native participation of the essential in the divine. The second, more profound element in his answer, lies in a sustained scrutiny of how the late Tillich came to understand the contingencies of history to contribute to the ontological wealth of Trinitarian life eternally.

Essentialization means for Tillich the return of the essential, immersed and enriched in and through historical existence, to its origin in divine life and specifically to its origin in the *Logos* in which the power of being gives primordial expression to the essences of individual and species. (Tillich 1963: 421, 422) Twice he describes this process in the history of individual and collective humanity as a line moving downward and curving through time ahead and upward in its return to its divine origin. (Tillich 1963: 400, 420) As the essential returns to its divine origin Tillich uses the poetic image of "*eternal* memory" to capture the idea that the enhancement of the essential in existence is remembered and so preserved as a real contribution to divine life. (Tillich 1963: 399) In this imagery the truth of a final post-temporal judgment becomes a disclosure situation. The only final failure would be that of having denied the essential any ingression into individual consciousness and existence in finitude. The penalty would be annihilation, but Tillich's understanding of the essential as grounded in God would seem to deny this as an ontological possibility. Rather the image of eternal memory implies that the divine retains and affirms eternally the individual's realization of the essential self in time and forgets all that was negative or non-essential in personal existential life. But it would appear that nothing of the essentialized can ever be entirely forgotten. All that has being, all that is essential, will endure because grounded in God. In Tillich's words the gates of non-being cannot prevail against it. (Tillich 1963: 415) This position grounds Tillich's qualified but ultimate option for Origen's *apokatastasis* (Tillich 1963: 416) and his own version of the containment of the macrocosm in the microcosm. What happens in the individual happens in all and what happens in all happens in the individual. If anyone is redeemed all are. (Tillich 1963: 409)

Tillich's mystical ontology is nowhere more powerfully evident than in these moving lines and themes among the last pages of his third volume of *Systematics*. Yet their power does not remove the obligation to look more closely at precisely how he understands history and processes of essentialization to contribute to the kingdom of God and eternal life in the eschaton. On closer examination he is found to be arguing that God drives the essential to actualization in existence. (Tillich 1963: 422) The resultant "creative synthesis" of the essential with the existential in its movement through time and history is preserved as the ontologically new in eternal life. (Tillich 1963: 401) Its preservation confers on the Trinity an ontological fullness and completion it would lack without this distillate of the essential realized in time and preserved in eternity.

In certain passages Tillich unequivocally identifies the realization of the essential in time as operative in every moment of current existential life and constituting the very "content of the divine blessedness". (Tillich 1963: 422) In his eschatology Tillich is even more explicit about the nature of divine blessedness than in his thought on God as Spirit. There, as seen, divine blessedness is simply the victory divinity achieves eternally in the resolution of its internal conflicting opposites. But now in his eschatology one side of Tillich shifts ground and argues that the "fight and victory" of divine blessedness were not achieved only in some primary sense in eternity as the basis of fragmentary victories in time moving to unqualified eschatological victory. Rather the victories in time become the very content of divine victory and blessedness in the eschaton. (Tillich 1963: 405) From this side of his thought history does indeed contribute radically to the fullness of divine life. In this context Tillich will explicitly deny the self-sufficient nature of divinity and revision divine life as a power both urging the realization of the essential in existential life and enhanced eternally by the contribution such essentialization makes to its eternal being. (Tillich 1963: 422) The urging of essentialization is presented as love in the creation of the free other, but, since God is realized in such love, love thus understood implies both necessity and divine self-interest.

Yet, in the end, Tillich can never bring this side of his understanding of Trinity and blessedness into harmony with his orthodox defense of the impassibility of God. First sensed in his theology of creation in his rejection of process theology and its God fated by real becoming, his denial of a God creating to be completed in history reappears in his eschatology. Here it takes the form of his rejection of the patripassian heresy that the Father suffered in the Son or, by extension in his own idiom, that God suffers in suffering humanity undergoing processes of essentialization. (Tillich 1963: 404) In his doctrine of creation a Trinity complete in itself nevertheless creates beyond itself a human freedom that falls in the very process of its actualization. In his eschatology a Trinity that remains somehow impassible is nevertheless fulfilled in human self-realization through the contribution that such essentialization makes to the substance of the eternal divine Pleroma. Tillich never resolves these tensions if not contradictions in his theology of Trinity, Spirit, creation and eschatology.

Let us turn now to Boehme on these issues. In continuity with his thought on creation Boehme's eschatology is less tortured in terms of its own logic and so more compellingly candid in its honesty to the experience that lies behind it. In fact Boehme's depiction of creation tends to coincide with his eschatology. A God compelled to create in order to recognize and reconcile its opposites in the creature completes both itself and created consciousness in one historical process at once creative and eschatological. This vision would not easily lend itself to Tillich's image of a curve descending from heaven moving forward and upward in time in its return to God. Using linear imagery, Boehme's first line would move vertically to a total identity with the nothingness of the *ungrund* preceding a downward line into existence describing an ongoing incarnation of the divine in human consciousness wherever and to the extent such consciousness brought about and was a product of the unity of divine opposites that engendered it. In this reciprocity God and creature would progressively share the victory and blessedness of conflict resolved in this world in an ever extending and deepening sense of the divine embracing an ever wider panoply of divine manifestation in finitude. In effect each side of the polarities latent in the *ungrund* would contribute their one-sided partialities through a newly won empathy for their opposites to the eschatological unities which complete the divine and the human in the one organic process of the religious and human development of historical consciousness as compassion. This compassion would be based on the heightened consciousness that all God grounded polarity is to be resolved not exacerbated in a humanity increasingly capable of embracing the perceived opposite or contradictor.

Catholic substance and the sacramental become, then, for Boehme the presence of divinity immediately experienced in nature and mind demanding conscious resolution of its contradictions there. More recent Boehme criticism rightly describes such extended sacramentalism as making all of nature and humanity consubstantial with the divine, extending, at least potentially, the unity of the divine, the human, and the natural from its more traditional confinement in exceptional religious personalities to every life and to all that is. (Walsh 1983: 13, 21, 64) This universal extension of the consubstantial grounds a wider sensitivity for the sacred wherever it might manifest in the human and natural realms. As evidence of this more encompassing sympathy for the holy Boehme will refer to the wisdom of the "heathen" as imbued with as profound an experience of God as is Christianity. (Weeks 1991: 50) His radical sacramentalism also enables Boehme to see the Spirit powerfully at work in Jews, Turks and the newly discovered native populations of North America centuries before the current enthusiasm for North American native spirituality as imbued with a more immediate and universal sense of the sacred than is current in the presiding Christian myth. (Weeks 1991: 133, 202)

One cannot deny the presence of these deeper and more inclusive sensitivities in Tillich but, as an orthodox Trinitarian whose theology is done in the service of Christianity, these themes are denied the broader implications they have in Boehme's imagery. Without ever denying the centrality of the Christ reality, Boehme gives to it a universal status as endemic to human nature itself. In this he anticipates Jung's position that the Christ image is an image of the self but one among many images possessed by each distinct culture as its culture hero. Such universality undermines the uniqueness of the Christ event and so removes the dangers, in Boehme's time and ours, that can attach to it the status of a final revelation to which all others are understood to be somehow ordered.

The form of future religiosity: Trinity or quaternity

Among the many questions the foregoing discussion raises, the most important one is whether Tillich and orthodox Christian theology could fully appropriate Boehme's more universal sense of God's presence urging an ongoing mutual redemption of the divine and the human in history and retain their recognizable identity. A related question is this. Could the new theonomy which Tillich's theology anticipated and to which it hoped to contribute accept any real version of Boehme's quaternitarian thinking and fully embrace the proposition that the Trinity must create to become conscious in the creature as its completing fourth? In the end the gulf that cannot be overcome between Tillich and Boehme is Tillich's central conviction, perhaps modified but never abandoned even in his late eschatology, that redemptive processes describe humanity's recovery of a pre-existing balance in divine life. Against this conviction stands Boehme's experience that divinity seeks the integration it lacks in itself in the historical humanity it was driven to create for this purpose. Both are to be thanked for the contributions they have made to humanity's appreciation of its ineradicable religious nature. Paradoxically Tillich's partial but significant reliance on Boehme to revive a compelling sense of religion in contemporary culture as the precondition for the reviviscence of Christianity in its relation to culture (Tillich 1959b: 29) has produced a picture of religious humanity more compelling than his Christology and the Christianity it was meant to serve. In the end his orthodoxy forces him to draw back from Boehme's even more compelling religious sense of an unconscious and conflicted divinity imbuing humanity with the inescapable vocation of cooperating in the redemption of the divine in history.

In an age when religious and political fundamentalism inform each other and threaten humanity's survival Boehme's broader sensitivity moves to a keener and safer perception of a common yet infinite power understanding itself through a multiplicity of religious and secular absolutes each representative of some aspect of the divine. Such sensitivity would undermine in principle the possibility of a final revelation with its ever present threat of a final solution. This newer sensibility would move toward broadened hope and more encompassing compassion grounded on the conviction that the God whose nature is to manifest or reveal could never be comfortable in one such revelation and would eternally transcend whatever concrete form its manifestation took in history. This feeling for religion would, on the one hand, evade Enlightenment critiques that would deny humanity's sense of a living God or reduce its content to bleak common denominators and, on the other, appreciate but corrode the claim of any manifestation to exhaust the divine plenitude. The way Boehme unites the inescapable nature of religion with the relativizing universalism of its manifestation may gain contemporary humanity the time it now needs to find the manner of uniting its divinely grounded but warring absolutes in higher forms of consciousness and compassion. His refusal to join the religious factionalism of his day and the intractable universal sensitivity of his thought which resisted even Nazi efforts at appropriation commend him as a bearer of a wider religious sympathy than can be offered by most current corporate religious bodies. (Weeks 1991: 129, 130) Failure in moving to this higher perspective would confront the religious impulse and its oft warring concretions in competing communities with the stark realization that, if religious or political conflict were to end humanity prematurely, divinity would also be the loser.

While the aforementioned differences would appear to stand between Boehme and Tillich, at best muted or disguised in Tillich's appropriation of Boehme, there is a sentence on the second last page of the *Systematics* to which both would give total consent. Tillich writes there, "for a world which is only external to God and not also internal to Him, in the last consideration, is a divine play of no essential concern for God". (Tillich 1963: 422) Boehme would only add, "Nor for man".

Chapter 5

The Goddess, mother of the Trinity

Tillich's late suggestion*

Preamble

The discussion to this point suggests that Tillich's late appreciation of the symbol systems of the world's religions would prompt a reflection on their common origin in the source of humanity's natural religious experience. Each religion would come to view itself as a precious variant of a common font. Yet in examining Tillich's appropriation of Boehme it became evident that Tillich, the Christian theologian, could not fully accept either Boehme's moment of mystical identity with the divine beyond the Trinity or its consequence, the unification of the divine opposites, not in the Trinity, but in humanity's historical religious maturation. However, the earlier discussion has also made evident that Tillich's mind was in a state of tension and growth to the end. One area of such development was his sensitivity to the religious implications of the then developing feminist movement. This almost prophetic interest led him to look for images of the feminine in the Christian Protestant tradition. In this context he points, in his fullest treatment of the Trinity, to the ground of being, first moment of Trinitarian life, as maternal in its role of generating, supporting and drawing consciousness back to itself. (Tillich 1963: 293, 294) In this passage Tillich adumbrates a cyclical process of birth, death and resurrection in terms as psychological as theological. He also approaches the gnostic realization that the first moment of divine life could be gendered as Mother/Father or beyond both to better describe its birthing of divine and human consciousness and, indeed, every form that proceeds from its womb.

When Tillich effectively identifies this power as maternal, termed "Father" in traditional Christian thought, he would relate it closely to Jung's understanding of the Great Goddess or Mother as a personalized description of the collective unconscious itself. In doing so he relates the first moment of Trinitarian life to traditions that precede and lie outside of Christianity. For

---

* A version of this chapter appeared in R. Bulman and F. Parrella (eds) (2001) *Religion in the Millennium: Theology in the Spirit of Paul Tillich, Proceedings of the International Tillich Conference, New Harmony, Indiana, June 1999*, Macon, GA: Mercer University Press, 79–95.

the name given to this power prior to and beyond Christianity when personi-fied is that of the Great Goddess or Great Mother. She might also be described in less personal form as that creative nothingness from which all particularity proceeds. Her lack of definition as the source of all definition explains why the ages have often described her as the One, the ocean, the desert, or matter, designations betraying the mind's efforts to capture the maternal formless-ness that contains and gives birth to all form.

The Goddess, understood in this extended sense, has little to do directly with gender, feminist, or womanist issues as they are usually addressed in contemporary discussion. Rather the question of the Goddess and the revi-talized religious consciousness that would accompany her return moves to the recovery of the maternal depths of the psyche, as the origin and ultimate source of the renewal of human consciousness lost when consciousness loses touch with its roots in her. (Dourley 2006) With little need for forced extension, Tillich's late theological speculation on a more profound recovery of the feminine by Protestant Christianity and by Christianity itself opens up the possibility of the recovery of a vital apophatic theology through the recovery of the experience of self-loss in the nothing from which the all proceeds. In the context of such recovery Tillich refers to one of his foun-dational symbol/concepts, "the ground" as imbued with a "mother quality" and as "an abyss". (Tillich 1963: 294, 288) The apophatic moment would be consistent with a moment of identity with the abyss dimension of this ground as the maternal origin of all that has or can have form, that is, of all that can or does exist.

The history of the apophatic experience, most evident in the lives of the great mystics, rests on two major moments in an ongoing cycle: first, a moment of dissolution into identity with divinity in a shared nothingness beyond all distinction including that between God and creature. This recov-ered identity is a prelude to the second moment, a return and renewed com-mitment to incarnate and worldly human consciousness now reconceived as engaged in the mutual completion of divinity and humanity in history. Such an understanding of the commerce between the Goddess and humanity would respect as it surpasses the family of orthodox monotheisms in all their variants as well as central positions in Tillich's theology which, never-theless, remain the inspiration of what follows. For the recovery of the Goddess affirms a moment of identity with her in her native presence to humanity as the precondition of her incarnation in the everyday consciousness of those who return renewed from her. Both of these movements are incompatible with the world's monotheisms. The first implies a residual point of identity between the divine and the human actualized in their shared nothingness beyond distinction. The second implies that divinity itself is diminished or enhanced in finite consciousness to the extent that the Goddess becomes or fails to become self-conscious in human consciousness.

The restoration of the Goddess would thus engage both genders in the

evolution of a cosmology effecting an appreciative undermining of conceptions of the divine–human relation still prevalent in today's monotheisms
and the wider cultures they continue to inform however surreptitiously. For
the experience of the Goddess would go to a point beyond the distinction
between genders and from that point enable a more compassionate relation
between them. Indeed, the reemergence of the Goddess might well raise the
question of the core compatibility of Christianity and the monotheisms with
her. For she makes her presence felt through a human depth from which
patriarchies in their defining allegiance to wholly transcendent Gods have
excluded themselves. This depth is the depth from which she gives birth to
human consciousness and to its ineradicable sense of the divine. In Tillich's
analysis as seen, this sense of God is vested with both a sense of alienation
from God and a drive toward God in the recovery of the essentially human.
The full cycle of intercourse with the Goddess would add that as she is
consciously recovered she and divinity are redeemed in the recovery. The
prelude to her own redemptive birth in humanity redeemed is the recall of
consciousness to a moment of dissolution in herself as the nothing from
which all energy, creativity and form derive.

Tillich's late Trinitarian speculation: quaternity and the maternal feminine

The wider context within Tillich's work dealing with the theological and
psychological possibility of the recovery of the Goddess is an unlikely one. It
lies in Tillich's effort in the third volume of his *Systematic Theology* to revitalize the symbol of Trinity for contemporary Christian self-understanding.
Since the symbol of Trinity is divested of an explicitly feminine or maternal
component Tillich is led to suggest the symbol could overcome the "male–
female" split by retrieving a dimension of divinity which precedes the split.
This dimension of divinity would point to the maternal as authoring the
gender split as well as all binaries and yet hold out the possibility of getting
behind and so healing the split by going to the common ground from which
gendered opposites emerge.

In the context of his total system, Tillich's need to engage in Trinitarian
restoration is less than fully urgent because his treatment of the living God in
the first volume of his *Systematics* presents a compelling picture of God as a
seething life force alive with those primordial opposites of dark power in
union with expressive light, naturally though dimly, experienced by humanity
as a prefiguration of the more precise Christian delineation of the symbol of
Trinity. (Tillich 1951: 241–252) In this theological masterstroke, Tillich makes
humanity's native sense of the living God the experiential foundation of
Trinitarian symbolism of later dogmatic development. The discussion of the
relation of the one God to the triune God simply becomes a difference of
nuance based on their common origin in humanity's primitive, but attenuated,

experience of a living divinity. Put succinctly Tillich is arguing that the experience of a living God is an experience of a Trinitarian God. In effect, Tillich extends the experiential basis of the ontological argument beyond God, simply sensed as absolute or unconditioned, to God sensed as living and so Trinitarian. With a remarkable affinity to Jung's grounding all dogma on the archetypal, Tillich can then affirm that only humanity's presentiment or "intuition" of a living and so Trinitarian God enables the gracious reception of the Trinity of dogma by believing Christianity. (Tillich 1963: 283)

This said, Tillich makes two fruitful suggestions, or two aspects of one suggestion, in his late efforts to revitalize the symbol of Trinity not prevalent in his earlier work. First, he engages in speculative play with the possible recovery of the symbol of quaternity, which would introduce a fourth dimension into the life of the Trinity itself. (Tillich 1963: 292) Again in remarkable affinity with Eckhart and Jung's appropriation of Eckhart, Tillich suggests that the fourth could be a divinity "above" the Trinity or that the "Father" be revisioned as a common ground from which the distinct persons proceed. (Tillich 1963: 292) In short Tillich is speculating on a dimension of divinity which precedes and authors all differentiation within divinity. In his speculation on this preceding dimension of divinity Tillich goes on to search for resources within Christianity and later, specifically Protestant Christianity, "which transcend the alternative male-female and which are capable of being developed over against a one-sided male-determined symbolism". (Tillich 1963: 293) In these remarks the search for a power which precedes and gives rise to Trinitarian differentiation and the search for the basis of a maternal Christian symbol, a fourth within divinity which gives rise to all differentiation including that of gender, become the same search.

When the search for the missing fourth and the feminine within the Christian world are seen to be identical, the mystical experience of identity with that which precedes all differentiation takes on added interest and value. For those who have undergone unmediated immersion in her power, the fourth becomes the origin or mother of the consequent moments and movements within the life of God, described as Father, Son and Holy Spirit, and of the emanation of such moments into creation beyond the inner life of God. Tillich frankly admits as much when he identifies the motivation behind the recovery of the lost Christian sense of quaternity in these terms:

> One of the reasons for the trend [toward quaternity] is the possibility of distinguishing the common divine nature of the three *personae* from the three *personae* themselves, either by establishing a divinity above them or by considering the Father both as one of the three *personae* and as the common source of divinity.
>
> (Tillich 1963: 292)

Though Tillich here does not address the emanation of the Trinity into creation, his dialectic of the movement of the essential, as initially expressed in the second moment of the Trinitarian life, into creation strongly suggests the necessity of such movement to complete the Trinity in the human through the human's cyclical return to a fuller participation in its origin in the Trinity and possibly beyond it in the fourth, the maternal origin of the Trinity itself. (Dourley 1990)

This text is rich with implication when elaborated through significant examples in the history of Christian mystical experience, especially that of the thirteenth century Beguines, of Meister Eckhart in the following century, and of Jacob Boehme in the sixteenth and seventeenth centuries. These mystics will be addressed later. But even in terms of his own amplification of quaternity Tillich goes on immediately to identify this "common source of divinity", the fourth, as maternal and the furthest reach of divinity, the ground of being itself, understood here as the first principle of divine life. He explains that the symbol/concept of ground is maternal because "it points to the mother-quality of giving birth, carrying and embracing, and, at the same time, of calling back, resisting independence of the created, and swallowing it". (Tillich 1963: 293, 294) He does not complete the cycle as would Jung in describing the dangers and the rewards in the return from such potential maternal swallowing.

The experience of the ground Tillich here describes as the furthest reach of divine life resonates with humanity's wider sense of the Goddess or Great Mother, the formless power who gives rise to all form and consciousness and renews them in the cycle of their return to her womb in what may well be the primary rhythm of all living religion. The Goddess gives herself expression in her progeny and in some sense remains distinct from them as an always surpassing potential, though she is always an ontological participant in all subsequent differentiation within and beyond Trinitarian life. Tillich's compromise that the originating power of the Goddess be somehow amalgamated with the Father understood "both as one of the three *personae* and as the common source of divinity" is self-defeating. (Tillich 1963: 292) For within his own systematic thought the Father is always in polar contrast with the *Logos* even when described in impersonal terms obviously borrowed from Jacob Boehme as an abyss and dark, chaotic, burning fire. (Tillich 1951: 250, 251) Here the Father, no doubt, precedes and achieves adequate expression of his divine/demonic power in the *Logos*. But the Goddess points to a dimension of divinity that precedes and gives rise both to the dark vitalities of the paternal power and to the more reassuring light of the *Logos*, even when, as Tillich's orthodoxy would prefer, these opposites are eternally reunited within God in and by the Spirit.

In the accounts of those fully absorbed in her power, she is the fecund nothingness pregnant with all polarity and form who remains herself beyond the conflict that polarity and form induce in consciousness. Yet it is her status as mother of the Trinity that enables the Goddess to give to those who lose themselves in her, fearful though such self loss be, her own deeper empathy. Such an extended sympathy works always to reconcile the power of her latent oppositions as they become progressively manifest and active, first within divine life and then within human life and psyche as divinity's externalization of its own polarities. In this sense, she both precedes and authors the conflicts of polar consciousness and, because she lies behind them and is deeper than they are, she is the greatest resource in urging and effecting their reconciliation in conscious life. As the ground of divinity, she dwells in the depth of humanity. Movement into her womb is as accurately expressed in psychological as it is in spiritual or theological language. The cycle of reentering her womb in the renewal of life is a clear description of a foundational element in all living religions and is the base meaning of the religious symbol of death and resurrection whose repeated rhythm is also the cadence of psychological maturation.

As suggested above, the experience of the Beguines, of Meister Eckhart, and of Jacob Boehme are significant resources for the recovery of a religious sense of the Goddess in the present. Their experience is pertinent to Tillich scholarship because Jacob Boehme's influence on Tillich is self-confessed. Boehme in turn was familiar, at least indirectly, with Eckhart's thought through Eckhart's disciples, Tauler and Suso. (Stoudt 1957: 80, note 5) Eckhart, in turn, was aware of the experience of a significant group of women mystics, the Beguines, of the previous century. Tracing Tillich's affinity with these traditions serves to identify resources in his thought and in its historical lineage that would dramatically enhance his search for the restoration of the maternal and feminine to Christian symbolism.

Tillich, the Beguines, and Meister Eckhart

Meister Eckhart, who died during his heresy trial in 1328, was a noted theologian at the University of Paris, administrator in his Dominican order, and mystic. Initially his preaching and teaching along the Rhine, after the conclusion of his academic career, drew the suspicion of the Inquisition and led to his trials first in Cologne and eventually in Avignon, then the seat of the Papacy. In this period, he became conversant with the Beguine tradition of women lay mystics, Mechthild of Magdeburg (1210 – c. 1285) and Hadewijch of Antwerp, in the thirteenth century and Marguerite Porete (d. 1310) in his own. (McGinn 1994: 4; 2001: 9) The first two use the symbol of physical intercourse with a virile Christ figure as a precedent to an unqualified immersion in and identity with divinity imaged as beyond the polarity which even sexual union cannot eliminate. (Mechthild 1953: 22–25; Hadewijch 1980: 281, 282) The latter is even more radical and proclaims that unless she can identify with the nothing she cannot be the all. (Porete 1993: 129, 193)

Eckhart's theology and spiritual experience have two sequential moments in his ingression into divinity and it into him. (Caputo 1978: 127–134) In a first moment, the Word of God is born in the human soul (the *gottesgeburt*), a moment that Eckhart identifies as the experiential and thus only significant meaning of the biblical Jesus' physical conception in his mother. In this, he makes of every Christian and human who undergoes this experience the mother of God. He will ask what good God's birth in Mary is if it does not also happen in himself. (Eckhart 1947b: 3) "What is the good to me of Mary's being full of grace if I am not full also?" (Eckhart 1947c: 216) In these words, Eckhart anticipates Tillich's modern sense of both the priority of personal religious experience of the truth involved in all elements of the Christ event and the necessity of symbolic discourse in the expression of such experience even in the necessarily distanced theological reflection upon such potent immediacy. In his emphasis on the connection between the experiential assimilation of the symbolic through its reenactment in the life of the individual, Eckhart is an early precursor of Tillich's and of Jung's in their shared enmity toward the literal, the historical, and the external in matters religious, spiritual and theological. What both Tillich and Jung will insist on is the experiential recurrence in the individual of the events foundational to the biblical story. For Jung, in support of Tillich, such biblical events as, for example, creation, fall, death and resurrection are expressive of the basic movements of the human spirit and psyche toward a more vital humanity informed immediately by the symbolic power of biblical mythology. Without such experiential appropriation biblical stories of any tradition remain descriptions of past events foreign to the inner life of those who read them in the present. As such they can be obstacles rather than conduits to the recurrence in the individual of the energies that gave these stories birth initially.

The second moment in Eckhart's experience, the "breakthrough" (*durchbruch*) draws Eckhart to a dimension of divinity clearly preceding that of the Trinitarian God and culminates in his unqualified identity with the divine beyond Trinitarian vitalities and urgencies. His ingression into deity culminates in Eckhart's recovery of that point where his humanity and divinity eternally coincide beyond the ontological possibility of total severance in eternity or time, that is, prior to creation and in creation. In this divine remove, Eckhart has effectively been drawn into the Goddess as that primordial power divested of all form and resting in herself. Identity with the Goddess, thus understood, grounds Eckhart's understanding of resignation. There is for a moment no urgency in the return from her to the status of his creaturehood and any form of created agency. Resting in identity with the source of the totality yet, paradoxically, beyond the need to express or do anything, would naturally lead to that self-possession content to "let be", to the questioning of rational questioning, and so to the final question, "Why ask why?", the question at the heart of Eckhart's spirituality. The experience based confidence that one is at one with the source of all that is sustains a resignation which, given Eckhart's lifestyle and accomplishment, would be far removed from any form of lethargy or indolence. If anything such moments of rest would enable rather than impede his great creativity and the legacy he left Western civilization.

Such immersion in her and in her rest is the basis of Eckhart's paradoxical prayer in one of his more famous sermons, which no doubt won the notice of his Inquisitors: "Therefore we beg God to rid us of God". (Eckhart 1978: 216, 219) Unpacking the unusual logic of this strange prayer illumines much of his experience of what can only be called two levels of divine life. Eckhart uses different German words to get at them. *Gottes*, a masculine noun, usually refers to the Trinity as creator and so as the source of the alienation inevitably constellated between God and humanity trapped in a mutual I–Thou or subject–object split. *Gottheit*, a feminine noun, refers to the Godhead beyond the Trinity and to that aspect of divine life that seeks no expression beyond itself. (Caputo 1978: 127, 128) Herein lies the Goddess. His prayer to God to rid him of God is a prayer to the Godhead to take him back to that identity with herself, which precedes the compulsion toward expression and creation that characterizes God as Trinity and as compulsive creator.

In Eckhart's experience, the Trinity's inability to constrain or contain its inner turmoil, termed a *bullitio*, "a boiling", necessitates an *ebullitio*, a "boiling over". (McGinn 2001: 72–74) For Eckhart, in the beginning the Trinity "boiled over" into creation. Such Trinitarian creative compulsion is profoundly ambiguous. It grounds Eckhart's theology of the divine necessity to create captured in his formulation "God speaks once and for all but two things are heard." (Eckhart 1981: 148) He goes on to explain that the Father in speaking the Word within the Trinity speaks the Word beyond it. Once the Word proceeds within the divine life, its externalization into creation and all the problems of a universal alienation necessarily follow.

Such compulsive need to create relates directly to another of Eckhart's more paradoxical utterances. "When I flowed out of God all things said, there is a God. Withal this cannot make me blest, for in it I acknowledge myself a creature." (Eckhart 1947d: 219, 221) This intriguing statement anticipates two of the problems at the heart of Tillich's theology as it reflects the temper of the nineteenth and twentieth centuries. For Eckhart here anticipates Tillich's affirmation that creation and fall or estrangement "coincide" in the movement of reality beyond God. (Tillich 1951: 44) Both are saying that to be human and conscious is to sense God, even if this sense is, to some great extent, one of tragic estrangement from the source of one's essential being in God. In Jung the equivalent experience is that of the ego born from the unconscious and so removed though never severed from the source of its energies and life giving truth in the self and destined to seek their recovery.

The second modern problem that Eckhart anticipates follows directly from the coincidence of creation and fall. It is that of freeing the experience of

God and theological reflection on it from the category of subject to object. For Tillich and other moderns the relation of a subject to another subject as object describes a relationship of alienation. The relation of divinity to humanity is not the relation of two subjects objectifying each other in the relationship. To be other is to be alien. To be wholly other is to be wholly alien. Tillich worked to overcome this problem through his understanding of God as ground of being and depth of reason. In this ground creator and creature naturally share a common point of being. In its depth the mind shares a point of identity with the divine prior to and as the basis of its perception of God as other. This shared point of being between the divine and human mind is the basis of Tillich's understanding of theonomy. This point of naturally shared being is all that prevents the relation between the divine and the human from degenerating into heteronomy, that is, the invasive imposition of a foreign and divine mind and power on the rightful autonomy of the human mind and spirit. As an adamant anti-theist, Tillich consistently affirms that the noblest spiritual response to theism, even or perhaps especially to biblical theism, based as it is on the subject–object split, is atheism. (Tillich 1951: 245; 1952: 185) It is Tillich's anti-theism which drives him in his search for "the God above the God of theism". (Tillich 1952: 187) Although he uses this dramatic phrasing explicitly only in *The Courage To Be*, a theistic God, imagined as a divine subject over against a human object or as divine object over against a human subject, is a major problem and concern he hoped to defeat throughout his entire corpus.

In his proposal that the recovery of creaturely happiness lies in an ingression into the Godhead beyond the Trinity as creator, Eckhart provides a radical and singular solution to the subject–object problem and the inevitable alienation of consciousness that occurs when the creator objectifies the creature in creating it and the creature returns the questionable compliment in relation to a transcendent God as wholly other. The consciousness or absence of consciousness in Eckhart's "breakthrough" obviously overcomes the subject–object split in the unqualified identity of the creature with the wellspring of its being and consciousness beyond all differentiation, including that of creator and creature. As such, it provides the only real solution to the removal of God from subject–object categories.

With this position, Eckhart may add to Tillich something that Tillich always approaches but never candidly states in his confronting the subject–object problem, namely, the frank admission that the problem can only be overcome if humanity and divinity share a point of ontological coincidence whose real and experienced recovery alone can heal the split. Tillich refers frequently to the principle of identity between the divine and human and to the mutual and ontological coincidence or interpenetration of the infinite and finite inspired in large part by Schelling's philosophy of nature. (Tillich 1967: 147, 148) Yet he seems to draw back from the simple, unqualified affirmation that divinity and humanity share a point of natural unity and being and that the culmination of the spiritual quest lies in a recovery of and living out of that natural identity, never, of course, beyond the ambiguity of its fragmentary realization in existence. Eckhart frames that recovery explicitly and candidly as the moment of identity with the Goddess beyond all differentiation and the need to differentiate.

In his 1957 dialogue with Dr. Hisamatsu Shin'ichi, Tillich does reveal a sophisticated knowledge of Eckhart's thought in the context of the discussion of the "formless self" and its meaning in Christian and Buddhist usage. In these passages Tillich refers to Eckhart's central positions on the birth of the *Logos* in the soul and the origin of the *Logos* in the abyss as preceding the "subject-object duality". (Tillich and Shin'ichi 1990: 88, 89) Much of what Tillich says in this revealing dialogue is latent in his wider work. Stating it as explicitly as it is stated here would clarify the Trinitarian pantheism that structures his thought with its sense of a divine abyss defining itself in the *Logos* and united with its origin through the same Spirit that leads the human into the eternal flow of this self-defining abyss. However, in his dialogue with Shin'ichi, Tillich seems to step back from Eckhart's implication that he proceeds beyond the difference between abyss and *Logos* to that dimension of divinity from which the abyss/*Logos* split itself derives. (Dourley 2005) To fully accept this position would validate the experience of the nothing as nothing and so without a necessary relation to expression in *Logos*. Tillich, the theologian of balance and of the unity of opposites in divine and human life cannot get beyond his Trinitarian bias to give to the nothing the autonomy it deserves as the fourth dimension of divinity prior to the urgencies of the Trinity itself. His reticence here seems based on his fear that the nothing standing in its own right is independent of its expression in *Logos* and possessed of a maternal fecundity that would relativize all expressions in a subsequent *Logos*.

One may speculate on Tillich's failure to grant to the nothingness of the divine its own realm by going back to Luther and the influence on Tillich of foundational themes in the religious experience informing Reform theology. Luther may have read Eckhart through Johannes Tauler, one of Eckhart's contemporaries and pupils, and concluded that the divine–human intimacy in Eckhart's spirit was offensive to his, Luther's, sense of the gratuity of salvation and of humanity's sinful separation from God. This sinful remove from divinity and humanity's helplessness in its face could never be overcome by accessing divine energies endemic to human nature even if they were to culminate in a moment of self-loss and total passivity in the nothingness of God. Eckhart's implication that the height of humility lay in the recovery and affirmation of one's native divinity through a letting go first of possessions, and then of mind, will and personal being even when framed in a conception of a resignation (*gelassenheit*) which could hardly be surpassed may have appeared to Luther as a disguised form of a works ethic based on a radical asceticism, in fact, wholly foreign to Eckhart's spirit. (Ozement 1978) For whatever reason Tillich's late dialogue with Shin'ichi reveals that to the end he was uneasy with the darkness of the divine nothingness and so had to link it always with the comforting light of the *Logos*.

And yet Tillich's late search to find an alternative to masculine symbolism in a Christian doctrine of God, his speculation about the maternal nature of divinity as ground of divine and human life, and his search for the God beyond the God of theism resonate with Eckhart's experience. The point at issue is that both, one in the fourteenth and the other in the twentieth century, uncovered the experiential basis of Goddess consciousness by locating such experience in the preceding dimension of divinity from which all differentiation within and beyond Trinity derives. As a modern, Tillich points back to Eckhart's mysticism as a contribution to the future religiosity and spirituality of the new millennium. Such expansion of the notion of the divine would deepen humanity's natural religious consciousness with the realization that the Goddess approaches humanity from its depths, leads it to a moment of interior coincidence with her, and so imbues humanity with powers of reconciliation and sympathy that transcendent but lesser derivative divinities cannot. They cannot because their singularity as distinct transcendent Gods lacks a universal embrace even if one of them were to win a unilateral victory in the struggle they engender between their human communities. This is unlikely though the struggle continues currently with a high cost in human lives and as a major threat to the continuance of the species. Union with the Goddess as the mother of the Trinity and of all forms of religious consciousness would become the ultimate religious strategy in the resolution of that conflict which differentiation, and especially religious communal differentiation, inevitably breeds between conflicting absolutes in history.

These resources in Tillich are also of great value in entering the post-supernatural epoch of theology. Tillich, in his extended effort to find a way between a dualistic supernaturalism and a naturalism unconscious of its religious depths, pays tribute to Franciscan pantheism and its immanental sense of God as ground of all nature, including human nature. In these passages, he remarks that the conception of God as ground worked in the long run to undermine "Catholic supernaturalism". (Tillich 1968: 182) Tillich is being modest. In fact, the conception of God as maternal ground undermines all supernaturalism. On this point Tillich described much of mid-century North American Protestant theism as "a supernaturalistic form of deism", implying that it had lost humanity's natural sense of God in its interiority. (Tillich 1967: 95) The resources for a post-supernatural spirituality and theology in the recovery of the Goddess would thus open up the deepest but shared ground of humanity and divinity to release a more universal compassion in those who enter or at least are sensitive to her depths.

At this point one might argue that the recovery of the Goddess as divinity's missing fourth demands so radical an immersion in her that concern for the world becomes secondary if not entirely removed. Would union with the

Goddess be compatible with catatonic schizophrenia? Perhaps it would, if it were not completed in the second major movement in the dynamics of commerce with her. Not only is she the fourth as the origin of the Trinity but also identity with her, however episodic as a moment in a fuller cycle, drives to a renewed commitment to worldly engagement in the conviction based on experience that humanity individually and collectively completes the Trinity in history. Full intercourse with the Goddess can be described only as a double quaternity. For the Goddess beyond the Trinity as its originating fourth is fully realized again beyond the Trinity in humanity as the Trinity's completing fourth. The mystic whose experience captures this side of the Goddess' dynamic is more apparent, though rarely footnoted, in Tillich's theological ancestry, namely, Jacob Boehme. The completion of the Goddess in humanity requires another look at this mystic from this perspective.

Tillich and Jacob Boehme: Christ, Sophia, and the androgynous spirit

Jacob Boehme's experience occurs almost three hundred years after Eckhart's. With good cause he is occasionally identified as the inspirational predecessor of Schelling and Hegel. (Darby 1982: 154) In his *History of Philosophy*, Hegel pays high tribute to Boehme's profound but "barbarian" formulations. (Hegel 1990: 112, 120, 121, 130) Yet, much of Hegel's philosophy can be construed as a sustained effort to give more precise philosophical elucidation to Boehme's more turbulent experience and expression.

Boehme, like Eckhart, writes of an experience of a divine ground as the fourth, giving rise to Trinitarian differentiation within and beyond God. (Boehme 1911: 2) He calls this source the *ungrund*. He will also call it the One and, like Eckhart, describe a moment of identity with it. Again reminiscent of Eckhart, Boehme understands the One to divide into the Father and Son within the life of God. However, two major related differences exist between Eckhart and Boehme. One is in the emotional tone of their writing and the second might be termed the directionality of the movement of divine life and of their personal participation in its movement. Eckhart describes a movement to the peace and rest of dissolution in the mothering dimension of divinity that enables a more vital return to worldly engagement. The affective emphasis is on the peace and resignation of identity with one's source. While this emotion is not absent in Boehme, his writing rings with the clash of opposites within the divine life and with the divine signature of such conflict imprinted on everything, including human consciousness, in creation. Where Eckhart can give a certain priority to immersion in the oceanic, preceding and renewing activity in the world, Boehme's experience is of divinity moving largely in a different direction. His divinity struggles with its own unresolved self-contradiction and is ultimately driven to create humanity as the only center of consciousness capable first of experiencing the divine antinomies and then suffering in itself the resolution of the divine failure to work its integration within its own life eternally. (Dourley 1995a) In Boehme's dialectic, maternal nothingness craves first for manifestation in human consciousness to relieve its antinomic nature there. In return human suffering seeks the curative power of reimmersion in her nothingness beyond the conflict as the greatest resource in resolving the conflict in human existential consciousness. (Weeks 1991: 193)

These characteristic notes of Boehme's experience couched in the intensity of mystical immediacy foreshadow foundational themes in Tillich's more measured philosophical and theological discourse, disguised though some of them may be. Boehme, like Eckhart, endorses the epistemic priority Tillich gives to immediate experience in matters religious, which is to be retained even in rational/theological reflection on the symbols such immediacy breeds. Tillich is also indebted to Boehme for his position on the necessity of creation as the universal waking from "dreaming innocence" and thus on the related necessity of universal estrangement characterizing the consciousness of all who exercise the will to be, that is, everyone. (Tillich 1957a: 33) Tillich's effort to evade the implication of the necessity of evil in creation by introducing the "irrational" in this one place in his system to describe the universal alienation attendant upon the transition from essence to existence mediated by the individual's will to exist remains in the end unconvincing. A less defensive Tillich would have to agree more fully with Boehme, not only on the necessity of creation but also of evil in creation as the divine becomes conscious of its own propensities in human consciousness and humanity becomes conscious of its role in uniting these opposites in itself.

One such propensity is unrelated self-affirmation, a characteristic Boehme attributes to the Father with whom he can then identify the hell of the fallen angels and so with the presence of evil in God. Put simply Boehme locates evil in that dark moment of the divine life itself which seeks affirmation unqualified by the restraint of reason, the *Logos*, and the relatedness of Spirit and Sophia. Tillich all but cites Boehme without a footnote when he first describes this dynamic of Trinitarian life in the first volume of his *Systematic Theology*. Here he understands the Spirit to unite and modify the "chaos", "burning fire", "absolute seclusion" of the first moment of divine life with its manifestation in the *Logos* or divine reason. (Tillich 1951: 251) Tillich's imagery is very close to Boehme's as the basis of their shared implication that a divinity without a demonic dimension is a pallid divinity. But Tillich's formulations do stop short of Boehme's experience of the first principle as hell itself, the locus of evil in the divine.

Tillich's very late eschatology continues its largely surreptitious affinity with Boehme's in his claim, a contradiction for a Trinitarian, that divinity's self-interest and enhancement in creation are all that prevent creation from being, in Tillich's own words, "a divine play of no essential concern for God". (Tillich 1963: 422) Carl Braaten performs a lasting service to Tillich scholarship when he points out that Luther's pervading influence on Tillich is significantly modified by Boehme. This modification is particularly true of what Braaten calls Tillich's "mystical ontology" and "mystical-ontological categories", which structure and enliven his entire system of thought with the sense of the dark and bright sides of God. (Braaten 1967: xxv, xxix) As seen above Tillich argues that humanity naturally experiences these tensions and the resolution of these tensions within the divine life. Admittedly, for Tillich, participation in the resolution of these tensions worked by the Spirit within divine and human life remains never more than fragmentary in time. But it is only late in the third volume of the *Systematics* that Tillich explicitly states that the integration of opposites in time enhances both the Trinitarian God and humanity in eternity. The early Tillich had argued against process theology. For Tillich the God of process theology was made truly dependent on the outcome of the human response to the divine overture. Such a God would be subjected to a fate and a process Tillich terms "an absolute accident". (Tillich 1951: 247) Boehme would have no problem with process theology and is, through Hegel, one of its remote ancestors. A divinity dependent on its creature to identify and resolve, at the insistence of divinity itself, the antinomy shared by divine and human life is certainly one whose fate is attached to the human response to its approach, a position Tillich resisted almost to the end.

In a cosmology depicting a conflicted divinity driven to creation to find a self-consciousness and integration in its creature it could not find in itself, where does and can the feminine and the maternal come into play? The feminine is prominent in Boehme's experience in the maternal from which all derives and in the Spirit of Sophia. Like Eckhart, Boehme refers to a dimension of divinity giving birth to the Trinity and its compulsions. Going beyond Eckhart, he calls this divine precedence "mother" and closely relates the word to "root" and "matrix" to describe her nature as origin of the Trinity and of creation, both born of her in all their faces. (Boehme 1909: 14, 54; 1958: 131–135; Weeks 1991: 62, 82, 188, 197; Stoudt 1957: 244) Yet, one feels that his overwhelming sense of God as an emanating antinomy makes her originating power less significant than her necessary manifestation and reconciling urgency in creation.

Because of the role she plays in creation as the unifier of opposites, the feminine is most prominent in Boehme's extended sense of Sophia, the principle of wisdom. Her many faces in Boehme's mythology make a systematic portrait difficult. She seems to function as a fourth within divine life distinct from, and possibly consequent to, the differentiation of Father and Son thought she is also the feminine side of the Christ figure. As such she is also engaged in the manifestation of divine wisdom in creation and revelation but in an ambiguous manner consistent with Boehme's position that divine life seeks clearer and progressive self-consciousness in the human. Hence, her function beyond the Trinity is much more important. Here she is effectively identified with the Spirit of Christ working out the resolution of the divine self-contradiction in the human through the kiss she bestows on the soul receptive to her. (Boehme 1978: 56, 57)

The role and symbol of Sophia as the androgynous Spirit of Christ strains the boundaries of Christian orthodoxy and undermines the foundation of Tillich's Trinitarian thought. For Boehme's conception of the Spirit denies the affirmation at the heart of Tillich's Trinitarian conception of God, namely, that the resolution of conflict within divinity has occurred eternally (Tillich 1951: 247, 251) and that participation in this accomplished victory, for Tillich the substance of blessedness (Tillich 1963: 403–406), is that toward which humanity is universally led by the Spirit. Rather Boehme insists that whatever resolution of the divine opposites takes place must take place in history and this gives to history as God's completion a meaning and importance that Tillich, or any Trinitarian, cannot. For this reason, more conservative but knowing critics of Boehme will identify his thought as the remote but real basis for the sacralization of various modern political/ utopian movements and so for the religious-like and murderous fanaticism that has informed them in recent centuries. (Walsh 1983: 34, 35, 93, 108) Tillich himself acknowledges this kind of analysis when he identifies Boehme as one of the more remote sources of his own religious socialism. (Tillich 1967: 235)

Of even greater significance in Boehme's understanding of Spirit as uniting divine opposites in history, is the implication that more, and eventually all, of the divine fecundity would have to go into the synthesis that the Spirit of Sophia would work in time as the enrichment of eternity. In this context, the Spirit as the eternal feminine working the unity of divine opposites in history, would be a Spirit more encompassing, and eventually all encompassing, in her embrace. Such a Spirit would have, then, to include the now largely excluded bodily and spiritual feminine as an element of a more inclusive spiritual harmony of opposites in which the Goddess would compel humanity to recognize fully as divine all of her creative latencies and polarities. In this newly emerging myth, all of creation would have to be sacralized or resacralized, including the earthly and the corporeal. Included too would be the demonic, too often currently projected onto competing religious or political absolutisms at odds with one's own personal or tribal commitment. At the end of a century of religious and political genocide, this now emerging Spirit would have to engage all extant religious and political traditions in the realization that their future preservation lies in whatever may remain of them after the Spirit of the Goddess works their self-transcendence toward a truly universal and all inclusive embrace to which none of them can currently give wholehearted or unqualified sponsorship.

Tillich's contribution to the religious spirit of the new millennium

Carl Braaten writes of Tillich's spirit, "He did not ask his theological students to look upon his system of theology as an achievement that could not be transcended." (Braaten 1967: xxxiv) This statement encourages the effort to preserve the substance of what Tillich had to offer by transcending so much of what he left through the exploitation of the undeveloped and very late potentialities of his theology. One such dimension was Tillich's ability to identify the residual and universal religious nature of humanity as the basis of a safer collective religiosity and spirituality in the new millennium. This effort relies on a recovery of the sense of the Goddess latent in Tillich and in his usually unnamed and undocumented mystical predecessors on whom he so heavily draws. This new religious paradigm would imagine her as presiding over a double quaternity. In this double role, she is the fourth who precedes and gives birth to all defined and definable deity, including Trinity, and then works through her Spirit, Sophia, to the completion and reconciliation in human consciousness of her divine offspring, largely imaged as deified males in still extant and warring monotheistic communities. In this second sense humanity is the fourth in which the opposing powers within the Goddess born into consciousness are united there in the co-redemption of both the divine and the human. In this process, humanity is ontologically engaged from the outset. Standing in the center of this double quaternity, humanity returns to the rest of the Goddess' originating power beyond all differentiation and returns ever more sensitive to her demand that her inexhaustible fullness be progressively realized in human history in ever greater syntheses of the many archetypal opposites that are her children.

What are the consequences of the restoration of the Goddess thus revisioned by the foregoing themes only latent in Tillich's theology? Her greatest resource is the possibility she holds out to human consciousness to recover that point in herself behind or before or deeper than conflicting archetypal opposites now so tragically obvious in conflicting religious or political convictions currently constituting the greatest threat to the survival of the species. In this, she is the ultimate bulwark against patriarchal aggression in either gender since she corrodes the dogmatic certitudes which feed ideological faiths and warfare.

Historians of theology sometimes state that the twentieth century began in 1914 with the First World War. (Zahrnt 1966: 15) At the end of the twentieth century war with genocidal overtones has broken out again at the same place and against the same religious background that authored the century's beginning. At the east end of the Mediterranean and elsewhere in the world, religious strife and loss of life go on. The Holocaust might well be described as the major religious event of the twentieth century and the culmination of the "shadow side", if not the substance, of Jewish–Christian relations whose consequences are yet to be absorbed fully by the religious mind. The immediate statistically verifiable benefit of the recovery of the Goddess would be the lowering of the religious body count. Only the experiential recovery of a common human faith, which works to make relative and safe the faiths necessary for so high a body count, will ultimately lower or eliminate it.

Tillich spoke frequently of God's fight within religion against religion, making this fight his fight. (Tillich 1966: 88) Today God's fight within religion against religion could be restated as humanity's common fight to survive its religions. The return to the Goddess as mother of them all could be an essential weapon in this fight. In the last paragraph of his last address delivered on October 12, 1965, Tillich confronted the challenge of the then emerging universal Spirit for members of particular or concrete religious communities. He writes, "Above all it [such universalism] lies in the openness to spiritual freedom both from one's own foundation and for one's own foundation." (Tillich 1966: 94)

Since he wrote these words, the religious and moral impact the Goddess currently sponsors would drive beyond what the early Tillich would term a "final revelation" to one which could never become the basis of a final solution. Such freedom from one's foundations would now appear imperative if humanity is to survive the very religious impulse Tillich so convincingly demonstrated resides in its common soul. The deeper and so wider and ultimately universal sympathy the Goddess fosters by her nature may become more than a luxury or speculative fantasy among theologians. Her extended sympathies could be a necessity in humanity's survival strategy, a moment of immersion in her embrace, the precondition of ushering her many divine progeny safely into a history in which all can live in mutual inclusion. Those concerned not only with humanity's survival but also with its spiritual enrichment can only hope in the extension of her allure and the freedom she offers from lesser religious foundations toward their transformation into an increasingly inclusive, and so richer, safer and yet still concrete religious Spirit. Tillich might well be happy to see his later theology contribute to her saving grace, even if the cost be the transcendence of much of his earlier thought.

Chapter 6

The problem of the three and the four in Paul Tillich and Carl Jung*

Preamble

Chapter 5 dealt with Tillich's search for a dimension of divinity that would point to the presence and power of the feminine in the divine. This concern prompted him to play with the idea of a fourth dimension of deity which would birth the dynamic and differentiation characteristic of the life of the Trinity itself. In this speculation Tillich approaches Meister Eckhart's understanding of the Godhead preceding the Trinity as the fourth dimension of deity. It was also suggested that Jacob Boehme completes Eckhart in his suggestion that the divine opposites seek their union in human consciousness which alone can discern the split within divinity and move to its resolution in humanity as the condition of its resolution in divinity. In this context historical human consciousness becomes the fourth in which Trinity and humanity redeem each other in time. And so a pattern of a double quaternity emerges. The God beyond God drives toward full consciousness in humanity. Since the sense of both quaternities derive from human experience the emergence of the sense of a double quaternity is as psychological as it is religious and theological.

When the dynamic of the double quaternity is subject to theological precision, it would mean that divinity immerses humanity in its formless depths to realize in its creature the totality of the divine creative possibility. The deepest meaning of pathological human suffering, psychologically and religiously, could then be seen as a stubborn one-sidedness that would resist the divinely based compulsion toward an ever extending conscious inclusiveness more adequately reflecting the divine as the source of all that is. Psychological conceptions of the realization of the self, in individual biography and the totality of human history, would then have to move toward the incarnation in consciousness of the total divine possibility. Any conception of the self or of

* A version of this chapter appeared in G. Hummel and D. Lax (eds) (2004) *Tillich Studien: Trinity and/or Quaternity – Tillich's Reopening of the Trinitarian Problem, Proceedings of the IX International Paul-Tillich-Symposium, Frankfurt/Main 2002*, Münster: Lit Verlag, 351–368.

God which would exclude significant domains of created reality would come to be seen as a truncated image of the divine working the same truncation of the human living under the symbol of so partial a God. Effectively this realization would currently present to the reigning monotheistic myths the challenge of the divinization of the bodily, the feminine and the demonic as the price of a now evolving image of God fostering a more complete humanity.

It is around these issues, basically the meaning and motivation of creation itself, that Tillich and Jung show profound affinities which in the end reveal an even more profound and insuperable distance. Both would clearly identify the approach of the divine to the human in and through the depths of the human in the interest of human enhancement and totality. In this they are at one. Yet an abyss opens between them over the manner and dynamic of this address from within. Tillich takes the position that the divinity that approaches humanity from within offers to humanity a deeper participation in the Trinity's eternally established integration or unity of opposites. Jung takes the position that the divinity that approaches humanity from within seeks its own integration in a receptive humanity created for that purpose. For Jung as for Boehme the unification of opposites in the divine and the human cannot be distinguished. This process of mutual redemption is ongoing. For Jung the urgencies of the unconscious and so of divinity work toward a far more inclusive sense of the sacred than informs contemporary Western religious consciousness at least in its institutional form. Thus for Tillich, in the burden of his corpus, the human still is to find its integration in the divine; for Jung the divine seeks its integration in the human.

This tension is at the heart of what Jung calls the problem of the three and the four. Briefly put Tillich's Trinity implies a self-sufficient divinity. Major segments of undeniably existent reality find no presence in the images depicting this self-sufficiency, most notably the feminine, matter and evil, though this divinity is allegedly the creator of all that is. This divinity is also devoid of any dependence on the human for its fulfillment, a position Tillich held till his very latest writings. Jung's quaternity points to a divinity engaged in its realization in the human. All aspects of the human and of nature are expressions of it and derive from such a divinity. From their real presence in creation and absence in divinity Jung's "missing fourth" points toward that which must be restored to divinity and sacralized in humanity in the now current stage of their mutual growth now understood as the base meaning of history. Because of their far-reaching religious and psychological implications the affinity and difference in the meaning of the symbol of Trinity for Tillich and Jung demand closer inspection.

Trinity in Tillich and Jung

The symbol of the Trinity is foundational in Tillich's *Systematic Theology*. It describes both the nature of the divine life itself and humanity's natural, though inchoate, experience of participation in that life. As such the symbol encompasses the entire relation of humanity to divinity cast as the support and integration of human life led by the Spirit ever more deeply into the flow of Trinitarian life. The symbol also illuminates the relation of divine life to human history and, as it functions in Tillich's late eschatology, suggests that processes of history contribute, in the end, to the wealth of divine life and to the blessedness of both the divine and the human in eschatological mutual completion. (Tillich 1963: 420–423) This late acknowledgment rests on Tillich's position that the essential is initially expressed in the *Logos* and given fuller expression in creation where its realization in human life enhances both divine and human life eternally.

Carl Jung was also highly appreciative of the symbol of Trinity. In his later writings he dedicates a lengthy essay to it. (Jung 1969b: 109–200) Like Tillich he too sees the symbol as describing the life of the Spirit urging always a unity of opposites, most generally, those of the unconscious with human historical consciousness in a single organic process mutually redemptive of divine and human life. This point will be amplified in the fuller discussion of Jung's work on Job in Chapter 7. Indeed, Jung gives to the Trinity the status of a symbol depicting, at least in preliminary form, the basic structure and dynamic of the total psyche in its movement to maturation understood as the realization of the unconscious self in consciousness. (Jung 1969b: 148–163) However, the symbol remains preliminary for Jung because of his conviction that the unconscious currently is sponsoring a myth of a quaternity as pointing to a more encompassing manifestation of the divine in creation and human consciousness.

Chapter 4 described Tillich's qualified appropriation of Boehme. Jung, too, writes extensively of Boehme. Both are thus consciously indebted to a common spiritual ancestor, and to the intensities of his experience of God as a living, seething antinomy whose conflictual opposites are united by the Spirit in the human. Yet it is precisely in their respective appropriations of Boehme that the beginning of their ultimately insurmountable differences are first and most clearly distinguishable. (Dourley 1995a) What follows is an effort to put forth Tillich's Trinitarian theology, drawing largely on the first and third volumes of his *Systematic Theology*. This exposition will put a certain emphasis on a significant shift in Tillich's view of the implications or consequences of historical humanity's participation in the life of the Trinity evident in the concluding pages of the third volume. Here Tillich does finally affirm the contribution of the historical process of essentialization to the wealth and being of the Trinity, dramatic witness to Tillich's grappling with the Trinitarian symbol to the end. (Tillich 1963: 422)

The chapter will then shift to an examination of Jung's appreciative under-standing of the symbol in itself and his movement from it to a quaternitarian view. Jung's quaternity undermines the symbol of Trinity by contending that the unconscious currently generates a myth whose Spirit would extend a sense of the sacred to realities excluded from the narrower embrace of the Christian Spirit and so corrode it by superseding it toward wider inclusion of all aspects of creation and so of all aspects of the source of creation manifest in creation. (Dourley 1994) In both thinkers the Spirit is understood as a unity of opposites. With Jung more opposites gain entrance to the synthesis the Spirit seeks in a now emerging myth imbued with a Spirit of greater inclusion.

Tillich on humanity's native sense of God as Trinity

In Tillich's theology of God there is little real need for the traditional distinction between God as one and God as three. There is such little need because Tillich opts for life as the primary description of God. Life, for Tillich, is, in all its variations, a unity of contending opposites united by the Spirit. As such life is always a triumph of the power of integration over against the tendency to disintegration and nothingness. Life as integration triumphant and disintegration defeated is evident in all of the major opposites Tillich introduces in his work but is dramatically so in his depiction of the conflict between power and meaning. The most general work of the Spirit as the unifier of opposites is to unite power and meaning and so to foster life. (Tillich 1951: 249)

From these positions Tillich will argue that humanity is vested with a latent awareness of this dynamic in its native sense of the divine. Tillich's profoundly immanental theology endows humanity with a natural sense of God as the ground of being and the depth of reason. What Tillich never ceased asserting was that his theology was not a static metaphysics but grounded on humanity's experience of God in its own depths. (Tillich 1951: 246) Tillich is explicit in giving to humanity's incipient but real sense of the immanental God a presentiment of God as living and so as Trinitarian. Put simply the experience of God as the ground of being is an experience of a life of opposites in union and so is an experience of a Trinitarian God. Humanity's native "intuition" of God is, for Tillich, an intuition of a Trinitarian God because this intuition is of the abyss of divine inexhaustible power and its exhaustive definition in the form of the *Logos*. (Tillich 1951: 250, 251) These potentially conflictual opposites are eternally united by Spirit. This human intuition of the Trinitarian nature of divine life as a unity of abyss and light becomes, then, a major anticipation and support, grounded in the human itself, for the specifically Christian doctrine of Trinity. In this context Tillich will write, when he returns to the Trinity in his third volume, that the formulation of the Trinity was a matter of epistemic necessity since the doctrine was from the outset native to humanity's universal experience of God as living. The Trinitarian symbols are a discovery, "which had to be made, formulated and defended". (Tillich 1963: 283)

In his identification of an underlying cognitive necessity as the basis of the specifically Christian symbol of Trinity, Tillich takes a position with discernible affinities to Jung's archetypal theory. In more general terms Jung would understand the archetypal unconscious always to seek fuller expression in its creature, human consciousness. In this context Jung identified more forceful or "numinous" archetypal expression with religious experience. He understood that by demonstrating the archetypal basis of any religious or metaphysical doctrine or dogma, far from reductively dismissing such affirmation, he was, in fact, giving it the greatest foundation possible by locating its origins in humanity's archetypal unconscious. (Dourley 1993: 20, 21) The loss of the power and meaning of any symbol or dogma, as well as any general diminishment in humanity's symbolic sense, would mean then a loss of a sensitivity for humanity's depths from which religion, symbol, and ritual reenactment rise to consciousness. The loss of the symbolic sense thus always entails a debilitating coarsening of the consciousness of individual and society in which such a tragedy would occur. Consequently Tillich, Jung and Boehme would share the position that the power of the symbolic derives from its emanation into consciousness from those depths where the human and divine coincide and that the symbol gives form to this "demonic power" through the agency of the Spirit expressing such power in symbolic form. (Dourley 1995a: 442–445) The symbols, the myth the symbols inform, and the reenactment of the myth work the union of the conscious mind with the life of its origins. The process is radically Trinitarian in that depth unites with form through Spirit and leads the mind through the symbol into the freeing and refreshing resonance with the life from which all consciousness derives. This is the basis of the ongoing renewal of spirit that all functioning religion works. In this sense the birth and function of symbol, myth and rite are profoundly and universally Trinitarian in a manner that cannot be reduced to the Christian variant.

Tillich on Trinity as power of integration

Tillich's work on existential humanity's search for courage paints a convincing picture of divinity alive in the fabric of human life as the ultimate answer to the negations of death, guilt and meaninglessness. (Tillich 1952: 186–190) These are indeed major threats to life, prompting the search for courage, but there is an equal if not more pervasive threat which runs throughout Tillich's description of existential life, namely, the threat of disintegration. Existential life made up of the balance of those opposites Tillich calls the "ontological elements" is constantly threatened with such annihilating disintegration. (Tillich 1951: 199, 200) In Tillich's response to this threat his Trinitarian theology is most evident and effective. For Tillich presents the Trinity as the ultimate and only counter to disintegration because in its life the conflictual opposites in human life are eternally grounded and eternally resolved. Their resolution in divinity then constitutes the possibility of their resolution in the human. (Tillich 1951: 244–249) Tillich's description of these opposites is transparently dependent on Boehme. The first principle is described as "chaos, burning fire . . . demonic, characterized by absolute seclusion . . . 'the naked absolute'". The second is that of *Logos*, structure, form, and objectification or manifestation. (Tillich 1951: 251) Without *Logos* the creative power of the first principle would fail to find expression. Without the power of the abyss *Logos* would become superficial, shallow, bland, as reason always does when severed from its depths. United in Spirit inexhaustible power attains exhaustive expression or meaning. A more cogent portrayal of Trinity is difficult to conceive.

On the basis of this portrait Tillich builds a pneumatology which would understand the Spirit to lead the individual in time into an ever deeper immersion in the flow of integrated or balanced divine life achieved eternally in Trinity. Such immersion in the Trinity in time can only approximate its eschatological fullness in eternity but is effectively the only process that prevents the disintegration and so destruction of human life and its polar tensions in existence. In this sense Tillich's understanding of the ontological elements which so structure the system are profoundly Trinitarian. The polarities and their function in existential life tend to split apart and move to pathological one-sidedness and eventually to nothingness unless integrated or led into more synthetic patterns of harmony by the Spirit. In the face of the ever present possibility of disintegration in existential life one must read Tillich to mean that whatever is held together in the interests of fuller life is held together by Spirit.

Put in greater detail Tillich's thought on Spirit as the unifier of human opposites, grounded on the opposites in divine life, would unite personal affirmation with relatedness, potential with its realization, and freedom with destiny. (Tillich 1951: 243) As the Spirit works their integration in human life in continuity with its role in eternal life it also works the unity of the most important dimensions of human life, namely, morality, culture and religion. Each of these is the fruit of the unity of one of the above polarities. Morality derives from the first set; culture from the second; religion from the third. The unities the Spirit works in human life relate closely to Tillich's conception of theonomy. For Tillich theonomy describes a religious state in which the Spirit unites existential consciousness with its divine depth and so works fragmentarily in humanity the integration it has perfectly worked in the divine. Thus theonomous consciousness is profoundly Trinitarian. Its basic movement is into the rhythm of Trinitarian life and so into the flow of opposites at the heart of that life. In the human it would manifest in individual life as moving toward ever greater and so vital unities of its opposites which would extend beyond the individual to the societal unity of morality, culture and religion. (Tillich 1963: 157–161) Religion becomes the "substance" not only of cultural but also of individual life as the collective and personal realms coalesce in the unities worked by the Spirit. (Tillich 1963: 158) This vision is no doubt utopian were it to be understood as a state that could be realized in human history. Nevertheless it does describe the teleology of a humanity uniting with divinity and so uniting the basic spiritual functions of humanity with each other in person and society. Tillich will point to certain periods such as the high middle ages when individual and society did enjoy a high degree of the unity of morality, culture and religion. Though defiant of an unambiguous and permanent realization in history, nevertheless, for Tillich, movement to such integration of God, society and individual is the direction toward which Spirit works in history.

Tillich and the essential self

Tillich's Trinitarian theology grounds individual life not only in the flow of Trinitarian life but also, more specifically, in the *Logos* in a manner that can unite theology, philosophy and psychology. As the primordial expression of all form, the *Logos* is the structural element in both the divine mind and in the human mind as it participates in the divine mind. (Tillich 1951: 238, 239, 249–251) This means that the human mind resonates with the divine mind and with the generative abyss which precedes and gives birth to all mind and form human and divine. (Tillich 1951: 79, 250) Each individual centre of consciousness inheres in the *Logos* as the principle structure of all that has form and so individuality, the primordial manifestation of the essential giving expression to the creative abyss within and beyond divine life. Both the essential components of universal reason, the universals, as well as the God-grounded truth of the individual inhere in the *Logos* expressing the abyss. Such primal inherence in the *Logos* empowers the drive of the individual toward the fuller recovery of one's essence in *Logos* empowered by the preceding abyss in every moment of existential life. (Tillich 1951: 255)

Processes of sanctification are effectively movements of the Spirit leading the individual within the confines of finitude into a fuller realization of one's eternally spoken essential self. Tillich describes the individual's temporal and ambiguous appropriation of one's eternal essence in the *Logos* as that moment of the "essential self shining through the contingencies of the existing self". (Tillich 1963: 235) More, he gives specific content to the emergence in existence of the essential self using psychological categories with explicit reference to depth psychology. (Tillich 1963: 231–237) These characteristics are a personal self-affirming spontaneity, neither inflated nor deprecatory, informed by an enhanced awareness, freedom, relatedness and sense of transcendence. While his idiom here is admittedly indebted to contemporary psychology, Tillich's theology adds a greater depth to most depth psychologies because he is correlating psychological growth through the above categories with an intensified inhesion in one's deepest truth rooted in the eternal flow of Trinitarian life. In fact this correlation moves to the point of identifying psychological maturation with participation in the flow of Trinitarian life. Through such appropriation the individual draws nearer not only to one's personal essence but also to the abysmal power which precedes such definition.

Put simply, through Spirit one moves ever toward a greater recovery of one's essential uniqueness uniting in itself divine power with divine meaning as the basis of an attendant psychological maturation to which Tillich gives precise content in these pages.

Though Tillich does not address the issue in this context he is also working here with the microcosmic/macrocosmic dynamic that runs throughout his system and its Trinitarian foundation. The process of the recovery of the essential self grounded in the second moment of Trinitarian life cannot be understood except in profoundly relational terms because the individual's personal essential truth is recovered in the *Logos* structure that supports mind and reality universally. Thus through an intensified inhesion in one's essential life in the *Logos* one participates both in the universal structure of reality and in one's deepest personal truth. Universal and personal truth move toward coincidence since both are grounded in the structure of the divine mind. The intensification of such inhesion can only result in an ever widening embrace for all that is as an expression of its Trinitarian source. In his late pages Tillich extends this perception to the contention that what happens in the individual happens universally with the consequence that no one is lost or saved individually and concludes that if anyone is saved then all of creation is. (Tillich 1963: 408, 409)

Processes of essentialization in Tillich's thought on creation, Christology and eschatology

Through his understanding of all of life, personal and collective, driven to recover its essence originally defined in the second moment of Trinitarian life, Tillich constructs an impressive and consistent doctrine of creation, of the Christ event and its consequences and of eschatological blessedness. Creation becomes for him the ecstasy or going out of the essential beyond its Trinitarian matrix into the distortions of existence, distortions never able fully to negate humanity's sense of a lost intimacy with the divine. (Tillich 1951: 61) The recovery of what is lost becomes humanity's universal ultimate concern and as such constitutes humanity's universal or formal faith. (Tillich 1963: 130, 131) Here Tillich's essentialism functions to depict human nature as vested with a universal religious sense that can never be evaded or lost as the basis of a credible and compelling argument for humanity as incorrigibly religious. All distinct or material faiths build on formal faith. All such faiths would be forms of a dehumanizing heteronomy were not formal faith endemic to human nature itself their preceding possibility and necessity.

In spite of this contribution to the understanding of humanity as religious certain problems in Tillich's doctrine of creation remain and become somewhat central in conversation with Carl Jung. Tillich, the Christian theologian, must deny that creation is necessary and that it necessarily entails evil. To do this he addressed the dialectic of the essential stepping out of its Trinitarian source from the viewpoint of human freedom. In the state of "dreaming innocence" humanity is at one with its source as expressed eternally in the Trinity. Such innocence is not fully real. The temptation is to exercise one's freedom and to become real, an option universally made, but at the cost of distancing the individual from an unqualified but dreaming and so unreal initial identity with the essential. (Tillich 1957a: 33–36) It is a brilliant ploy. The fall becomes the universally exercised individual choice to become real even though the choice inevitably brings on an existential remove from the divine ground of the individual with the attendant suffering of existential alienation, anxiety, and potential disintegration, never wholly devoid of the memory of the essential and the drive to recover it.

Yet Tillich's description could be understood from a reversed perspective with closer affinities to the experience of Jacob Boehme. The Trinity as creative would be itself the subject of dreaming innocence and only awake to its unrealized potential, namely the essential, when the essential expresses itself beyond and over against Trinity in human consciousness. This reversal would imply that divinity gains whatever self-knowledge it has in humanity. Such a reversal would insert an element of necessity into creation because only in creation would the creator realize the essential beyond a divine dreaming innocence of unexpressed divine potential. Though Tillich draws on Boehme extensively in his understanding of the distinct moments in Trinitarian life, he draws back, as we have seen, from the conclusions of Boehme and Jung who are explicit in their positions that the creative source of human consciousness must create human consciousness so that it can itself become conscious in the consciousness of the creature.

This problem in the procession of the essential into existence continues in Tillich's treatment of evil. Evil, in its deepest and most extended sense, becomes for him the distancing of the creature from its divine ground through freedom responding to the temptation to become real in existence. Here Tillich stands in continuity with Augustine and Augustine's understanding of evil as *privatio boni*, that is, as privation of or removal from the essential, a synonym for the good in all essentialist perspectives including Tillich's. In his adoption of a variant of the *privatio boni* argument Tillich avoids another conclusion his Christianity forbids him, namely, that creation could not occur without evil since, in his own terms, it is always a departure from unqualified unity with God which he conveniently attributes to the individual's self-creation through the will to be. This position also enables him to avoid Boehme's and Jung's position that evil is simply an externalization of a power native to its divine source. Tillich further steps around the necessity of evil in creation by confessing that it is the only place in his system where the irrational is operative. (Tillich 1957a: 91) In so doing he admits that the evil involved in the transition from essence to existence remains simply unintelligible in his system. The implication that creation necessarily entails evil is divested of any real metaphysical foundation, surely Tillich's forte, and dismissed as "a story to be told" with all the irrationality of a "leap" worthy of Kierkegaard himself. (Tillich 1957a: 29, 44)

Were Tillich faithful to his thought on creation as the expression of the divinely grounded essential in existence he would have to admit that the reality of evil in creation has its ground in God or, at least, that evil could not be avoided if creation were to step out of its essential divine matrix. Both Boehme and Jung do not step back from this conclusion and argue that a divinity possessed of a dark and light side must express its total reality in creation and seek the resolution of its polarities in human consciousness. This counter position would imply that divinity not only had to create to know the potential of the divinely grounded essences in creation over against itself but also had to rely on human consciousness as the sole theater in which its own eternal divisions could be clearly differentiated and resolved at the insistence of divinity itself. Among these divisions would certainly be that between good and evil.

Tillich's essentialism is also brilliantly operative in his Christology where it functions to establish the Christ event (at least in his early writing) as the unqualified realization of the essential in existence against all human expectation (the paradox), and yet in response to humanity's deepest need and quest. (Tillich 1957a: 91, 94) As with all claims to an exhaustive and final revelation, the particularity of the expression of the essential in an historical moment and individual life is in some tension with Tillich's universalism. Identifying the Christ event as the definitive moment of the realization of the essential in history comes into serious tension with humanity's universal search for the essential as expressed in other religions as thoroughly examined in Chapters 2 and 3. This tension between the particular and the universal is most evident in his late insistence that Christianity through the symbol of the crucifixion is endowed with a self-critical principle not to be found in other religions and in secular forms of commitment. (Tillich 1963: 154) Tillich's late confession of provincialism without denying his essentialism could allow him to pay greater tribute to the realization of the essential in other manifestations, religious or secular, and would support a relativism which would not be offensive to a Christianity seeking to supersede its provincialism. In some later writings he may have done so, as seen in Chapter 1. Yet in his magisterial third volume he seems impelled to argue that the Christ event is somehow definitive or cumulative of humanity's religious history, a shadow side of his provincial theological commitment all the more disappointing in the light of the universalism and relativism Tillich had at his disposal in his thought on religion as the expression of the essential in history. In contrast Jung's understanding of figures, such as the Christ, as varied depictions of the self bonding various societies by providing them with their diverse culture heroes can at once respect the Christ figure while giving archetypal value to other self figures and symbols of religious and cultural substance. (Jung 1968a: 68)

However, a close reading of the latter pages of the third volume reveals that the late Tillich was more sensitive to the implication that divinity as a "separated self-sufficient entity" undermined the meaning of historical human life making of it "a divine play of no essential concern for God". (Tillich 1963: 422) In fact divine self-sufficiency is explicitly denied. In affirming that divinity seeks the essentialization of all that is Tillich attributes to this process an ontological contribution to the life of the divine itself completed as it were through processes of essentialization in creation and history. Such completion would "contribute to the Eternal Life in each of its moments" and donate ontologically to "the content of the divine blessedness". (Tillich 1963: 422, 423) These passages are certainly reminiscent of Whitehead's consequent God and conception of divine memory. They can only be read to mean that essentialization contributes to the final being of Trinitarian life.

Nor should these passages be surprising because their foundation is laid as early as the first volume of the *Systematics*. There Tillich grounds the essential in the *Logos* and understands the *Logos* as the structure of the divine mind and of the existential human mind which participates ambiguously in it. The expression of the essential beyond the *Logos* and the Trinity is the self-manifestation of God in which the divine is residually present. Tillich does not identify his total system as "pan-en-theistic" till the second last page of his massive *Systematics*. (Tillich 1963: 421) But already in identifying all epistemic structure as grounded in the *Logos* Tillich is engaged in a sophisticated panlogism however disguised. Unless this panlogism in creation and history contributes through its fuller realization in human consciousness to the divine then nothing is really at stake for God in history, a point Tillich comes to admit only at the very end of his system though it is implicit from the first. In effect Tillich's last description of God is of a God in processes of self-creation through the essentialization of all that is in nature culminating in the essentialization of human nature as contributing to the eternal fullness of God. In the end, then, Tillich acknowledges humanity as the fourth through whom the Trinity contributes to its own blessedness and completion. What Tillich concedes toward the end of his system is prominent from the outset in Jung's understanding of the Trinity and of humanity as the vessel of its completion, the fourth in which the three fulfills itself.

Jung on the Trinity and quaternity

In marked contrast with the rest of the boring process, Jung recounts in his autobiography that he had actually anticipated his minister father's instruction on the Trinity in his youthful preparation for confirmation. He was dismayed when his father simply confessed that he would skip the matter since he understood nothing of it himself. (Jung 1965a: 53) Apparently the fascination lingered in Jung's mind because he was to return to the symbol in a major essay in his maturity, an essay which not only gives archetypal validation to the symbol of Trinity but also implies that the unconscious urges its supersession as a quaternity in an now emerging myth. (Jung 1969b: 164–192) In an earlier section of the essay Jung pays high tribute to the symbol as pointing to the psyche's most foundational and all encompassing movement to maturation. (Jung 1969b: 129–138, 148–163) His appreciation of the symbol is based on his functional equation of the archetypal unconscious with the generative source of consciousness universally. The procession of consciousness from its archetypal origin, when recast in religious terms, describes the procession of the Son or *Logos* from the Father. This procession accounts for the tension between Father and Son as conflicting opposites whose conflict is intensified by the recognition, in the consciousness of the Son, of the Father's questionable competence as Creator because of the all too present reality of evil in a flawed creation. Here Jung is signaling his later remarks in the essay on the origin of evil in the divine. Jung then introduces the self as the Spirit which unites the opposites of Father and Son, unconscious and conscious (Jung 1969b: 133–136), toward the forthcoming age of the Spirit to which, in the footsteps of Joachim di Fiore, Jung hoped his psychology would contribute. (Jung 1975a: 138)

In this paradigm the union of the unconscious origin of consciousness with consciousness is the work of the self or Spirit which is itself born into consciousness through the union. Here Jung's thought has marked affinities with certain medieval and modern theologies of Trinity in which the Spirit as connecting power would both unite opposites and be born from their union in both divine and human life. (Dourley 1975: 125, 126) This unity in which the self becomes increasingly conscious through the union of consciousness with its creative origin is the basis of Jung's thought on the divine child born into the mind from beyond the mind as the basic meaning he gives to incarnation. So appreciative is Jung of the inclusiveness or totality of the symbol of Trinity that he applauds conciliar history for its formulations of the symbol. He does so because the councils attribute divinity to Father, Son and Holy Spirit and so validate the agencies of the unconscious, consciousness and their union in the tripartite processes of maturation he calls "individuation". (Jung 1969b: 194, 195) More, in his conclusion to his essay on the Trinity, he describes the Spirit worked unity of opposites as leading the individual into nothing less than "a unity with the substance of God". (Jung 1969b: 194, 195)

Jung does not endorse a static understanding of substance. The full import of his remarks here is that the basic meaning of time and history is one in which the unconscious basis of consciousness becomes increasingly conscious in human consciousness. Cast in religious language human development becomes a progressive incarnation of its origin in human consciousness. This process assumes that humanity is latently divine from the outset and experiences this divinity in divinity becoming real in consciousness. In this context the meaning of human development is the progressive realization of humanity's native divinity universally in individual and collective consciousness. Divinity and humanity are organic poles in this development and are mutually realized in a human consciousness ever more pervaded by its source.

The problem of the missing fourth

Having paid such high tribute to the symbol of Trinity, Jung goes on immediately to undermine it by contending that currently the unconscious moves beyond it toward a symbol yet to be given highly defined form. The newly emerging symbol would embrace more of what is evident in the only creation humanity knows and, by extension, reveal more of God as its creator. (Jung 1969b: 164–192) He begins this section citing Plato's *Timaeus* and Goethe's *Faust* around the theme of the missing fourth. (Jung 1969b: 164) This reflection leads on to the contention that divinity as the source of reality must be a creative power which contains in itself all significant opposites that exist in reality. This position, in turn, leads to the observation that creation manifests undeniable realities which are excluded from the divine as their alleged creator. In this essay Jung largely confines himself to the absence of evil in the divine and its obvious power in reality. He responds by locating the reality of evil in God or the unconscious in which all opposites are present but undifferentiated because of the absence of discriminating reason of the kind possessed by the human ego. (Jung 1969b: 175)

The pleromatic One or Father, the container of all opposites as undifferentiated, becomes the first moment in the life of the quaternity. Reason as it rises from the unconscious increasingly differentiates the opposites or archetypal polarities in its unconscious origin. The historical process of reason's discrimination of the opposites of good and evil reached a certain culmination in the Christian tradition which would then, for Jung, differentiate Christ and Satan as the light and dark sons of the same Father. (Jung 1969b: 175) Christ and Satan as opposites then would be the second and third moments in the life of the quaternity when viewed from the focus of good and evil. But the differentiation of opposites is never more than penultimate in Jung's total understanding of the movement of the psyche. Whatever is differentiated drives to its conscious reunification in the interests of a wealthier and healthier consciousness. In this process the undifferentiated in the divine is differentiated in humanity and then reunited there in a consciousness immensely extended and enlivened by bringing together in itself elements currently excluded from divinity and so from presiding conceptions of human wholeness. In terms of good and evil their mutual embrace in and by consciousness would be the fourth moment and completion of the opposites in a synthetic symbol which the absolute distancing of Christ from Satan anticipates and demands. The union of these and all archetypal opposites in the fourth moment is the work of the Spirit or self and the Spirit or self is born into consciousness in this work. (Jung 1969b: 176–179)

To expand on this vision, the Spirit of the quaternity does not limit its extended inclusiveness to the integration of good and evil in the more encompassing synthesis it seeks. It also would include the admission of the feminine and the bodily or material in the fourth and completing moment of quaternitarian life. In effect Jung is contending, when his quaternitarian thought is widened to include its total implications, that the Spirit of the quaternity includes not only the demonic, but also the feminine and the material whose only common trait is their joint exclusion from the presiding Christian symbol, the Trinity. Such exclusion effects the consequent and still current devaluation of all three as sacred in themselves. His perception that the unconscious is currently engaged in the making of a myth that appreciates and depends on the Christian myth even as it supersedes it would locate the reality of the demonic, the feminine and the bodily in the divine as creator, to be differentiated in historical consciousness from their opposites, the good, the masculine and the spiritual and reconciled in human consciousness moving to an eschatology, the age of the new Spirit working a more inclusive fourth characterized by the union of good and evil, male and female, body and soul. (Dourley 1995b: 239)

The new age: the Spirit of the fourth and the Answer to Job

In another late essay, "Answer to Job", Jung further spells out the implications of his quaternitarian view. Here he again identifies the experience of God with the experience of the archetypal unconscious. Job's experience of Yaweh points to that moment in the evolution of religious consciousness in which the instability of the ground of consciousness is becoming dramatically evident to the world of consciousness. (Jung 1969a: 428) With this emerging awareness comes the stark realization that humanity is more conscious than its unconscious origin (Jung 1965a: 220) and is imbued with the task of first differentiating and then uniting in itself the self-contradictions or unrelieved polarities that defied resolution in the eternal life of the divine. (Jung 1969a: 461) In these positions Jung is most obviously indebted to a more total Boehme than any form of orthodox Trinitarian thought including Tillich's can accommodate.

Jung appreciates the symbol of the crucifixion as one of his favourite depictions of the human plight in history. (Jung 1969a: 408, 455; 1969c: 225; 1968a: 44; 1968b: 255) Christ dies between archetypally based opposites of a yes and a no in the figures of the criminals crucified on either side of him. This interpretation of the crucifixion implies that the opposites between whom the Christ figure dies are themselves grounded in the archetypally divine. Further Christ's dying cry of despair at being abandoned by the Father expresses his consciousness that no help can come from a divinity wholly external to the psyche. The suffering of Christ is that of humanity universally caught between divinely grounded polarities and charged with uniting them in itself through the suffering to the point of death of the consciousness crucified between legitimate archetypal opposites. Only through such death can a resurrected consciousness arise now able to bring together the lethal conflict of the conflicted consciousness it transcends. The psychic dynamic here symbolized as death and resurrection is the same dynamic involved in what Jung terms the "transcendent function". The conscious suffering of divinely grounded opposites leads to an always more inclusive and synthetic consciousness. The transcendence involved does not point beyond the process itself but to the process itself, a process in which humanity suffers the divine contradiction to conscious resolution as the base meaning of human existence. Unlike the biblical story of the death and resurrection of Christ, the process can never end because of the infinite fecundity of the unconscious. As states of more inclusive consciousness succeed each other historically or individually they are challenged even as they appear to include yet more of the underlying divine wealth seeking consciousness in the ever broader patterns of synthesis such extended inclusiveness and compassion achieve in consciousness.

Significantly Jung calls such suffering of the divine opposites through psychic death toward their unification both "psychological" and "eschatological". (Jung 1969a: 408) It is psychological because only in the personal suffering of that side of the divine conflict most prominent in one's unique life are processes of wider history moved toward the eschatological union of all opposites in the age of a more inclusive Spirit. In this sense the psychological movement of the individual caught up in the suffering of the divine is eschatological because the redemption in consciousness of the divine opposites operative in an individual life is the greatest contribution the individual can make to the movement of history and to the eschaton now cast as the ongoing resolution of the divine self-contradiction in universal human consciousness. Only when the totality of divinity becomes conscious in human consciousness through this psychological and eschatological process will God be all in all though this situation remains ever an ideal or direction and never a possibility that can be realized. This religious and psychological situation appears to be one which can never be realized and yet never abandoned because the wealth of the unconscious will always surpass its constant realization, but that wealth itself will never cease demanding entrance into consciousness.

The moral imperative endemic to the quaternitarian myth imbues humanity with the task of perceiving and uniting in its consciousness the living antinomy which is the life of God in its depths. Jung will state that now everything depends on the human ability to usher divinity into consciousness in humanity at the insistence and with the help of divinity itself. (Jung 1969a: 459) The dynamic of this drama entails the rhythmic or repeated cycle of conscious entrance into the Pleroma, the infinite fullness of the unconscious, as the necessary prelude to the Pleroma being redeemed in consciousness upon the return of the traveler to consciousness from dissolution in its origins. (Jung 1969a: 425) Jung's appreciation of mystical, gnostic and alchemical experience rests solely on the movement of consciousness into its divine depths as the precondition of divinity becoming increasingly conscious in humanity through the reconciliation or atonement of its opposite in historical psychic processes, individual (psychological) and collective (eschatological).

Conclusion

Both Tillich and Jung give to Christianity's central but most arcane symbol of Trinity a new and pulsating life as something endemic to humanity's deepest experience of itself. For Tillich the Trinity is adumbrated in humanity's universal intuition of divine life as the ground of human life and itself a unity of opposites. The presiding opposites Tillich identifies in the natural human intuition of the divine are those of the infinite and overwhelming abyss giving expression to itself in the *Logos* and so united as power with meaning by the Spirit. For Jung the Christian symbol is an adequate but now preliminary description of the agencies and their energies operative in the foundational movement of the psyche toward maturation. He would follow Tillich in Tillich's understanding of divine and human life made up of a unity of opposites, even those of power and meaning. For Jung the power is that of the archetypal unconscious as the source of the numinous and so of humanity's ineradicable sense of God. Meaning resides in the ego as the centre of consciousness ideally to be united with the power of its source by the Spirit of the self.

In this sense both Tillich and Jung understand the Trinity to be a description of life as a coincidence of opposites in which Spirit functions to integrate polarities which, unchecked in their one-sided drive to ascendancy, could lead to life's disintegration and fragmentation. For both, Spirit thus contributes to an ever growing fullness of integrated life understood as a conscious unity of opposites. More, both take up a somewhat traditional but a highly sophisticated dialectical position on how Spirit works the unity of opposites and itself becomes incarnate in consciousness through the unities it works. While Spirit makes life possible then richer by uniting life's opposites it is itself made more real in the life it makes possible and enhances. It is born in the union it works. For Tillich this means a progressive ingression of existential life into the flow of Trinitarian life. For Jung it means a life in which the Spirit of the self unites consciousness with the unconscious in the personal integration of archetypal opposites accompanied by an ever greater sympathy for reality beyond the individual. These seemingly opposite effects of the work of the Spirit flow from the fact that the Spirit works to unite the individual with what Jung calls "the eternal Ground of all empirical being" (Jung 1970: 534) and with what Tillich calls the "ground of being" in patterns of personal integration moving to the embrace of all that is. With both Tillich and Jung it is only because the unification and integration of the multiplicities that make up the individual is worked by the power that underlies all that is that greater personal integration and an extended compassion become two sides of the same process. The false dichotomy between a developing individuality and an extended concern for the wider totality is defeated. The greater the individuality worked by the Spirit or the self the wider the relatedness.

These common positions do not extend to Jung's movement to a quaternitarian paradigm, a paradigm in his view currently prompted by the spirit of the self toward the completion and so supersession of what is contained within the confines of the Christian symbol of Trinity. This paradigm shift revisions the divine–human relation itself. With Tillich humanity is led by the Spirit to an ever greater participation in the integration of divine life worked from eternity and symbolized in Trinity. For Jung divinity is forced to create humanity, first to perceive and then to suffer the eternal divine self-contradiction toward its progressive resolution in historical consciousness. In Tillich's spirituality, an eternally integrated God shares this integration with the creature. In Jung's spirituality a yet to be integrated God seeks integration in the humanity created for that purpose. Though Tillich, largely without footnotes, draws the qualities of the moments in Trinitarian life from Jacob Boehme, Jung is more faithful to their common ancestor in his insistence that divinity effectively unites its opposites not in itself but in the human driven by the divine imperative and need to do so.

Jung understands this divine insistence currently to demand that the demonic, the feminine and the earth be included in the wider synthesis the Spirit now seeks. Jung can envision the unity of male and female in androgynous imagery from various cultures including the West. He saw the unity of heaven and earth, the spiritual and the bodily, as the deepest motif in the symbol of Mary's Assumption proclaimed in 1950. Christianity had at last its compensating goddess who united in herself heaven and earth and in so doing brought the Trinity to completion. (Jung 1969a: 465) But in terms of the union of good and evil Jung was unable to be precise on how the symbols of Christ and Satan would embrace in a symbol beyond their split. He left only statements that the battle between these opposites must continue till such a symbol emerged and urged those he addressed to appreciate the unresolved conflict the Christian myth presents at its core. This conflict was not to be superseded by being dismissed. In fact in a personal passage, in which he related his psychology to Joachim de Fiore's vision of an imminent age of the Spirit, he confesses that only the Spirit that has given rise to the Christian myth can lead humanity beyond it. At the same time he was convinced that this was how the Spirit currently worked but only through suffering to the full the conflict symbolized in the separation between Christ and Satan and not through any form of evasion or jettisoning of the current conflicted myth or myth of continued conflict between Christ and Satan. (Jung 1975b: 137, 138)

Jung's perspective presents many difficulties to Christian and to mono-theistic theology. Can they abandon the conception of a Trinity or of any God that is at least in principle self-sufficient for one whose being and enhancement is at stake in worldly processes, a point Tillich seems to at least hold up for consideration in the final pages of his system? Can orthodox theologies move to a pneumatology and eschatology in which the Spirit would drive to an eschaton in which all aspects of divinity found inclusion including the satanic, the earthly and the feminine? Tillich toward the end of his career was aware of a significant aspect of the problem when he faced the question of the place of the feminine in the Christian myth as seen in Chapter 5. His most compelling speculation on the problem was latently Trinitarian. He pointed to his foundational symbol/concept of God as ground of being as maternal, supportive and yet potentially consuming, all attributes Jung would lodge in the Great Mother. (Tillich 1963: 293, 294) As argued the ground, for Tillich, was alive with the Trinitarian pulse. Effectively, in his late speculation, the Father became the Mother or matrix of consequent reality divine and human. This was a brilliant stroke on his part but one wonders how conscious he was of how close he here came to identifying the Great Goddess or Mother as the more remote power in the divine, preceding even Trinitarian movement toward form and creation. In this matter Tillich's speculation could posit a fourth beyond Trinity as it maternal source. Here Tillich approaches the experience of Meister Eckhart in the latter's apophatic experience of identity with the Godhead beyond all Trinitarian definition. (Dourley 1990: 41–68) Both Tillich and Eckhart seem to describe a moment of identity with the Goddess as a prelude to a heightened engagement with the world. It is to be regretted that Tillich never exploited the affinities of his theology with Eckhart's experience and so open up the possibility of identity with the maternal source and so creative precedent of the Trinity and its differentiation within and beyond divine life.

Turning to Jung, his appropriation of the mystics points to a double qua-ternity. The mother goddess, the nothingness of mystical experience, adds a fourth in the life of divinity prior to the Trinity itself. In this position Jung was fully aware of Eckhart. (Jung 1971a: 241–258) This side of Jung's psych-ology points to dimension of psyche beyond even archetypal impulse where the drive of the archetypes to consciousness cedes for the moment to a rest in that nothingness which is at the same time the source of all form and definition, even that latent in the archetype. It is also regrettable that Jung, in spite of his frequent citation of Eckhart in his works, never elaborated this side of his psychology. Psychologically it might well point beyond the archetypes as theologically it posits a fourth dimension of psyche and divin-ity preceding Trinity and creation. Boehme completes Eckhart by adding humanity to Trinity as the sole theater in which the Trinitarian drama is played out in creation. When Jung's appropriation of Eckhart and of Boehme is put together he is found to be arguing that the deepest ingression into the psyche is the precondition of the psyche's greatest realization in historical consciousness. When this is put in a religious idiom the double quaternity would mean that the unity with the fourth as the God beyond the God of Trinity and creation fosters the realization of God in humanity as the Trinity's completing fourth. Can Christianity with its foundational symbol of a self-sufficient Trinity embrace either side of the double quaternity? Eckhart died in 1328 during his trial for, among other things, his views on the possibility of a human identity with the Godhead beyond the Trinity. Jacob Boehme (1575–1624) was harried by clerical officials throughout his life over the implications of his religious experience identifying the human as the sole locus in which the divine contradiction was to be healed. History points to the fact that neither aspect of the double quaternity is acceptable to the mainstream Christian tradition.

In effect Jung challenges traditional Christianity, as it moves into the future and the need to face its own self-transcendence, with the question of whether the recovery of its health and wholeness, will have to involve the recovery of what it has lost or excluded, frequently as heresy, in reducing itself to its current limited spiritual resources and too often truncating intellectual and so meaningless dogmatic formulations. Tillich, in treating of symbols, often referred to the fact that they grow and die but never explicitly considered the death of the Christian symbol. (Tillich 1951: 128, 240) Would Jung's vision of a more adequate image of God as author of the totality and of the human as living into this totality call for a supersession of presiding Christian symbols which would no doubt be somehow preserved in their being surpassed toward a more encompassing image of God urging a wider human sympathy for all that truly is? Probably it would. These are questions only time will answer but the dialogue here construed between Tillich and Jung contributes greatly to their answer by pointing to the immensity of what is at stake, possibly nothing less than the emergence of a new myth which would transcend and complete Christianity in much the same manner that Christianity claims to transcend as it includes its own immediate religious precedent. (Stein 1985: 186)

Chapter 7

Bringing up Father

Jung on Job and the education of God in history*

The background

Just how radical the myth embedded in Jung's psychology is in both its appreciation and supersession of monotheistic mythology in any of its variants becomes evident in his work on Job. If this work is read in the religious language in which it is cast it would contend that an unconscious God necessarily creates human consciousness as the only agency that can perceive divinity's unresolved eternal conflict and contribute to its resolution in time, finitude and history at the insistence of divinity itself.

Spelling out this extreme position did not come easily to Jung. He was fully aware that it corroded the reigning Western religious myth. He confesses that he had to overcome, "the greatest inner resistances" before he could write his "Answer to Job". (Jung 1965a: 216) Many theologians and their constituencies failed to overcome theirs in their response to this work. For it is an extreme statement and Jung candidly admits he fearfully anticipated "the storm" its publication would unleash. (Jung 1965a: 216) It was, indeed, a stormy text well equipped to provoke the theological tempest which followed. Two texts capture much of the spirit and substance of the work. The first is not from the work itself but from Jung's autobiographical description of the personal psychological forces that led him to write the work. Jung interprets the meaning of one of his major dreams to stand him in the same position before his father's religion, Christianity, as Uriah stood before a betraying David and as Job stood before Yaweh. (Jung 1965a: 216, 217) For both Jung and Job the unquestioning capitulation to the divine demand laid on them from beyond would mean the betrayal of their humanity as Uriah was betrayed by David, Yaweh's royal agent. We shall shortly return to the text of the dream. To Jung the dream spoke of the "idea of the creature that surpasses its creator by a small but decisive factor". (Jung 1965a: 220) The second foundational text, from the work on Job itself, deals with the reason

---

* A version of this chapter appeared as "Bringing up Father: C.G. Jung on History as the Education of God", *The European Legacy*, 4, 2, 1999, 54–68.

for creation and by extension with the meaning of incarnation, human suffer-ing and the direction of human history itself. It reads, "The inner instability of Yaweh is the prime cause not only of the creation of the world, but also of the pleromatic drama for which mankind serves as a tragic chorus." (Jung 1969a: 428) This "pleromatic drama" at the heart of Jung's work on Job is a drama based on the movement of the ego into the fullness or Pleroma of its origin for the purpose of making that fullness conscious in humanity.

Jung describes his "Answer to Job" as an amplification and extension of a previous work, *Aion*, in which he had criticized the figure of Christ as an incomplete image of the self because severed from his shadow in the figure of Satan. (Jung 1968a: 41, 42, 44) The criticism easily extended to the adequacy of the symbol of the Father in whom, like his divine Son, there was allegedly no darkness. One might say that, for Jung, the problem seemed to run in the family. To meet his own inner need to elaborate these positions and to satisfy the external pressures of his public and of his patients to make them explicit, Jung wrote his commentary on Job. (Jung 1965a: 216, 217) He more than fulfilled both inner and outer demands. Yet the explosive nature of the text well explains his resistance to so daunting a task and his need for the help of his dreams in rising to meet it.

Toward the end of his life Jung had a series of dreams in which his father, a minister in the Swiss Reformed Church, appeared. (Jung 1965a: 213–219) As a youth Jung had argued at length with his clerical father, especially over the meaning of a faith and its dogmatic expression devoid of any immediate experience of its truth. (Jung 1965a: 91–94) Jung intimates a faith stripped of experiential immediacy had soured his father's life and possibly contributed to its untimely ending. (Jung 1965a: 95, 96) The late dreams in which his father appeared imbued Jung with a renewed sense of vocation. Jung was to inherit the karma of an insipid Christian spirituality and to contribute to the birth of a myth which would provide relief to the suffering of the Christian Amfortas wound, the wound of the fisher king and the consequent spiritual impotence which so burdened his father and the wider Christian community. Jung was to be the Parsifal seeking the grail to heal Christianity itself. (Jung 265a: 215, 216)

Now, to return to the crucial dream steeling him for his work on Job, he and his father kneel before a higher door behind which is Uriah, King David's faithful general. In the dream Uriah personifies a faith betrayed, a faith in a divinely established king who murdered Uriah out of lust for his wife. Jung's father kissed the floor before Uriah in submission to Uriah and to his God. Jung bowed to within a millimeter of the floor but did not kiss it. (Jung 1965a: 219) Had he done so he would have capitulated to the pathology of his father's faith and become, in his terms, another Christian "dumb fish" (Jung 1965a: 220), one of those "unconscious souls" (Jung 1965a: 216) whose suffering is non-redemptive because unrelated to the only legitimate form of suffering, the suffering attached to redeeming divinity by resolving its conflicts in human consciousness. In this case the opposites to be suffered were those of divine authority and human autonomy, the same clash Tillich constellates in the battle between religious heteronomy and rational autonomy. His father as a symbol of non-redemptive suffering points to a faith severed from human experience. Such faith originates beyond the psyche and is imposed on it. The cost of such faith is the repression of all doubt about what Jung calls the "sacrosanct unintelligibility" of symbols when symbolic expression is understood literally, or historically and not psychologically and experientially. (Jung 1969b: 109, 110) In his rejection of faith understood as obedience to an external divinity, Jung recasts faith as obedience to the self and to the demand it makes from within the psyche on the consciousness of the individual, a demand for the mutual redemption of both the self and the consciousness in which it seeks to become progressively incarnate.

The millimeter that separated Jung's forehead from the floor before Uriah *is* the "small but decisive factor" by which the consciousness of the creature surpasses that of the creator. (Jung 1965a: 220) The maintenance of conscious autonomy preserves the very possibility that its origin, the divine, can become conscious in it, admittedly through the cyclical reimmersion of consciousness in its divine and maternal source. The wholly intra-psychic dialectic of the creation of consciousness and its return to its source in processes of the ongoing incarnation of the self in consciousness is the foundational dynamic inspiring the wholesale revisioning of the divine–human relation informing Jung's "Answer to Job", making of that work a myth superseding its Jewish and Christian precedents and, indeed, appreciatively undermining any form of monotheism. To a brief telling of that myth let us now turn before concluding with a discussion of what Jung, with considerable justification, identifies, as prominent among its harbingers, namely, key moments in the historical development of Western Christian mysticism.

Yaweh wed to Israel: a troubled marriage

Jung's work on Job is really an extended metaphor in which the history of Western religious experience is understood as the developing history of consciousness in relation to its creative origin, namely, the archetypal unconscious. As Jung opens the drama Yaweh, purportedly the creator of consciousness, is himself profoundly unconscious. (Jung 1969a: 367–372) He has forgotten Sophia, his feminine wisdom, with whom he played initially in the creation of the universe. (Jung 1969a: 395) Thus reduced, he is engaged in a patriarchal marriage with Israel, his submissive wife. (Jung 1969a: 395) As with all patriarchy, power outstrips wisdom and perfection, wholeness. Yaweh, the unconscious patriarch, has no doubt about his omnipotence. In fact, his naked power becomes his trump card and, in the end, his only card in his confrontation with Job. Yet, on his behalf, he has a well founded and Satanic doubt about his omniscience and wisdom. (Jung 1969a: 375) His doubt is projected as suspicion on his wife, Israel, whose spokesperson Job becomes. Yaweh's self-doubt and accompanying unconsciousness become, then, the psychological basis for the testing of Job. As a divine narcissist Yaweh's only self-assurance lies in his constantly being the object of the nation's undying adulation. Should it vanish, so would Yaweh. Yet, as is the tragedy with all narcissists, the reassurance is never enough and never ultimately convincing. Job becomes the victim of Yaweh's narcissistic need for the ongoing but self-defeating testing of those who provide such dubious praise, in this case Job as representative of the nation/wife, Israel. (Jung 1969a: 372)

In some passages Jung describes Yaweh as "amoral" (Jung 1969a: 424) like an impersonal natural force, reminiscent of the incessant but unconscious energies of evolution, devoid of all rational discrimination yet pushing blindly toward consciousness as the only agency in which it can come to know itself and in the knowing become morally responsible. (Jung 1969a: 383) In fact, in a footnote beyond all symbolism and metaphor, Jung simply denies in box car letters that the creator could be a "conscious being". Writes Jung, "The naive assumption that the creator of the world is a conscious being must be regarded as a disastrous prejudice which later gave rise to the most incredible dislocations of logic." (Jung 1969a: 383 note 13) In other formulations Yaweh moves from an amoral to an immoral force too unconscious to be moral. (Jung 1969a: 372) The confrontation with Job thus symbolizes a then developing religious consciousness shocked into the numinous recognition of the creator's continuing unconsciousness and the role of the creature in educating its creator into the creature's own superior consciousness and heightening moral sense. But while Job's consciousness is superior to a Yaweh divested of wisdom and balance it is no match for his overwhelming power. Job clearly perceives Yaweh's instability in swinging from one extreme to the other; just, loving and good on Mondays, Wednesdays and Fridays and free from all such restraints including his own covenants or bargains on other days of the week. Here Jung first sounds the theme that Yaweh's instability necessitates the creation of human consciousness which alone can perceive such instability and eventually, at the ambiguous insistence and help of Yaweh himself, work towards its resolution in human history and consciousness. (Jung 1969a: 406)

Job's conscious superiority to Yaweh marks, for Jung, the end of the credibility of all forms of monotheism. In the precise context of his work on Job, Jung means by "monotheism" the conception of divinity in whom there is no evil, a claim jointly made by all three currently competing one and only Gods. (Jung 1969a: 385) Expanding on this thought, it would not be an undue extension of Jung's mind to include in the graveyard of the one and only Gods, their revealed self-depiction as potentially self-sufficient divinities living in independence from the psyche which, as their creature, they can at will address and manipulate from without and beyond. Recent Jungian scholarship has well argued that Jung's understanding of the psyche leaves only two options for the approach of the divine to the human. Either the unconscious itself gives rise to the sense of the divine or the divine, understood as somehow beyond the psyche, works to consciousness through the unconscious. (Corbett 1996: 6–8) Given its superfluous nature, the latter option might well fall before Occam's razor in the hands of Carl Jung. With the fall of the option for a transcendent God working from beyond the unconscious through the unconscious would also fall the current threat posed by the competing monotheistic communities to the survival of the species whenever they meet geographically or share the same territory, a point which finally is dawning even on geopoliticians and the social sciences when they now speak of the next stage of warfare as the battle of religiously grounded civilizations. (Huntington 1996)

To return to Jung's story line, Job walked away from the argument, bludgeoned into silence by the sheer power of his divine conversant, but victorious as the possessor of a consciousness greater than that of his heavenly adversary now reduced to a vanquished victor by the exchange. The consequences of the victory took a while to register on both Job and Yaweh, that is, on humanity's collective conscious and unconscious. Especially in the unconscious were the effects slow but profound as they moved toward Yaweh's conversion experience. Like Augustine who prayed to be chaste but not yet, Yaweh, after the exchange with Job, wanted to become human but not quite. (Jung 1969a: 456) Yet as his embarrassment grew over Job's triumph, Yaweh came to envy the defeated who had defeated him. Such envy eventually became a major factor in his wanting to become as conscious as his conqueror, and not only as conscious, but also as moral and as embodied. (Jung 1969a: 424) This movement of the unconscious to become conscious in its creature becomes, for Jung, the divine motive for the incarnation. (Jung 1969a: 406) In the extended sense that Jung gives to the term, "incarnation" becomes the never ending process of divinity becoming self-conscious in individual and collective human consciousness. Such an understanding of incarnation would make it difficult to confine its occurrence to a single outstanding individual. (Jung 1969a: 462) Rather incarnation, the recovery of one's native divinity in and through one's humanity, would become a universal developmental possibility and maturational demand.

The recovery of Sophia and the Answer to Job

At this point in the drama Sophia reappears as Yaweh's missing feminine and her gentle urging pushes Yaweh further toward becoming an embodied human, even if the cost be the surrender of his infinite unconscious power and self-indulgence to full entrance into the suffering of finite humanity. Sophia's influence is many-sided. Her love for material creation impels an isolated Yaweh to become real as human. On his part Yaweh's humanization makes him more compassionate as he enters consciously into the suffering of humanity which in its deepest meaning is really his own suffering now becoming fully conscious in humanity. (Jung 1969a: 397) Of utmost importance in Jung's version of Job is the realization, that becoming real by clothing his thoughts and himself in matter at Sophia's invitation involves Yaweh and humanity in suffering together the resolution of Yaweh's self-contradiction in the only place where it can be perceived and redeemed, that is, in embodied human consciousness.

The redemption of divinity through the pain of the unification of its opposites in the human is, for Jung, the substance of the answer to Job. In a breathtaking, outrageous and not a little sardonic passage, Jung points out that the biblical figure of Christ by and large shows little sign of reflective self-knowledge, an abiding characteristic of all forms of messianic puerility. The notable exception and corrective to such impenetrable unconsciousness is his death in despair, abandoned by his transcendent and omnipotent Father, between the divinely grounded opposites of a yes and a no spoken by his fellow criminals on either side of him. (Jung 1969a: 408, 455; 1969c: 225; 1968a: 44; 1968b: 255) Jung loved and repeated throughout his works the symbol of the crucifixion as the classical psycho-spiritual hang-up redemptive in one stroke of both the divine and the human. (Jung 1969a: 455; 1969c: 225; 1968a: 44; 1968b: 255) In the image of the crucifixion, divinity tastes to the dregs in suffering humanity the cost of the resolution of divinity's eternal irresolution that necessitated the creation of human consciousness in the first place. From the human viewpoint, in the image of crucifixion, humanity realizes that its deepest meaning in history is to be redeemed by suffering the progressive unification in itself of the living unresolved conflict that is the eternal and universal life of Yaweh in the depths of the human, whatever name this life be given.

Toward a new eschatology

To reduce the symbol of the crucifixion to an individual redemptive historical event is simply to miss the universal implications of the imagery. Jung describes the event as both "psychological" and "eschatological". (Jung 1969a: 408) As psychological the image describes the dynamic of the meaningful suffering at the heart of every life, namely, the healing of whatever side of the divine self-contradiction is most prominent in that life. But as eschatological, the image describes the movement of history itself and gives to Jung's psychology the status of a philosophy of history. By using the term "eschatology", here and elsewhere, Jung is taking to himself a theological category that describes history's movement toward its culmination in God. For Jung this movement would be humanity's ongoing, conscious identification, differentiation and unification in itself of the archetypally contesting powers that swirl about in the divine vortex of the unconscious. These are the powers that underwrite lethal conflict when they incarnate as possession in individuals or the bonds of faith in communities. In history these powers are easily perceptible in the elevated body count that accompanies them, grim tribute to their reality and power. What is more difficult to understand and suffer is that each opposite, in such conflict, is divinely grounded and so would truncate a more total human consciousness expressing a more total divinity if either or any were to win an unlikely unilateral victory. In terms of Jung's eschatology all of God's archetypal complexes must become conscious and unified in humanity before the drama can end and since the divine complexes are infinite in variation the psychological and so religious drama can probably never end.

One dramatic instance of the integration of opposites is the resolution of good and evil as history moves toward this final but distant synthesis. Jung explicitly places the reality of evil in God. He makes the telling psychological point that a God in whom there is no darkness is a one-sided God who, like Yaweh and the biblical Christ figure, pathologize their devotees with an impossible demand to imitate such goodness. Such efforts at perfection, as evidenced in the revelation of John, not infrequently flip into a psychotic hatred. The lamb of God returns as the ram of God in seeking revenge against all those who have denied him or his followers in the course of their efforts to live out such impossibility. (Jung 1969a: 437, 438)

What are the alternatives to such one-sidedness? Jung credits Christianity with an absolute differentiation of good and evil in the separation of Christ and Satan, the light and dark brothers of a common Father. (Jung 1969b: 174, 175) Yet in his more comprehensive understanding of the psyche, all differentiation of opposites is a preliminary moment on the way to their reintegration, at a higher level, painful though such reintegration be. This process is at the heart of what Jung calls the "transcendent function". (Jung 1969d: 67–91) By it he means that the conflict the psyche constellates in any life and in the life of the species is in the interest of the reunion of the opposites involved in a more inclusive consciousness of wider compassion and more inclusive embrace. This higher union becomes the deepest psychological meaning of atonement, the putting at one in human life of the eternally unresolved polarities in the divine life.

But how are the figures of Christ and Satan, once differentiated, ever to embrace? And if they do not, what will ever prevent those who live out of any variation of a good in whom there is no darkness from projecting their darkness on others, then attacking their projected darkness in the working of the atrocities which fill the pages and airwaves of today's media? On the other hand, who and how many are able to sustain the suffering that would reunite Christ and Satan and redeem the one-sidedness of both in personal and then societal life? Jung will concede that the Christian incarnation is of the good side of God, the side to which Job rightly appealed against the darker side, but goes on to suggest, if not insist, that now the other side must become incarnate and unite with its opposite in the interest of a more total and safer realization of God in human history. (Jung 1969a: 456) He leaves us with little specific directives in this respect, perhaps an instance in his own thought of what he meant when he would occasionally say, "Ultimately we all get stuck somewhere . . .". (Jung 1975c: 297.)

Toward a newer and holier Spirit

Nevertheless, one might well move through this sticking point by simply reflecting more deeply upon the wider implications of what Jung has left us. Throughout his work he develops an understanding of Spirit that is to be the Spirit of the future now taking form. This emerging Spirit will be of wider embrace than the understanding of Spirit currently abroad. Jung follows much of traditional religious thought in understanding Spirit as a unity of opposites, for instance, in its Christian variant as the unity of Father and Son in the Spirit of the Trinity. His thought on the quaternity, however, offers a much more inclusive understanding of Spirit because it includes in the life of the Spirit certain opposites whose divinity is denied in traditional and ortho-dox religious conceptions of Spirit. The exclusion of these polarities from prevalent notions of the Spirit of God devalues them in reality and accounts for the contempt, or, at least, devaluation with which they are held in societies where the traditional sense of Spirit yet prevails. In Jung's vision, the Spirit of the future will unite the lowly body with the spiritual, the earth too often excluded from heaven with heaven, the feminine now denied divine stature with the masculine strangely more at home in the current sphere of the divine, and finally evil with good, and so Satan with Christ. Through including and so sacralizing the polarities of body, the earth, the feminine, and the demonic, currently excluded from the divine, the Spirit of the quaternity would bring to birth in human consciousness a far more encompassing and adequate expression of its creator. And this is the myth Jung foresees as the myth of the future.

And just here the plot thickens. The birthing of a Spirit of such extended embrace is a psychologically complex process. In his work on Job, Jung describes this process as one worked by the Spirit, the self, leading conscious-ness into the Pleroma as the precondition of the Pleroma becoming conscious in humanity. (Jung 1969a: 424, 425) Pleroma means fullness. Jung probably borrowed the term from gnostic literature where it has connotations of an original or creative fullness from which all creation derives. Effectively Jung uses the term as a synonym for the unconscious and implies that in this Pleroma all archetypal opposites are present but undifferentiated because the Pleroma is wholly divested of a point of conscious discrimination even though it is the mother of all consciousness. (Jung 1969e: 495, 504, 505) The pleromatic drama at the heart of the mutual redemption of humanity and divinity describes the reimmersion, Jung says, "baptism", of consciousness into its unconscious source and its return to life renewed and broadened by such immersion. (Jung 1969a: 425) This cycle is one which can never end because of the infinity of the unconscious but whose direction is the progressive redemption of the matrix of consciousness in historical consciousness itself. This redemption would take the form of a consciousness ever more informed by the wealth of its conflicted source now energizing that consciousness in which the conflict is recognized and overcome. Put simply the process of God becoming increasingly conscious in history is one of humanity entering ever more deeply into God in resolving the divine self-contradiction in subsequent human consciousness. Jung perceived this rhythm as the deepest psychological and spiritual rhythm in those mystics to whom he points as precedents in living the pulse he here grounds in the process of individuation itself.

Toward a new morality

The current developmental demand on the evolution of religious consciousness to assist in the birth of the new Spirit brings with it a new morality. Jung will write, "Everything now depends on man." (Jung 1969a: 459) It is something of an overstatement in the context of his own wider work in so much as it could be read as exclusively lodging such dependence on humanity's use of its conscious resources. Jung would be the first to affirm that everything depends on conscious dialogue with the unconscious mediated by the self in generating a broader and deeper human sentiment. The self remains always the presiding agency regulating the conversation between consciousness and the unconscious especially through the medium of the dream as its spokesperson. Jung is more faithful to his own thought and to the role of the self in it when he rests the moral imperative of the new Spirit or self on the demand that humanity resolve in time and history the divine antinomy that defied divinity's resolution in eternity. (Jung 1969a: 461) This resolution can take place only in a human consciousness resonant with its own depths. No appeal to an apocalyptic divinity, in the imagery of an omnipotent reliever, striding to the mound from a transcendent bull pen in the bottom of the ninth to strike out the evil side is any longer morally responsible. To affirm that it is is to miss the redemptive meaning of Christ's final despair over the God who abandoned him. Only consciously suffering the divine into consciousness from its eternally conflicted presence in the depths of the human will effect the completion of the divine and human in one organic psychic and historical process, a mutual completion that is to be the imperative of a new human morality. A corollary of such a newly emerging morality would be the individual's obligation to listen to the voice of the self as it works for the incarnation of a more universal compassion. The cultivation of such individual sensitivities would encourage archetypal powers to embrace rather than destroy each other through the communities who are their embodiment in time and history.

The Second Coming

In both his works *Aion* and the "Answer to Job" Jung is simply stating that the symbols of the Jewish and Christian Gods and the latter's messiah were historically understandable, even necessitated by the psychological laws of compensation. Male and forbidding Gods were a psychological and historical necessity in the face of the mayhem they opposed. As such these divinities and their mythologies are to be appreciated and, like all truly archetypal expression, once surfaced, will never be forgotten in the collective memory. Yet currently they cry out for their missing wholeness. The demand for their supersession arises from the same energies and Holy Spirit that created them. (Jung 1975b: 138) The foundational image of this supersession Jung fittingly takes from the Revelation of John, the last of the Christian canonical books and certainly the most eschatological. The image is that of the endangered birth of a child from a woman clothed with the sun, the moon and the stars. (Jung 1969a: 438–441) Here persona imagery is much more than a surface impression since the woman is clothed with and so is the natural universe.

In Jung's hands this hallucinatory material becomes much more than simply a second reprise of the birth of Christ, the obvious, though mistaken, meaning for the author or authors whose consciousness had been recently impacted by the myth of Christ and so rendered incapable of imagining the seeds of its own need to be surpassed buried within it. (Jung 1969a: 440, 441) So important is this second birth described in the Book of Revelation that the newborn is immediately whisked to heaven and his mother to the protection of the desert against the threat of a devouring dragon. These dramatic events are a variation of the motif Jung describes earlier as the precautions taken to insure the sinlessness of mother and child in the birth of Christ, the psychological basis of the Catholic doctrine of the Immaculate Conception. (Jung 1969a: 397, 398) So also must this second mother and child be protected since they carry humanity's future. Rather than see the second child as a simple though conclusive reoccurrence of the birth of Christ, Jung sees it as compensating that one-sided and less than fully human birth and so surpassing the pure, bright, luminosity of the sun by including the moon and the stars, images of night and of earth and so of the maternal origin of all consciousness in the unconscious. In uniting sun, moon and stars, consciousness with the unconscious, the second mother and son complete the first birth of divinity in humanity as humanity moves toward the New Jerusalem in which there is no temple because the ever fuller birth of the unconscious into consciousness is sacred in itself working always a more total incarnation of the divine in the human extending the sense of the sacred to all that is. Put briefly Jung is here contending that the compensation of a pathological Christianity imbalanced toward the spiritual already occurs within the Christian revelation in the imagery of a total woman giving birth to a total son destined eventually to carry the future.

At the end of the day Jung believes that such compensation is now occurring. He is contending that the spiritual future of humanity and the survival of the species will depend on its success in ushering the total God into an ever more total human consciousness, the only consciousness that exists, in a process mutually redemptive of the divine and the human. The conclusion is not compatible with any form of monotheism and, in those monotheistic traditions given to the identification of heresy, would surely qualify as such. And yet in the text of his work on Job, Jung appeals to a number of Christian mystics, two of whom appear widely throughout his work. In Jung's view they anticipate his efforts historically and he implies that his work, prefigured in theirs, gives to their experience a psychological precision and endorsement that they could not. Both have been dealt with in previous chapters but foundational elements in their experience provide for Jung a strange precision to the radical processes of the psyche as it moves current Western religious sensitivities toward the Spirit of totality and inclusion that Jung sought to describe in such late works as the "Answer to Job".

Meister Eckhart and the breakthrough

Jung cites Eckhart over thirty-five times throughout the *Collected Works* and describes him in one complimentary passage as someone who had experienced the reality of the unconscious six centuries before it was more formally identified and addressed in nineteenth century Europe. (Jung 1968c: 194) As seen earlier in the work contemporary Eckhart scholars identify two discrete but related experiences in his mysticism. The first is the birth of God in the soul. The second is the famous breakthrough. Jung appreciated both events because he understood mystical experience to be an immediate experience of the archetypal, the origin of all religious experience. (Jung 1976a: 98, 99) Such unmediated experience would give to the mystic a certain priority or privilege in the religious realm and make of mysticism a sort of proto-religion.

What then would Eckhart's experience of the birth of God in the soul be? From Jung's perspective it would point to an experience of the self, often imaged as the divine child even in contemporary dreamers. It would thus describe the incarnation of the self in the individual imaged by the birth of God in the soul. Indeed, Eckhart was of the opinion that the historical birth of Christ in the virgin Mary would be an interesting but remote historical, gynecological event, perhaps to be included in Ripley's *Believe It or Not*, unless he were to experience it in himself. (Eckhart 1947c: 216) For Jung, this passage is clear evidence that the man possessed an appreciation of symbolic discourse and as the prime language of immediate religious experience and as the basis of so called "revelation". Furthermore it would point to Eckhart's awareness in the fourteenth century of Jung's point in his "Answer to Job" and throughout his work that divinity approaches humanity immediately from within making of such experience a personal revelation in which divinity and humanity are naturally implicated and mutually redeemed.

Eckhart's experience did not stop there. As seen in previous chapters the birth of God in his soul served as a prelude to the event he described as the "breakthrough". In the breakthrough God's birth in Eckhart's soul culminated in a total and unqualified moment of identity with the Godhead. Such identity is a human potential residual or native to Eckhart's humanity and so is universally human. Effectively this moment of identity is the actualization of a native capacity which would follow Eckhart in his return from it to the affairs of the world convinced that his natural divinity was irrefrangible. Its residual effects are evident in his assurance that in his deeper humanity he and God shared a common point of being which could never be lost. Though he much admired Eckhart, Jung is judicious in giving a psychological interpretation to this aspect of Eckhart's experience. Obviously it depicts a psychological situation in which the ego and the unconscious are wholly one, dissolved into each other. I have been able to find only one text in Jung in which he clearly alludes to this psychic state of unqualified identity of ego and unconscious. In his interpretation of this dimension of Eckhart's experience Jung writes, "God disappears as an object and dwindles into a subject which is no longed distinguishable from the ego." (Jung 1971a: 255) In turn about when Eckhart is used to amplify Jung such a state would have to be a moment in which the ego dissolved into its source beyond even latent imagery and any urge to act, as the precondition to an immensely invigorated return to consciousness. This would have to be the case even in terms of Tillich's search for the way beyond the subject–object split in the divine–human relation. Such a moment would have to be wholly beyond any differentiation an active ego could make between itself, God and the world of other discrete beings. Jung treats this moment with caution because of its obvious psychotic potential. Such a moment raises the question of what then would move the ego back from such identity with its origin to its engagement with the world and would also raise the psychotic possibility that such a return could fail. In terms of his own psychology only the power of the self could work the unqualified identity of ego with its unconscious source and the return of ego to a conscious life after such a moment of identity. As such the moment stands as evidence of how deeply into the unconscious the self stands ready to plunge the ego in the interests of its renewal and transformation.

Jung is less reserved in appropriating Eckhart's experience for what Jung calls "the relativity of God". Again confessing his dependence on Eckhart, Jung here describes the divine and the human as "functions" of each other within the containment of the psyche. (Jung 1971a: 243) He could hardly be more explicit in his contention that humanity's experience of the divine is wholly intra-psychic. Such experience engages a conscious function, the ego, impacted by the function of the archetypal unconscious generating from within the psyche the experience of the numinous as the basis of all religion, personal and collective. Nor could Jung be more insistent on the point, when he accuses those who are not aware "that God's action springs from one's own inner being", of ignorance of the nature of religion itself. (Jung 1971a: 243) In these words Jung could hardly be more precise in denying the origin of religion from a point or agency somehow beyond the psyche.

Jacob Boehme (1575–1624)

To return once more to Boehme, he is an even more frequent visitor to the pages of Jung's work for reasons that become obvious in an account of Boehme's experience. To recapitulate he was a largely self-educated shoe-maker and merchant living in Silesia in the turbulent century following the Reformation. He too ran into trouble with the official Church now in the form of his Protestant pastor. The trouble was over his recording and sharing mystical experiences undergone at discrete moments in his life in 1600, 1612 and 1619. Like Eckhart, Boehme also experienced a moment of total identity with the divine described as the "One" or the *ungrund*. (Boehme 1911: 2) Differing from Eckhart's emphasis, identity with the One was not the high point of Boehme's experience. Rather his experience of the divine, as he moved away from this moment of identity with it, was that of a conflicted power whose conflict was mirrored throughout nature and humanity and sought resolution in human consciousness. The central imagery of this unresolved divine conflict depicts a dark, angry burning fire, the Father, over against a warming, somewhat androgynous Christ figure, the bearer of light and con-scious manifestation. (Boehme 1958: 25–27; 1911: 46–49) The father power is also the hell where the fallen angels dwell, an image anticipating Jung's iden-tification of the dark side of God, the *deus absconditus* of alchemical fame. (Boehme 1909: 49) Sophia as wisdom is also present in divine life and closely related to the Holy Spirit but she does not unite the divine conflict in eternity. Instead, again as Jung understands her in his work on Job, she urges the creation of human embodied consciousness where God becomes first aware of his inner division. Historical consciousness becomes the only theater in which this division can be perceived and healed. (Boehme 1911: 48)

In the history of Western thought the idea of the ground of history resolv-ing its conflicts within history was given philosophical formulation in con-scious dependence on Boehme by Hegel and rendered operational by Marx. Thus the philosophical and social history of Boehme's imagery is not without its own ambiguity as it develops in his successors. Jung himself and Jungian scholarship tend to emphasize Jung's claimed dependence on Kant. There is some basis for Jung's claims. The archetypes do structure human perception and behavior, what Kant would call pure and practical or moral reason. Indeed, the structuring role of the archetypes does have affinity with Kant's categories which Kant understood to determine the boundaries of legitimate human thought and to prompt morality. However, some question might well be raised as to whether Jung violates Kant's prohibiting to the mind a licit knowledge of the noumenal which lies behind or beyond the phenomenal world. Jung's understanding of the numinous and its manifest power in dreams and other psychic phenomenon could well be understood as providing experiential access to Kant's forbidden world of the noumenon. Jung's conception of the numinous and Kant's of the noumenon could have the same referent with the major difference that with Jung the noumenon are knowable in the numinous. Indeed, Kant may have himself evaded his own proscriptions on reason's access to the noumenon when, in his moral reflections, he speaks of the impact of the voice of conscience on consciousness. The experience of the numinous that Kant denies to the thinking mind seems to reassert itself in Kant's understanding of the moral mind in the form of a voice or injunction of the ought resounding unabatedly in the soul making of the experience a revelation directly from God clad in moral guise. (Kant 1960: 40) Kant would also be among the first to identify the figure of Christ as an "archetype" of the morally perfect man and so anticipate in a narrower moral sense Jung's understanding of Christ as a symbol of the much more inclusive self. (Kant 1960: 54, 55)

While Jung's affinities to Kant are well know the affinities of his thought with Hegel are less known and only admitted by Jung himself late in his life. (Jung 1975d: 502) Their deepest affinity lies in their shared conviction that the ground or origin of human consciousness redeems itself through the conquest of its conflicts in human consciousness through humanity's coming to perceive and to cooperate with the process. Hegel could see the process externally. He could, for example, identify the hand of God in history with the French Revolutionary army marching through Jena at war with the pre-revolutionary *ancien régime*. For Hegel conflict could be externalized on the field of battle as the theater of that archetypal enmity through which God and humanity become mutually conscious in history. It is a vision with its own compelling attraction and does give meaning to human conflict as it moves the direction of history to ever greater freedom. Jung, of course, could never agree with Hegel's provincial conclusion that the ultimate archetypal difference, that of God and humanity, was resolved in the symbol of Christ as the symbol of the definitive unity of the divine and the human. But Jung might have more to offer the current situation than Hegel on even deeper grounds. Jung has more because he departs from Hegel when he removes the conflict of absolutes from projection into historical events understood as outside the psyche and relocates the process within the psyche. Thus contained humanity is to suffer the union of divine opposites in an internal psychic war that would eliminate the carnage which always results when these opposites escape inner containment and seek resolution in war in the external forum.

In this sense Jung's understanding of the psyche holds out greater promise for the survival of the species. While it maintains a vital dialectic, based on warring forces within the psyche, Jung's psychology provides something of a prophylactic to the mind preventing that kind of divine fecundation which has created the religions, their transcendent Gods, and their now secular, ethnic, and political equivalents so often depriving their members of consciousness and so of moral responsibility in their mutual interface. Jung's psychology provides such a prophylactic by giving to the individual the possibility of identifying the archetypal energies which bond communities, including one's own, in mortal conflict and which bond the individual member to such communities in support of the conflict. The identification of such energies is the first step in freeing the individual from their suasion toward a freer, and more conscious relation to those archetypal forces manipulating the masses in one's immediate social surrounding. The moral defeat suffered by humanity universally in the wars in the Middle East when coalition leaders could induce an archetypal bonding from their constituencies reminiscent of Jung's description of events in Germany in the 1930s speaks to the necessity of coming to terms with the societal power of the archetypal and of how little time humanity may have left to do so. In this context Jung's psychology, though always intimately individual, is profoundly political and latently subversive because it forbids the possibility of the appearance of the absolute in unqualified identity with any specific revelation, mythology or other manifestation of the archetypal in history. If this sensitivity were to come to inform a newly emerging societal myth it would become increasingly difficult for archetypally bonded communities to kill in the name of their bonding power.

Jung's myth of an emerging quaternity would offset the threat that archetypal conflict based on faith in religious or secular form poses to contemporary humanity because it is grounded on the conviction that the goal toward which the Spirit leads history must be one in which the totality of the divine resource and all of its polarities are surfaced and resolved in human consciousness. It is something of a paradox then that Jung sees in specifically Christian mystics the seeds of the expansion and ultimate supersession of Christianity itself. If we are to listen to Eckhart and Boehme and to Jung's psychic appropriation of them we are faced with a double quaternity at the core of now emerging myth. Eckhart leads to what Paul Tillich has called the God above the God of theism, the Christian Trinitarian God, to a fourth in God beyond all division and so capable of healing such division within and beyond God. (Tillich 1952: 186) Psychologically this movement is to the point where ego and unconscious come into an identity beyond the distinction between creature and creator, consciousness and the unconscious. Boehme adds to this moment its completion in humanity as the fourth, namely as the only place where the implacable opposition implied in the symbol of Trinity can be resolved in the human Spirit impelled by the divine Spirit. These are the ground movements in what Jung in his interpretation of Job describes as the pleromatic drama in which each of us and our epoch are engaged. The major moments in this drama are the recurrent sacrifice of the ego through its dissolution into and identity with its divine origin and the sacrifice of that divine origin as it becomes human, and so limited but increasingly responsible and compassionate in its ongoing incarnation in humanity.

Conclusion

The pleromatic drama Jung describes in his work on Job is the substance of the glory and tragedy of being human. The drama can never be completed. It has no final act because divinity, the wealth of the unconscious, will always surpass the concrete historical stages of its always limited incarnations and so corrode them toward patterns of ever greater inclusiveness in ever richer harmonies. To deny this side of the human plight would be a form of lethal idolatry which would proclaim as ultimate and final that which can be no more than permanently preliminary. This is true for any claim to a final revelation be it religious, political, or ethnic or any combination of the foregoing. Such claims in the name of whatever divinity pit themselves against a divinity which always lusts for ever greater and deeper incarnation in the human. Efforts to close the religious canon and so the ongoing process of revelation put themselves in conflict with the deepest powers of the psyche itself and so with the unfolding of history.

On the other hand to forgo the challenge to cooperate with the divine in its incessant demand for greater incarnation in history is to give up on life and on life's universal vocation to redeem the divine in humanity. Where this sense dies the spirit grows coarse with a superficiality breeding despair, and a meaninglessness that ultimately loses the will to live. But living with the gift and burden of the redemption of the divine in history as a task which can neither be accomplished nor abandoned does take definitive turns for the better in the evolution of consciousness. Such a turn is Jung's understanding of the deeper psyche as the common and human matrix of all archetypal expression and conflict. This understanding in and of itself can only work a consciousness with a deeper compassion for the other. The clear identification of the common origin in humanity of the divinities and absolutes that conflict in history should work to dissolve their still murderous power. Such realization should lead to an embrace that would move, through the suffering of the loss of lesser faiths in provincial and tribal commitments, to a wider, ultimately universal sympathy. Jung's "Answer to Job" contributes immensely to the hope for that "afternoon" of humanity he envisaged where conquest would cede to an empathy for the other as other completing and complementing a divinity only partially realized in ourselves and in our or any culture. (Jung 1969e: 493)

Chapter 8

Memory and emergence

Jung and the mystical anamnesis of the nothing

The problematic: why ask the question of the mystics and the nothing at all?

Chapter 7 presented evidence that Jung understood the process of individuation to entail not only a return to the unconscious as the origin of consciousness but also an immersion of the ego into the unconscious beyond all difference and differentiation. It is this side of the individuation process that aligns Jung's psychology with the mystical experience of a loss in a formless nothingness which the mystics take to be a moment of identity with the divine. Such mystical consciousness and its relation to the nothing seem an exotic indulgence, when Jungian psychology seriously faces the question of what it has to offer current processes of humanization. On closer examination, however, the relevance of mystical consciousness becomes quickly evident as Jung's ultimate corrective resource to the blight he consistently identified at the heart of the psyche and soul of Western society in his time and, by extension, in ours. Jung described this social and individual pathology as a consciousness reduced to "a rootless will o'the wisp" (Jung 1966a: 205) that is, a consciousness severed from that maternal nothingness from which all consciousness and its capacities are born. Such a state of mind had cut itself loose from the universal "root of the whole human race" (Jung 1966a: 202) and so from the mother of consciousness herself who creates and, having created, renews all conscious life.

In the individual, this "soul sickness" manifests as the "uprootedness, disorientation, meaninglessness" of a life devoted to the surface levels of psyche. (Jung 1969f: 415) In the collective, the disease manifests as those currently all too obvious "psychic epidemics" compelling archetypally possessed communities to kill for their bonding faiths often along the territorial fault lines that divide them. (Jung 1968d: 126, 127; Dourley 2003) The unconsciousness informing archetypal conflict makes the continuation of the current and future "clash of civilizations", now a familiar phrase in the mass media, psychologically inevitable. (Huntington 1993) For Jung meaningless superficiality and murderous faiths are joint products of a humanity torn from the universal ground and source of its life and so from the more encompassing compassion conscious rerooting in that ground would afford. (Jung 1964a: 248)

Much, if not all, of Jung's mature psychology was an effort to reconnect the currently uprooted mind and soul of the West with their deeper stabilizing roots in their intra-psychic maternal "origins". (Jung 1966a: 429) He uses many idioms and images to depict the dynamic of this crucial reconnection and to name the power that is its sponsor and goal. Sometimes it is the Great Mother or Goddess (Jung 1966a: 222, 223), sometimes the Pleroma or original fullness (Jung 1965b: 379), sometimes the One of Plotinus (Jung 1966a: 138), sometimes the sea (Jung 1966a: 218, 251) and sometimes the prime matter from which all is born. (Jung 1970: 18) Perhaps Jung reserves his most cogent description of the universal mother of consciousness for those occasions when he makes of her the basis of a truly modern spirituality. Here the rerooting of the uprooted modern, who may know the Western tradition but can glean little spiritual sustenance from it, takes the form of an unmediated contact with "the Nothing out of which All may grow". (Jung 1964a: 75) In this formulation the mother is herself the nothingness.

In this passage Jung makes explicit that the radical resolution of contemporary uprootedness lies in the reconnection with that nothingness, itself divested of mind and form, which is the source of mind and of all archetypal impact on the mind. The most profound form of baptism is the ego's dissolution in and return from this nothingness with a consciousness now more able to embrace the all beyond through reimmersion in the maternal nothing within from which the all is born. (Jung 1969a: 425) It is a baptism, unlike lesser forms of baptism, which cannot guarantee the return of the initiate. The mother devours as well as renews. This risk is why such dissolution in the origin is the substance of the hero's journey and one the hero undertakes not once but repeatedly in the renewal of life and consciousness. (Jung 1966b: 169, 170)

In large part, it was their experience of their dissolution in and return from the nothing that drew Jung to those mystics who people his pages. They were his predecessors in heralding the cyclical rebirth of the "I" through the recurring moment of identity with its wholly intra-psychic source. These women and men were not arbitrarily drawn to the original and originating nothingness. Rather they and Jung seemed residually sensitive to its natural psychic allure. Effectively their memory of the nothing, the source of the divine image in and for which they were created, empowered their return to it and from it in processes of ever growing realization of a divine fullness in their individual person.

As they returned from dissolution in their origin they experienced themselves as more intensely imaging God in what Jung describes as a personal apocatastasis, that is, in a greater approximation of their totality, not as in a pre-temporal paradise or in a post-temporal heaven but in the eternal now as the basis of their developing consciousness within time and finitude. Put succinctly Jung's most forceful expression of his sustained efforts to reroot individual and society in their native divinity takes the form of the intensification of the memory of the nothing that precedes the all and seeks its fullness in the all. Here Jung's critique echoes Heidegger's of an uprooted society that has forgotten and then forgotten that it has forgotten. Neither Jung nor his mystical predecessors had forgotten or could forget. The considerable social significance of Jung's psychology lies, then, in his efforts to stir up the memory of a common human origin funding a more integrated individual possessed of an extended compassion both for differing individuals and for differing archetypally bonded communities.

The anamnesis of the Nothing and apocatastasis

Anamnesis means a recalling or recollection. Throughout Jung's work the term "anamnesis" usually refers to the entirely conscious recall of a personal history, ordinarily in the early stages of an analysis. (Jung 1961: 230, 231) Yet in one telling passage he confesses that the real analysis, the experience of the deeper unconscious through the dreams, begins only when the more superficial biographical anamnesis concludes. (Jung 1954: 100) Thus, in rare but incisive passages, Jung greatly expands the meaning of anamnesis when he extends its inward reach to the memory of the individual's pristine nature and so to the individual's experience of one's native divinity. Writes Jung, "As a result of this 'anamnesis' the original state of oneness with the God-image is restored." (Jung 1968a: 40) Jung elsewhere equates the memory of one's divinity with the experience of the "incorruptible" and "eternal" self as "pre-existent to consciousness". (Jung 1969c: 265) The realized memory of the self then becomes "the most immediate experience of the Divine which it is psychologically possible to imagine". (Jung 1969c: 261)

Such an anamnesis brings the individual closer to one's totality in the present, and so always carries with it "the restoration of an original condition, an apocatastasis". (Jung 1968a: 40) Apocatastasis, especially in the epistles of Paul, usually refers to the reunion of the totality of creation with its origin at the end of history in a post-temporal situation. When Jung equates the recovered memory of one's totality with apocatastasis, he is stating that such wholeness is experienced as worked by the memory itself and in the here and now. Both paradise and the end time are to be approximated and experienced in the present as moments in natural processes of maturation or individuation, for Jung, no longer distinguishable from divinization.

When Jung connects such memory with the experience of immortality, he understands the experience of immortality as the individual's experience of continuity with the total human, past and future. (Jung 1968e: 188) More, he contends that the recovery of the sense of immortality linking the individual to the total temporal human experience is the goal of functional ritual when it serves the anamnesis of the origin. (Jung 1970: 419) Such ritual activation of one's living memory of the ancestral or divine origin carries the participant to that dimension of the psyche where opposites unite and so restore to the individual the sureness of one's spiritual and instinctive roots which discriminating consciousness can divide and turn against each other. (Jung 1966c: 122, 123) In this context ritual anamnesis bears the power of the *anthropos* symbol, the sense of the identity of each individual human with humanity itself and with the total proclivities that contribute to the total human. (Jung 1970: 420) When the ritual is privatized, as in alchemy, it carries the initiate back to unity with the origin of consciousness, an origin to be made increasingly conscious as the realization in the here and now of that eschatological reality, recovery of the divine, toward which all consciousness moves. (Jung 1968f: 1169) Put briefly, Jung understands the psychodynamics of the eschaton driving both collective and individual life to be the intensifying memory of the origin now seeking ever greater ingression into human consciousness as such memory moves consciousness into its present and future fullness.

As suggested, the recovery of the past divine origin in the present as the direction of the future is, for Jung, vested with great social import as the only real resource in reconnecting the uprooted individual with a sustaining meaning and society with the energies of evolution needed for its ongoing survival and enhancement. Jung describes the peril of individual and collective uprootedness in stark terms. "Nevertheless, when a living organism is cut off from its roots, it loses the connections with the foundations of its existence and must necessarily perish. When that happens, anamnesis of the origins is a matter of life and death." (Jung 1969f: 180) And so for individual and species the stakes in the recovery of the memory of the origin in the service of her current incarnation as redeeming the present and enhancing the future could hardly be higher.

Jung, the mystics and the Nothing

The foregoing discussion establishes, then, the link between the mystical experience of the nothing with the experience Jung personified in the figures of the Great Mother or Goddess and so with the furthest realm of the archetypal psyche. Effectively the nothing, the Goddess and the depths of the archetypal unconscious become synonyms. Jung was to dramatically illustrate the psychodynamics of cyclical immersion in and return from such nothingness through the experience of a series of mystics prominent throughout the *Collected Works*. This series extends from the thirteenth century Beguines through Meister Eckhart to Jacob Boehme, who greatly influenced Hegel and so modernity. In a spontaneous interchange in his Tavistock lectures, Jung unqualifiedly identified unmediated mystical experience with archetypal experience. (Jung 1976a: 98, 99) Since Jung undeniably underwent such experience in his own life his own comments identify Jung as a mystic himself, his frequently expressed Kantian reservations notwithstanding. More pertinent to this discussion, the equation of mystical experience with archetypal experience means that such experience charts the further reaches of the archetypal psyche and, in the phenomenon of apophatic experience, may even point to psychic geography uncharted or, at best, cautiously sketched by Jung himself.

Currently what is called apophatic mysticism, the mysticism that culminates in the mystic's total dissolution in the nothing, is enjoying a heightened interest in the scholarly community. Jung, in his choice of mystics, would appear to have anticipated the current scholarly renewal of interest in the apophatic. For all the mystics of Jung's interest include in their experience the moment of identity with and return from that nothingness generative of mind and so of the knowable. A scholarly consensus is currently forming around the conclusion that the mystics of apophaticism experience a *unitas indistinctionis*, a union of identity, between the divine and the human at the height of their experience. (McGinn 2001: 47, 148; Cuppitt 1998: 106–122) Such unity is distinguished from a *unitas spiritus*, a union which maintains the distinction between the divine and human spirits throughout the entire commerce of the mystic with divinity. (McGinn 1998: 217)

Of even greater interest in the contemporary appreciation of the apophatic experience is a still inchoate but developing realization that in the end such experience is as psychological as it is religious. For instance, a prominent commentator will state that the moment of identity of the mystic with the divine is not of the "existential I of our subjectivity" with a contrasting divine ego. Rather such identity is attained through a so called "transcendent I", which is that virtual or residual divine dimension of the human in the divine ground beyond divine–human distinction. (McGinn 2001: 111,138) This language bears patent affinity with the Jungian paradigm of the self orchestrating the ego's dissolution in the creative nothingness of its origin as a prelude to a deepening and broadening of consequent consciousness.

The following analysis of the mystics whom Jung appropriates to elaborate his psychology and the implications of such appropriation deepen the affinity between mystical experience and archetypal experience, even as such analysis serves to illuminate the further reaches of the ingression of the ego into its intra-psychic origins. Effectively this analysis could suggest an extension of the boundaries or depths of the psyche and encourage the value of plummeting them beyond the parameters of the psyche that Jung more usually establishes throughout his corpus. Looking at the historical sequence of the mystics Jung introduces into his work does a number of things. It illuminates the psychological nature of mystical experience and moves to the conclusion that at this depth the distinction between psychological and religious/mystical experience vanishes. More importantly Jung's understanding of the evolution of the psyche would insinuate that certain streams of mystical experience and their historical development in the West serve a religious consciousness based on an immediate experience of the ultimate currently urging a new societal/religious consciousness much more fully expressive of the resources latent in the origin of consciousness than extant religions can comfortably mediate to their constituencies.

The Beguines and Mechthild of Magdeburg, Hadewijch and Marguerite Porete

The Beguines originated in the twelfth century and moved toward effective extinction in the fifteenth. (McDonnell 1954; Hollywood 2004; Babinsky 1993: 6–20) Today they might be termed a "lay" movement. They sought their place in the area between the religious life of those living in permanently vowed communities with formal ecclesial support and protection and those living simply as members of the laity. Their life took on many forms including that of the solitary and wanderer. However, they are best known as self-supporting communities of women bonded to celibate life as long as they remained in the community. Such communities were dedicated to a variety of good works including caring for the ill and teaching. Because they never received the unqualified approbation of the Church as did the regular orders of men and women and were even looked on with suspicion by the ecumenical Council of Vienne (1311), their status remained vulnerable throughout their existence. (Denzinger 1964: 282) Frequently they were or were perceived as threats to ecclesial order. Tenuous though their status was, three of their more prominent members brought an acuity and depth to apophatic spirituality not previously seen in Christianity. Jung refers to one of them, Mechthild of Magdeburg, in his *Collected Works*. Her apophaticism will here be amplified by two of her Beguine colleagues, Hadewijch and Marguerite Porete, neither of whom are cited in Jung's texts but do serve to amplify the psychological implications of Mechthild's experience. So original was the experience of these three women that a leading scholar of the period describes them as evangelists and extends to the novelty and substance of their writing, "a status comparable to that of the Bible itself". (McGinn 1998: 199)

Mechthild's imagery centers around the archetypal theme of sexual intercourse with an 18-year-old Christ figure. (Mechthild 1953: 20–25, 237–238) The love-making moves into an immersion in the flow of Trinitarian life which, in turn, brings about the mutual completion of Mechthild and the Trinity. In a key passage she depicts the members of the Trinity driven to create her and to kiss her to relieve their eternal self-sufficient unfruitfulness. (Mechthild 1953: 74, 75) She proclaims that of this "intercourse with the soul" the divine cannot have enough. (Mechthild 1953: 105) From a Jungian perspective the Trinity's lust for Mechthild is the divine lust for consciousness itself. In this imagery Mechthild distantly anticipates the Yaweh of Jung's Job, who was driven to incarnation in human consciousness as the sole theater where he himself could become self-conscious and morally responsible.

Mechthild's tryst with a teenage Christ figure is set in the trope of courtly love. As she moves to the moment of consummation she sets aside her senses but asks them to wait for her upon her return. (Mechthild 1953: 24) Jung also would have it that the senses cannot go where God is experienced. Mechthild also refuses the blandishments of various virtues as cheap substitutes for the intensity of immediate physical love here functioning as a symbol of an intensity and immediacy surpassing what the virtues can offer. (Mechthild 1953: 22–23) Her own lust for the divine enables her to affirm that she is divine "through nature" and to enter naked, stripped of all virtue, into "the blessed stillness" of sexual intimacy with her young divine lover. (Mechthild 1953: 24, 25) The apophatic moment of identity with the divine is captured, then, by the image of the stillness of sexual love wholly satiated.

Jung mentions Mechthild early in his work in his efforts to differentiate his understanding of libido from Freud's. The God with whom Mechthild sought and achieved identity becomes the height of archetypal energy itself. Jung writes, "To carry a God within oneself is practically the same as being God oneself." (Jung 1966a: 87, 89, 90) He mentions her again in a case where the God image was being projected on himself by a patient. The patient's recovery of the projection became the occasion of her coming to live her own divinity under the immediate suasion of the self. (Jung 1966b: 134) Elsewhere Jung describes the imagery of Mechthild's love for the Christ figure as a form of the *hieros gamos*, the marriage of the ego with the archetypal inner opposite (Jung 1968g: 176) expressed in a "quite unabashed Christ-eroticism". (Jung 1971b: 232) One can hardly imagine a more supportive animus at once divine and human, and so uniting the sexual and spiritual in its embrace of the feminine.

However, Jung does not identify in Mechthild that moment of rest in the nothingness of God that he so clearly describes in Eckhart. This aspect of Mechthild's experience, though there, is made explicit in the very similar imagery of Hadewijch, a fellow thirteenth century Beguine. Hadewijch leaves little to the imagination. In one of her most powerful visions, the Christ figure appears sequentially as a shape-shifter, first as a 3-year-old child and then as an adult at the age of his crucifixion. (Hadewijch 1980: 280–281) After offering her the sacrament as an external embodiment, "he came himself to me, took me entirely in his arms, and pressed me to him: and all my members felt his in full felicity, in accordance with the desire of my heart and my humanity". But this image of unqualified intimacy was soon to fade so that her lover was no longer beyond her nor within her. Her description of this state reads "Then it was to me as if we were one without difference." (Hadewijch 1980: 281) Here she describes a state of identity with the divine as beyond all othering and so forces the question whether, from a Jungian perspective, she is describing a recovered identity of ego with the unconscious prior to all differentiation between them.

The third Beguine in this sequence, Marguerite Porete, was burnt in public in Paris on June 1, 1310. She was executed by the secular arm to whom a church court committed her after convicting her of heresy. Throughout her trial she had remained totally silent, witness to her well-founded conviction that the men who condemned her had little capacity to understand or sympathize with her experience. (Babinsky 1993: 21–24) Though her single work, *The Mirror of Simple Souls*, somehow escaped the flames and became a classic through the centuries following her execution, her authorship was established only in 1946. (Babinsky 1993: 1; McGinn 1998: 244, note 237) Her importance both in the history of mystical experience and Jung's appropriation of it lies in the fact that current scholarship has established thematic and possibly literary continuities between her formulations and those of Meister Eckhart, a major figure in Jung's work. (McGinn 1998: 246, note 253) During his second teaching period at the University of Paris (1311–1312) Eckhart lived with her inquisitor, William Humbert or William of Paris, an English fellow Dominican. In this period Eckhart likely read a copy of her condemned work. (McGinn 2001: 9) Some speculate a major sermon of Eckhart's, "Blessed are the poor", containing most of the foundational elements of his mysticism, reflected and affirmed Marguerite's experience. (McGinn 2001: 136) Eckhart may have written the sermon in later life when he was defending himself at his own heresy trial or had been already condemned and so was less concerned with orthodoxy. (Sells 1994: 183)

Marguerite is also indebted to the courtly love tradition but is less explicit sexually than Mechthild or Hadewijch (McGinn 1998: 260) in her occasional references to the divine "Spouse of her youth". (Porete 1993: 193) Rather she is much more explicit about the culmination of her psychological and spiritual development in that state she calls the "annihilated soul". (Porete 1993: 102, 120, 135, 169, 174, 185) The annihilated soul achieves an identity with the divine in a nothingness that is at the same time the all. In this radical apophatic state the achievement of the nothing and through it the relation to the totality are but two aspects of the same psychic event. She writes, "Now this soul has fallen from love into nothingness, and without such nothingness she cannot be All." (Porete 1993: 193, 129) Nor does Marguerite attain annihilation as a passing moment. Rather she is "established" in it. (Porete 1993: 90, 144, 194) Her establishment in the nothing means such consciousness cannot be lost. Her consequent life remains then "unencumbered" by all forms of will and desire as a residual consciousness. (Porete 1993: 127, 129, 159, 167–168, 171) From a Jungian perspective it would seem that when the self leads back to annihilation in the nothing it is an unforgettable experience and can become one which benignly possesses its willing victim for a lifetime leading into an intensely active passivity and a life lived in Marguerite's and Eckhart's terms "without a why". (Porete 1993: 167)

Like Mechthild the annihilated soul is naked of whatever clothing the virtues can provide. Yet the annihilating identity with the divine nothing does not preclude the virtues. Indeed it presupposes them, even as it lies beyond them and defies attainment through them. (Porete 1993: 169) Her position here resonates with Jung's. No doubt individuation requires the virtuous effort of the ego, but the ego never writes its dreams or works their effects and remains throughout subject to the self experientially indistinguishable from "God". (Jung 1970: 546) For Marguerite souls whose spiritual journey terminates in the virtuous life, the life of ego activity for Jung, are "sad" souls. (Porete 1993: 130, 134, 153, 166) For the hopelessly "lost", the depression of leading a virtuous life goes unnoticed because they can imagine nothing beyond its sterility. (Porete 1993: 132) With others the disappointment of virtue attained is the strongest suggestion and prompt that there is something more. The depression of living a virtuous life itself prompts the search for more. For Marguerite the more becomes the living out of a fixed identity with the nothing which mothers the totality. (Porete 1993: 134)

Especially in her understanding of the will and its role in creation, fall, and return to God does Marguerite reflect the psychology that attracted Jung to Eckhart. Her thrust on these foundational religious themes is this. In the use of the will she has severed herself from the divine with whom she enjoyed an identity, "where she was before she was". (Porete 1993: 218) Marguerite's logic is foreign to our modern mindset yet is consistent on its own presuppositions. It argues that, if the alienation between the divine and the human is due to the will and the knowing of two distinct subjects, this knowing and willing makes them opposites in a creation now fallen from their prior identity. If this alienation is to be defeated it demands the recovery of identity with the divine in that state Marguerite enjoyed prior to her willful removal from this identity.

This cosmology and psychology would then endorse the annihilation of the faculties of consciousness, never more than temporarily, so that between the human will and the divine will there could be only a total fusion. Abstracting from the historical question of Eckhart's literary dependence on Marguerite and approaching the two through thematic affinity, it cannot be denied that the dynamic of the annihilation of will as well as intellect is at the heart of Eckhart's own experience of his return to the nothing. Nor can it be denied that Jung's attraction to Eckhart rests on the dynamic of the ego as a child of the Nothing, Pleroma or Great Mother, name it as you will, re-entering the womb, the creative nothing, as a precondition to a return to a greatly enhanced consciousness. The process, taken in all its moments, effects a more residual and mutually redemptive marriage of ego with its eternal and maternal ground and lies at the core of the individuation process itself.

Jung, Eckhart and the relativity of God

Eckhart's continuity with Marguerite rests on her description in a religious idiom of the universal dissociation which occurs when consciousness is born from the unconscious and seeks to overcome the split occasioned by its birth. In his thought on the relativity of the God concept, Jung transposes the religious dynamics Marguerite and Eckhart describe into a psychological idiom which nevertheless bears an identical content with their religious formulations. (Jung 1971a: 241–248) However, the elevation of their religious experience to the psychological plane endows their experience of the nothing and Jung's own psychology with a greater intelligibility and power for the religiously and psychologically sensitive contemporary mind.

No doubt Jung cites Eckhart extensively in connection with the gnostic/ alchemical (Jung 1968h: 135; 1968c: 189, 193–194) and Zen traditions. (Jung 1969g: 543–544, 548) Yet his thought on the relativity of God is the center-piece of Jung's interface with Eckhart throughout the *Collected Works* because in these passages Jung effectively equates the dialectic between the ego and the unconscious with the dialectic between the human and the divine. Further, in doing so, Jung contains the dialectic within the psyche, forbids external intervention in the process, and so eliminates all supernatural residue in the commerce between the divine and the human. Jung thus fuses the realms of psychic and religious experience in a synthesis which forces neither and enriches both.

At the core of his thought on the relativity of God, Jung makes the daring statement that God and the human are "functions of each other", effectively caught up in a single, organic and universal process of mutual reciprocity and redemption. (Jung 1971a: 243) In this process the soul as mediator between the divine and the human loses all substantial connotations. The soul as "receiver and transmitter" simply becomes the very symbols (Jung 1971a: 251) and the energies the symbols mediate to consciousness from the depths of the psyche beyond the soul. (Jung 1971a: 247) The greatest energy is the energy that gives rise to images of God. Just as the soul is the experience of the energy the images carry to consciousness, the soul becomes God as the image and energy of God come alive in it. To speak then of God is to deny substance to God. Rather to speak of God is to speak of the experience born in the soul as it mediates the libido carried by images of God to consciousness. And what is this experience? In all the master images of God throughout Jung's works, the experience the image of God conveys to consciousness is that of the synergy between the integration of the personal complexes within an individual with an ever greater embrace of and compassion for the totality beyond the indi-vidual. This personal integration and extended sympathy are consistent with the dissolution of the ego in and return from its source in the maternal nothingness of the apophatic moment because this nothing mothers the all. Immersion in her within the psyche can only sponsor an encompassing sympathy for all her faces beyond the individual.

With this understanding of soul Jung amplifies Eckhart's statement that the soul is not blissful when she is in God. (Jung 1971a: 246) The soul is unhappy in God in two ways. The more common peril of the soul's loss of bliss through a destructive identity with God takes the form of the soul's identification with its projection of God beyond the psyche into matter. In this situation the soul must sacrifice its idolatry and recover the divine energies which have turned an entity, physical or spiritual, external to the soul into a God. (Jung 1971a:

247–248) But then the soul faces a second and even great danger to its bliss. For, in its retraction of the projection of those energies, which create the Gods beyond the soul, the soul runs the risk of identifying with the inner God or with the archetypal power which gives birth to all external Gods. Beyond his specific discussion of Eckhart, Jung understands the current evolution of religious consciousness, at least in the West, to be at that point where the conscious return of the transcendent Gods to their common psychic origin is the foremost demand the psyche presently makes, a demand on which the survival of the species may now depend. (Jung 1969h: 85) However, his discussion of this process in specific relation to Eckhart does clarify the risks and challenges of this stage in humanity's current religious evolution. The recall of the Gods to their psychic origins must face and evade the danger of identifying with an inner God and losing both ego and soul to such identification.

For the return of the Gods to their psychic origins demands the descent of the ego and soul to their origins in the *dynamis* or "flood and source" of the unconscious as the mother of all consciousness. (Jung 1971a: 255) This is the descent to what Jung terms the *deus absconditus*, the hidden God, the raging, chaotic nothingness from which all form derives. (Jung 1971a: 253) Jung is as aware of this psychic experience as was Eckhart himself. In modern philosophical or theological terms this is where the subject–object split is definitively overcome through the identity of the profundity of human subjectivity with what had been commonly perceived as a wholly other God. Jung could hardly be more explicit about this psychic state than in his restatement of Eckhart's experience in Eckhart's terminology,

> But when the "breakthrough" abolishes this separation [between the human and the divine] by cutting the ego off from the world, and the ego again becomes identical with the unconscious *dynamis*, God disappears as an object and dwindles into a subject which is no longer distinguishable from the ego.
>
> (Jung 1971a: 255)

Jung goes on to identify Eckhart's breakthrough even more succinctly as simply the reestablishment of "the original state of identity with God". (Jung 1971a: 255)

Jung takes Eckhart's use of the term "breakthrough" (*durchbruch*) from Eckhart's sermon, "Blessed are the poor". (Schurmann 1978: 214–220) Like Marguerite and Mechthild before him, in this sermon Eckhart makes the point that true poverty has little or nothing to do with various forms of virtuous self-denial. (Schurmann 1978: 215) Rather poverty means the forgoing of mind, will and even autonomous existence through what Eckhart calls the "breakthrough" to that identity with the divine which he enjoyed in his own words, "as he was when he was not yet". (Schurmann 1978: 216) In this sermon he twice utters his paradoxical prayer. "Therefore we beg God to rid us of God." (Schurmann 1978: 216, 219) The prayer is to the Godhead beyond the Trinitarian God of creation. It implores the Godhead to reestablish that pristine identity shattered when creatures removed themselves from their source to know and love God as other than themselves. In this, the current state of the human psyche, states Eckhart, all proclaimed God but none were happy because of the universal sense of alienation from their source. (Jung 1971a: 254, 255) For both Jung and Eckhart only a recovered identity with the nothing can alleviate this bifurcation and the alienation creation spawns.

That Jung understood Eckhart's breakthrough as a moment of the ego's unqualified identification with the original nothingness which, then as now, violates the always to be maintained distance orthodoxy places between the divine and the human, is confirmed in his statement, "The characteristically Eckhartian assertion that 'God is nothingness' may well be incompatible in principle with the contemplation of the Passion of Christ, with faith and collective expectation." (Jung 1969g: 548) Jung here joins Eckhart in a joint assertion that the furthest ingression of the ego into the unconscious, of the human into the divine, goes beyond all imagery and especially collective imagery. This realization can be a hard one for therapist and religious minister since both make their living through such imagery, the therapist at the personal level and the minister at the collective.

But the moment of the loss of difference between the divine and the human, ego and unconscious, is not the whole story for Jung or for Eckhart. This is so because in the completion of the cycle of the ego's entry into and dissolution in the Goddess its return is implied. Jung picks up on the return with the other half of Eckhart's expression. The soul is not blissful when she is in God but is blissful when God is in her. (Jung 1971a: 251–252) For Jung the bliss of the soul when God is in her describes the soul as returned from her perilous moment of dissolution in the origin, to her role as mediatrix of the energies derived from a divine source preceding herself to the ego in the interests of the renewal and expansion of conscious and affective life. Here Jung goes to Goethe and describes the flow of psychic energies in an extended analogy with the flow of blood in its diastolic and systolic pulsations to and from the heart. (Jung 1971a: 253) The image makes explicit that for Jung, using Eckhart's experience, the residual rhythm of individuation is one of the ego's othering from the divine, followed by a return to an identity with the divine culminating in the ongoing "renewal of life". (Jung 1971a: 252) This dialectic describes the most foundational movements of psychic and religious life which, with the help of Jung's amplification of mystical experience, now can be seen as one.

The predominant focus in Eckhart's apophaticism and Jung's appropriation of it lies in the moment of identity of the human and the divine, the ego and unconscious, though the completion of the cycle in the recreated ego's return to consciousness is certainly there. The far-reaching consequences of the ego's return from the nothingness is the central focus in the experience of the only mystic more cited in Jung's works than Meister Eckhart, namely, Jacob Boehme.

Jacob Boehme and humanity's redemption of the divine

When Jung refers to an age-old human premonition, namely, "the idea of a creature that surpasses its creator by a small but decisive factor", he was probably referring to the consciousness of Job. (Jung 1965a: 220) He could equally well have been referring to Jacob Boehme, the first Western Christian mystic to make explicit that divinity can become self-conscious only through the reconciliation of its eternal self-contradiction in human consciousness. Like Eckhart, Boehme too had the experience of immersion in the ground, or the *ungrund* in his quaint German, the one, the nothingness, the mother of the all, herself beyond all differentiation even that of the Trinity. However, it was in his return from identity with the source to what he terms "the grossest and meanest matters of the earth" (Boehme 1911: v) that Boehme's experience takes on the characteristics that distinguish it in the history of Western mystical experience. For, in his return from the point where psyche and divinity coincide, Boehme became painfully aware that the powerful opposites which constitute the eternal life of the divine have not been resolved in eternity as a resource for their resolution in time as orthodox Trinitarian thought, typically represented in Tillich's thought, would have it. Rather the divine antinomies can only be perceived and resolved in human consciousness created out of divine necessity for that purpose. (Dourley 1995a: 434) Obviously these foundational themes in Boehme bear dramatic affinity with Jung's mature understanding of divinity, made explicit in his late work on Job. In that work Jung defines a divinity seeking the unity of its opposites in a humanity burdened with the suffering of their unification in personal and collective history. (Jung 1969a: 455, 459, 461)

As with Jung, so with Boehme, two of the predominant opposites are that of evil and good. Boehme locates these opposites in the Trinity itself. The first power becomes a dark fire, a masculine, angry figure, the reality of hell itself to which the fallen angels were consigned. Effectively Boehme is here experiencing evil as the power of unrelated assertion. The second power is a relational principle of light and loving communication, a Christ figure closely associated with the feminine figure of Sophia and so possibly androgynous. These are the powers which war eternally in the divine and seek their redeeming embrace in the human. (Dourley 1995a: 434–435, 438–439) Boehme's images of this reconciliation are filled with a sense of the suffering such reconciliation entails. Such images make it evident that the deepest meaning of human historical suffering is the resolution of whatever aspect of the divine contradiction is most operative in the suffering of the individual and of the historical epoch in which the individual lives.

The broader implication of Boehme's experience is that human consciousness is a necessary creation of a divinity which could become self-conscious only in it. Human consciousness thus experienced is in ontological and living continuity with its divine source. Effectively it is the fourth person in the Trinity. In this sense the emergence of human consciousness becomes an historical necessity as the sole locus in which its creator can become conscious through the human perception and resolution of its opposites. The process brings redemption to a conflicted divinity through the resolution of its conflicts in a humanity itself redeemed wherever and to the extent such resolution is effected. (Dourley 1995a: 439)

In his work, "Answer to Job", when Jung answers Job's question directly he describes the answer as both "psychological" and "eschatological". (Jung 1969a: 408) Jung's answer to Job is the crucified Christ dying in despair between the opposites of a divinely grounded yes and no without the possibility of intervention from beyond. The scene is a symbol of universal human consciousness suffering the divine self-contradiction to the point of death as a prelude to the embrace of the opposites in a resurrected consciousness enriched by their synthesis. By uniting in this process the deepest movement of the psyche and the eschatological telos driving history itself, Jung is simply following Boehme's mystical intimation that humanity is charged by the divine with the progressive redemption of the divine through the resolution of its archetypal contradictions in the life of humanity itself. The moments in this process are the suffering of the opposites into an identity with the divine in a death which leads to the resolution of the divine antinomy in the resurrected but always historical consciousness such death entails.

Conclusion: journey inward, journey outward

And so at the end of the day we come to a deepened appreciation of Jung's psychology and the myth it bears, when looked at through the prism of those mystics whose experience both anticipates Jungian psychology and is made more conscious for the contemporary in and through it. The mystics are the predecessors of the mythic substance of Jung's psychology understood as one major contributor to the emergence of a societal myth of greater depth and inclusive extent than contemporary Western monotheisms can proffer. In Chapter 7 this myth has been described as the myth of a double quaternity. This twofold quaternity centers on the priority of the nothing and on the full cycle of the ego's commerce with her. The double quaternity could be reconceived in more traditional terms as a journey inward toward a profound wisdom correlated with a journey outward of vastly extended compassion. The thirteenth century women mystics whose experience culminated in a moment of identity with the nothing are now known to have influenced

Eckhart in his clear movement to identity with the Godhead beyond the Trinity and beyond its boiling lust to give itself expression within and beyond itself. Effectively Eckhart's experience places a fourth in the divine beyond all form and even tendency to form. This is the God whom Eckhart identifies with in his "breakthrough" and whom Paul Tillich identifies as the "God above God". (Tillich 1952: 182)

When the light of Jungian psychology is brought to bear on this furthest reach of divine life it would point to a dimension of the psyche beyond the archetypal and free of the archetypal compulsion to create consciousness and become incarnate in consciousness thus created. This moment of rest might well moderate the possessive urgency the archetypes exert in their creation of patterns that can so easily congeal into ideological absolutes hostile to individual and to collective life. The pacific power the mystics exert may well flow from their having gotten behind the archetypal energies that inform the murderous faiths, religious and political, of their time and ours. Getting behind the archetypes into a preceding nothingness would contribute to the more harmonious relations between archetypal concretions in human history and consciousness because their common origin in the depths of the human would become increasingly obvious to collective consciousness. This gain in consciousness would make it increasingly difficult to kill for ideological or religious variants of a common human origin.

Yet it cannot be denied that the moment of nothingness, however liberating and broadening, could foster a sterile solipsism unless it completed itself in the consciously and politically human. This completion of the nothing in human consciousness is at the heart of Boehme's experience. As such it constitutes the second quaternity. In this quaternity humanity is the Trinity's natural and completing fourth. The human psyche becomes the theater of history wholly encompassing the divine–human drama. For only in the psyche can the divine antinomies be perceived and find relief in a humanity broadened and deepened by suffering toward a full consciousness of its divine ground in the resolution in time of divinity's eternal failure to integrate its life in eternity.

The dynamic of the two quaternities, and their wisdom and compassion, when combined yields a myth in which divinity and humanity, the archetypal powers and human consciousness, are poles in an all encompassing, all inclusive organic totality. The first quaternity leads consciousness to a point in the psyche beyond the need for any expression or activity, and yet this moment of rest in the God beyond God, serves as a prequel to a more gracious ushering of the divine contraries into the embrace they seek and can enjoy only in humanity. In short the deeper the ingression into the depths of the divine or the psyche, the greater humanity's ability to unite their conflicting opposites in the world. The compassion such penetration enables carries with it into the world the ability to bring those real but always partial and preliminary expressions of archetypal ultimacy, especially in religious and political commitment, into ever richer harmonies within the confines of human history itself.

The ground dynamic of the myth of the double quaternity would, in the end, present humanity with stark alternatives. Either the divinely based opposites will move toward those unities that redeem divinity and humanity as two agencies in the same process, or the opposites will continue to harden into individuals and communities possessed by truncated archetypal compulsions whose drive is to destroy each other. Currently in so many places in the world it is not difficult to identify this sad scenario in the destructive nature of archetypal hatred turning community against community. At this point the mystical values of the myth of the double quaternity move beyond idle socio-logical, psychological or religious speculation. The myth takes on survival value. If we cannot get to a point of rest beyond the inner archetypal wars between those archetypal combatants who spawn external war, then such wars between individuals and communities are likely to proceed from psychic necessity and continue to threaten the species. Jung died in the Cold War when, then as now, archetypal absolutes pitted communities against each other in potentially lethal interface. In the end Jung quite frankly proposed the loss of faith in these truncated archetypal and bellicose personal and social con-figurations in order to avoid the end of the species toward which they moved. He writes, "We are threatened with universal genocide if we cannot work out the way of salvation by a symbolic death." (Jung 1976b: 735) That Jung thought such a loss of current faiths toward a more encompassing universal sentiment was a real possibility is evident when he could still write of a distant afternoon of humanity in which conquest had ceased to be the dream. (Jung 1969e: 787) For Jung, and the mystics who inform his work, only humanity's recovery of its deepest and so common ground made real in living memory will enable it to move beyond archetypal enmity to the embrace of the archetypal other as other and to the wealth such embrace could yield if humanity is, indeed, to enjoy that "distant afternoon".

Chapter 9

Tillich's theonomous naturalism and its relation to religious and medical healing*

The problematic

Chapter 4 contended that Tillich stepped back from a full embrace of Boehme's experience of divinity and humanity as polarities engaged in an organic and all encompassing process of the mutual conferring of consciousness upon each other as the base meaning of both historical and individual human life. Boehme's categories would make it impossible to separate the religious, philosophical and psychological dimensions of his experience of a divinity driven to create and to become conscious in humanity through humanity's recurrent and cyclical return to its origin in divinity. This vision would imply a divine need to create, the possibility of a divine aggrandizement or loss within the vagaries of human history and a divine dependency on human consciousness for its own conscious growth. All of these positions would be forbidden to Tillich's Christian orthodoxy, at least, until very late in his life.

Moreover, a Jungian psychological interpretation reveals that Boehme is arguing that the source of consciousness seeks to resolve its primordial conflict in human consciousness and that human consciousness engages in this process through a return to a moment of identity with its origin. In his own quaint formulation the I or ego and the nothing from which the ego comes seek each other in a complementarity in which the I is created by the nothing and seeks its healing in a return thereto. Again the theological implications of this psychology fall beyond the borders of Christian orthodoxy.

Despite these difficulties in fully accepting the religious and psychological implications of Boehme's experience, Tillich did remain interested throughout his working life in setting the boundaries between psychological and religious experience and the healing that each could legitimately claim as its own. Though unable to embrace Boehme without serious restrictions,

---

* A version of this chapter appeared as "Issues of Naturalism and Supranaturalism in Tillich's Correlation of Religious with Psychological Healing", *Studies in Religion*, 26, 2, 1997, 211–223.

Tillich's own rejection of supernaturalism and religious naturalism proved of immense help to him in this side of his theological project. Out of his concern to relate religious to psychological healing Tillich eventually did build a bridge between the worlds of religious and psychological experience that quite clearly and precisely spelled out the fact that medical or psychological healing could be the agency or occasion of what theologians call "salvation". In this achievement he provides a specifically theological foundation for Jung's effective identification of psychic with religious healing. When addressing this problem Tillich, with his usual philosophical and systematic precision, came to embrace and endorse the real and radical possibility that psychological healing without a specific religious referent could be in and of itself salvific. In the context of his discussion of the relation of what theologians called *salus* or salvific healing to therapeutic healing Tillich tended to group under the latter category medical, psychological and psychoanalytic healing. At least three times throughout his English corpus he attempted formally to delineate the relation of religious salvation to the health that the medical/psychological/psychoanalytical tradition could proffer. (Tillich 1952: 64–78; 1963: 280–282; 1959c: 112–126)

In these formal treatments of the question he quite explicitly and consistently laid out the principles which should determine their relationship. A summation of these principles will be forthcoming. However, to understand and critique Tillich's position on the relation of religious to psychological healing one must understand that Tillich, ever the systematic thinker, implicates two of the foundational elements of his system in establishing the relationship between these two kinds of healing. The foundational elements are first, his methodology of correlation itself and, second, his understanding of the relation of essence to existence.

Tillich's method of correlation

Tillich's method of correlation seeks to avoid the opposite pitfalls of supranaturalism and a shallow naturalism as well as a third position, an unhappy combination of the first two failures. Supranaturalism would imagine a heteronomous God wholly other than humanity addressing humanity from beyond it "with a sum of revealed truths". (Tillich 1951: 64, 65) Such supranaturalism, argues Tillich, informs orthodox Protestant conceptions of revelation and all forms of theism which implicate divinity in a subject–object split with humanity. (Tillich 1962a: 30) This critique means that Tillich rejects any relation of divinity to humanity based on the interplay of a divine subject of consciousness over against a human subject of consciousness engaged in processes of mutual objectification. Tillich's response to such theism engages his critique of heteronomy, namely, a conception of a God who imposes its power from without on the human only to elicit from the autonomous mind the legitimate rejection of such imposition. In response to such intrusion,

Tillich counsels a purgative atheism on behalf of a more sensitive human spirituality. (Tillich 1951: 245; 1959b: 18, 25)

Naturalism, which Tillich closely relates to certain streams of humanism and, on occasion, to Enlightenment rationalism, would affirm that humanity in effect is capable of conferring its essential nature on itself out of its own native capacities. Put simply salvation lies within the resources of natural humanity. (Tillich 1951: 65) In his critique of naturalism Tillich has to be cautious because his own thought actually supports a sophisticated form of naturalism in which nature is understood as grounded in God and self-conscious human nature is understood as universally aware of this grounding. Such intensified realization of the conscious intimacy between the divine and the human is the basis of Tillich's understanding of theonomy and is a form of naturalism which makes the experience of the divine natural to humanity. When Tillich does critique naturalism it is a naturalism that is insensitive to the experiential intimacy that exists between nature, human nature, and the divine. Such a critique targets the truncated human sensitivity resultant in the loss of the immediate sense of the divine, an inevitable consequence when the total human cognitive capacity is reduced to the realms of rational, scientific or technological perception.

The third position Tillich rejects would give to reason the ability to work "a natural revelation", taken to be the sum total of what the natural mind can know of God, then to be supplemented by a heteronomous supranatural revelation. This dualism is obviously related to Tillich's rejection of all forms of Aristotelian Thomism and especially its furtive efforts to prove the existence of an invisible object, God. As such this ploy is not so pertinent to this particular discussion. (Tillich 1951: 65, 66) It is not pertinent to a discussion on healing because for Tillich such a position is fragmenting and itself needs to be healed. It splits the cognitive capacity into a natural ability to achieve a limited knowledge of God supplemented by revelation as divine information to which assent is then given through the coercion that the theological virtue of faith works on the victimized intellect through the grace enabled violence of the will. (Tillich 1957b: 35–38)

Rather, it is Tillich's critique of naturalism and, to some extent, of humanism that would come to the fore in the way in which he relates religious to psychological healing. His rejection of psychological naturalism is in the first instance a rejection of those traditions that would deny that the essential, which he relates so closely to the divine, does indeed address humanity from its depths. Nearly all forms of behaviorism and exclusively conscious therapies would take this position and so be Tillich's target in this side of his critique. Again in tension with Tillich some traditions would admit the inner address but contend that humanity can and must respond to this address with its conscious faculties in a process which effects the natural gracing of the human. Most forms of British and American humanistic psychology and nearly all forms of existentialist psychology that grant to the human the power to confer the essential upon itself take this position. Are these latter psychologies, then, to be rejected by Tillich's rejection of naturalism or do they, in fact, describe in naturalistic terms the dialectic Tillich establishes between essence and existence, between the divine and the human? They would indeed appear to do so but let this question hang for the moment.

Tillich's own solution to the problems that he seeks to address in his theological methodology rests on a compelling picture of humanity driven to quest for or ask after its essential nature from which it is separated in existence but whose memory it cannot extinguish as the basis of its universal drive to recover what it has lost. With this theological anthropology in place Tillich can argue that existential humanity must ask after its essence but that the essential, whether it be called revelation or salvation, can only be given as grace from beyond the questioner. "The answer cannot be derived from the analysis of existence." (Tillich 1951: 64)

What Tillich is obviously defending here is the Christian theological ideology of the gratuity and priority of divine action in the gracing and healing of humanity. It leads Tillich into tortured and devious formulations. In his initial effort to relate human question to divine salvific answer he gives a priority to divinity. "Symbolically speaking, God answers man's question, and under the impact of God's answers man asks them." (Tillich 1951: 61) In this opening gambit God would seem to take the initiative even in provoking the question. But on the next page Tillich writes, "Man is the question he asks about himself before any question has been formulated." (Tillich 1951: 62) Revelation now responds to the nature of humanity as living question. Here Tillich reverses his original position. The question precedes the revealed answer and demands it. In these same passages Tillich refers with apparent approval to both philosophical and theological traditions grounded on the "mystical identification of the ground of being with the ground of self". (Tillich 1951: 62 note 19) Here he makes one of the earliest statements in his *Systematic Theology* that the depths of religious and psychological experience coincide in the ground from which both experiences proceed to consciousness.

If humanity is universally addressed by this ground and if the recovery therein of humanity's essential nature or self is, in fact, the concern empowering humanity's universal religious quest, the inability of humanity to usher this ground into consciousness remains a strange incapacity in the face of the ontological intimacy Tillich himself establishes between the essential self and the existential quester. However, Tillich's Christianity forces him to maintain just such an incapacity evident in his statement "revelation is 'spoken' to man not by man to himself". (Tillich 1951: 65) Otherwise humanity could author its own healing revelation and so salvation, or, at least, cooperate out of its natural conscious powers with the incursion into them of its equally natural divine ground. But these options are not readily available to Tillich, the Christian theologian. Were Tillich possessed of the kind of distinction that

Jung makes between ego consciousness and the archetypal dimension of the psyche which transcends the ego but on a wholly intra-psychic basis, he could argue that when the ego cooperates with the archetypal impress it is not a case of the individual speaking revelation to oneself. Rather it is a case of the transcendental powers within the psyche speaking to the ego from beyond the ego's limited capacity and asking or demanding of the ego entrance into consciousness. Such a concept of intra-psychic transcendence is by and large absent in Tillich though it may be implied in his later work on the presence and effects of the Spirit. Its absence forces him into an uncomfortable tension between the experiential intimacy he establishes between the divine and the human and the Christian affirmation that revelation is spoken from beyond to the human and not to the human from a dimension native to it but beyond the realm of consciousness and its executive faculties of intellect and will.

Tillich's philosophically nuanced and precise understanding of the existential plight is thus operative in his own methodology and the theological ideology that informs it. The methodology demands that the theologian formulate the questions of existence, contextually the deepest questions that any culture is asking, and then answer them out of a revelation " 'spoken' to human existence from beyond it". (Tillich 1951: 64) This methodology assumes that the Christian revelation as final has the answer for all questions in all cultures. The honest theologian then correlates the questions of each culture and epoch with the Christian answer. For all the intimacy Tillich establishes between God and the ground of the self, in the end, existential humanity must seek a healing revelation which comes from "somewhere else" (Tillich 1959c: 125) a revelation that an authentic and functioning theology must then relate to the deepest questions society would address to the Christian community. Or so one significant side of Tillich would have it. Another side, evident in his reflections on the ability of psychology to mediate the essential, may well compromise or corrode his theological ideology when he suggests that purely natural psychological healing through purely natural processes might indeed mediate the essential and in so doing serve as a means of salvation.

Essence, existence and their relation to healing

Tillich's categories of essence and existence are, by his own admission, the "backbone" of the theological system and operative in every part of it. (Tillich 1951: 204) As seen above they determine his method of correlation which relates the questions of existence to their resolution in the definitive, that is, Christian manifestation of the essential. These categories also determine the way he relates religious to psychological healing. Though Tillich brings philosophical precision to his conceptions of essence and existence, he also locates them against the background of his version of the more encompassing Christian myth. The essential is grounded in the dynamics of

Trinitarian life, and especially in its second moment, the *Logos*. Trinitarian life, understood as a primordial and ongoing act of self-creation is the locus of actual or first creation, since everything that can be beyond the Trinity is expressed in its inner dynamic. Tillich clearly distinguishes this actual creation, the pristine expression of the essential within the Trinity, from fallen creation or existence as experienced by current humanity. (Tillich 1951: 80, 204, 251)

As the drama of the divine life unfolds Tillich implies that such initial creation was somehow deficient in that, in its state of "dreaming innocence" or potential for existence, it lacked the full reality which only existence could confer upon it. (Tillich 1957a: 33–36) The question becomes who the dreamer really is in the state of "dreaming innocence"? If it is God it would undermine the self-sufficiency of the initial Trinitarian differentiation by suggesting that essence without existence remains somehow unfinished. It would also imply that Trinity could not mediate the transition from essence to existence without the necessity of the fall. If the dreamer is humanity, Tillich's own position, the consequences are much the same. In actualizing one's freedom the individual comes into existence but is keenly aware of a fallen state or distancing from an essential expression in the Trinity to which the individual belongs and toward which the individual is driven to recover more fully one's unqualified essential nature. The original sin of freely willing and so actualizing oneself is thus both universal and personal. Original sin carries with it the tortured consciousness of an existence which is somehow more real than the innocence of the essential confined to a preliminary expression in eternity but which is also informed by the anxiety of finitude removed from but incapable of either forgetting its divine ground or recovering it out of its own resources. (Tillich 1957a: 44)

These categories of essence and existence then serve to illuminate the universality and depth of human anxiety. Self-conscious finitude is anxious because of its removal from God as the ground of its essential self. To name but a few of its vicissitudes, humanity is universally anxious in the face of death, guilt and meaninglessness. Reflection on these negations is the substance of Tillich's work, *The Courage To Be* (1952). Existential humanity is also threatened with disintegration, the inability to hold together the opposites which constitute the dynamics of life. (Tillich 1951: 174–186) These anxieties turn existential humanity toward its Trinitarian ground as the saving answer to its plight. And yet, in terms of Tillich's relation of essence to existence, the ground of courage and of integration, though universally demanded as the answer to humanity's existential anxiety, can only be given as grace.

In thus grounding existential anxiety on the ontology of humanity's removal from its essence Tillich possesses the categories which are foundational to the way in which he first distinguishes and then refines the areas of competency belonging to religious and psychological healing. These categories enable Tillich to do two things: first, to distinguish clearly between existential and pathological anxiety. Existential anxiety is ontologically endemic to humanity universally. It is a consequence of removal from the essential in all existential life. To be a self-conscious human is to be anxious. Clearly distinguished from existential anxiety, pathological or neurotic anxiety then becomes an exaggerated and self-defeating or self-reducing response to existential anxiety. (Tillich 1952: 72–78)

Second, on the basis of the above distinction to assign to religious healing the role of the removal, however fragmentary, of existential anxiety, and to the doctor/psychologist/psychoanalyst the role of the removal or reduction of pathological anxiety. In this context pathological or neurotic anxiety becomes a life-limiting response to the inescapable fact of existential anxiety in fallen existential human life.

Principles of determining the relation of religious to psychological healing

Thus the anthropology that informs his methodology of correlation and his philosophy of essence and existence determine the distinctions that Tillich makes between the roles of the priest/minister and psychologist in alleviating human suffering in the three places in which Tillich explicitly addresses the problem. The following six positions constitute a compendium of Tillich's treatment of the issue.

First, the priest/minister's formal role or vocation addresses existential anxiety directly through mediating the essential. For Tillich the recovery of the essential self is the substance of religion and religion is only functional when and to the extent it can access the essential self. The process is one that can never be completed. Nor can it ever be avoided due to the insistence of the essential to become real in the existential. Tillich remains deeply aware that the mediation of the essential self is always fragmentary and that the total defeat of the existential structures of anxiety remains an eschatological hope. Obviously this position shares much in common with Jung's understanding of the commerce between self and ego within the psyche.

As such the priest/minister is not primarily concerned with, and not usually competent in, the removal of neurotic or pathological anxiety, though it would be logical to assume that the diminishment of existential anxiety would carry with it a curtailment of neurotic anxiety. Tillich does point to such possibility through his conception of the multidimensional healing of life understood as the Spirit's elevation of the center of a personal life to unity with the center of the divine life, the ultimate source of human courage and integration. Such elevation by implication would exercise a healing influence on the totality of a life thus united with its divine center. (Tillich 1963: 280) Tillich is probably referring to this conception when he writes out of what sounds perilously like the very religious imperialism his whole effort, in this discussion, is to avoid: "Therefore the ministerial function comprehends both itself and the medical function." (Tillich 1952: 74) In an ideal world no doubt the ministerial mediation of the essential self would also heal psychological pathologies. Nevertheless, though psychological disturbance may be operative in its earlier or initial stages, as William James was to affirm, mature sanctity excludes the neurotic. Tillich is very aware that the impact of the Spirit does not mechanically or automatically remove pathological anxiety nor neurosis. If it did religious healing would swallow psychological healing and obviate the need for serious reflection on their boundaries and interaction and on the nature of the agencies involved in each.

Second, the psychologist/therapist/medical practitioner, on the other hand, addresses and can remove neurotic anxiety as a pathological response to existential anxiety. The psychological practitioner does this with the competencies acquired through training in whatever variant of the psychological disciplines one practices. Many such traditions have a proven efficacy in addressing pathological anxiety. As such the practitioner in these traditions is not concerned with nor able to alleviate existential anxiety, at least as a primary goal or capacity of therapeutic endeavor, and so is not involved with the specific religious function. However, the practitioner could legitimately become involved with the religious function if the patient was using religion as a neurotic response to existential anxiety and so demeaning one's humanity and limiting one's freedom in doing so as critics from Karl Marx to Erich Fromm have contended. Tillich is quite frank in admitting not only the possibility but also the frequency of the connection of neurosis with religion. Such connection would occur whenever religious belief or practice constrained the individual in a fuller engagement with life or denied to the individual the courage, integration and wider compassion that are the hallmarks of the assimilation of the essential self. This side of Tillich's analysis would quite clearly expose religion as neurotic whenever religion denied the reality of existential anxiety or provided a false relief from it. But Tillich's thinking here could also be very positive to psychological healing because it identifies a religious element surreptitiously at work wherever a specifically medical or psychological approach effectively engages the essential self even if such an approach refrained from identifying the power of the self, theoretically or therapeutically, as religious. Frankl's logotherapy comes to mind as an example of this possibility. The restoration of a healing meaning such therapy seeks is not far from Tillich's understanding of *Logos* as structuring both the divine and human mind and serving as the ultimate resource for the alleviation of the suffering of existential consciousness.

Thus in these first two points Tillich establishes the legitimate fields of operation of religious and therapeutic healing. The third makes more explicit their relative autonomy as the basis of their legitimate relatedness. This autonomy then constitutes Tillich's response to the conflict that can arise when one tries totally to absorb the other.

Third, neither priest nor psychologist, acting within the boundaries of their own competencies, should subsume nor deny the validity of the other's role which must remain permanently distinguishable at least in principle. Tillich is here obviously attacking those positions which would see religion as pathogenic in and of itself or argue, along Freudian lines, that therapy can now do what religion has done and so leave it behind as an historical monument, a response to human suffering which a mature humanity has now outgrown. On the other hand the religious response might argue just the opposite, namely, that religion has in itself all the resources that the therapeutic community has to offer and reject the efficacy of the therapeutic endeavour in favor of a supernaturalism adequate to all forms of human suffering including the psychological pathology which such a view so often produces in its holders. For Tillich a unilateral victory of either position would either deny the depth of the human disturbance that religion directly addresses in the name of therapeutic omni-competence or extend to religion a universal efficacy insensitive to the areas where therapy has proven it can touch and heal what religion cannot. In passing, Tillich does point to the possibility of one individual assuming both roles of religious minister and therapist if trained in both domains. (Tillich 1963: 281, 282) In this position Tillich may have foreseen the tendency of those working in ministerial or pastoral situations to qualify as therapeutic practitioners and in not a few cases to relinquish their previous ministerial roles. This constituency would currently seem to be increasing as testimony to a growing perception that therapeutic approaches to human suffering have more to offer than does religion, at least, in its current institutional form.

Fourth, but then, in a point he consistently makes, in apparent contradiction or, at least, significant modification, of the preceding tightly drawn delineations of their relative realms of competence, Tillich acknowledges that the role of the priest can bring relief from neurosis and that the psychologist can mediate the essential and so alleviate existential anxiety. In the light of this substantial concession it would appear that Tillich's precisely drawn allocation of the relief of existential anxiety to religion and of pathological anxiety to therapy serves simply to establish the continued validity of each form of healing. Once each has been granted its enduring realms of competence, Tillich gladly concedes that the essential can be mediated through medical/therapeutic agency and that specifically religious access to the essential could and, perhaps, should relieve psychological pathology.

His extension to therapy of the capacity to mediate the essential and so resolve existential anxiety may be, in the current context, the most radical and fruitful of the points Tillich makes in relating the two modes of healing. (Tillich 1952: 77) It is so because Tillich is here clearly affirming with metaphysical precision that medical and psychological healing can, in principle, mediate the substance of what theologians term "salvation". In the contemporary situation Tillich's position here addressed and confirmed in the mid twentieth century what is, in fact, occurring in Western society. Many who have turned away from ecclesial access to a fuller humanity, and to the essential self, are finding greater access to the healing self in a therapeutic context. Tillich's reflections here should be taken up as providing a late but still necessary theological validity and understanding of this now widespread phenomenon. Effectively it would identify a significant constituency of those who turn to a therapeutic healing for access to the healing power of the essential self which their previous or even continued ecclesial association could not provide.

Fifth, again consistent with his methodology and the apologetic or answering theology he builds upon it, Tillich is grateful to Freud, to the psychoanalytic tradition and to depth psychology in general for providing significant contemporary existential questions about the distortions and inner conflicts of humanity as valued foils for the theologian's response out of the latter's possession of the "final revelation". (Tillich 1959c: 123–125; 1957a: 53) Taking this stance Tillich reverts to a certain degree to his position that questions provoked by significant cultural phenomenon, in this case the distortions and healing of psychic life so well documented, for example, by Freud, are to be appreciated and answered out of Christian resources. The imperialism latent in this position – Christianity has the answer for all cultural problems – is profoundly modified by the position taken in point four above. In conceding that therapy can bear salvific power Tillich compromises the neat distinction he draws between cultural question and Christian answer. In fact he admits that the question of or quest for psychological/spiritual health can be both asked and resolved through purely psychological and natural processes as long as the natural mediates, knowingly or not, the energies of the divine as its ground and ultimate healing resource. Full acknowledgment of what he implies here should impede Tillich's inclusion of the yield of depth psychology's analysis of the human situation as the basis of a cultural question that Christianity would then answer. Rather he could simply follow what he previously makes explicit and grant that for many depth psychology is the answer and is as effective or more effective an answer than the Christian or any institutional tradition might proffer.

Finally, Tillich pays tribute to the psychoanalytic tradition for removing Christianity from a too conscious moralism by showing Christianity that humanity's legitimate spirituality can never be removed from its instinctual vitality. (Tillich 1957a: 53, 54) This point reflects Tillich's concept of the multidimensionality of life which would deny a hierarchy of *soma* (body), *psyche* (soul) and *pneuma* (spirit) in processes of healing or becoming whole. (Tillich 1963: 11–29) No longer would spiritual or psychological maturation be understood in the upward movement from body through psyche into spirit. Rather movements to maturation would be to that point in the individual where body, psyche and spirit coincide with each other and with the individual's divine center as this oneness came progressively to inform the maturing consciousness. In the movement toward such a maturational centeredness the exclusion of body, psyche or spirit would maim the entire development. Again, Tillich's thought here lends a religious and psychological weight to the current recovery of the body and of soul as correcting a long pathologizing religious distortion toward the spirit at the expense of body and soul.

In this position Tillich also anticipated developments after his time. Currently those concerned with the interaction of a mature spirituality with psychological development are seriously examining the traditional Christian suspicion of the bodily, the instinctual and especially the sexual. What Jung writes of Catholicism might well be extended to Christianity itself, "The arch-sin the Catholic Church is ever after is sexuality, and the ideal *par excellence* virginity, which puts a definite stop to life." (Jung 1976b: 742) Jungian psychology, in particular, is sensitive to the devastating psychological consequences of the Christian exclusion of matter and the body from the sacred both in nature and in God as the ground of nature and endorses a newly forming societal myth in which the bodily, material and the sexual would be restored to the dignity of the sacred. (Dourley 2001) Tillich's conception of maturation as movement toward a center in which body, soul and spirit unite with each other and with the divine has profound affinities with Jung's understanding of a movement toward a conscious wholeness which would progressively embrace all three in the process of the self incarnating in an increasingly integrated and related consciousness manifest in patterns of a more unified personality and greatly extended compassion.

Response from psychologies of the self

In today's climate Tillich's principles for the differentiation and relation of religious to psychological healing might well seem somewhat too clear, too cut and dried, at least as they lead up to the point where they identify psychological maturation as in and of itself salvific. The principle holding out most promise for the present and future is Tillich's concession that, on occasion and in principle, the psychologist can be a mediator of the essential, that is, of salvation. In the interest of a happier integration of religious and psychological healing this pregnant remark could spark the search for psychological traditions and practices which would in principle be capable of mediating the essential. The following are the minimum features such psychologies would have to embody.

First, they would meet Tillich's concerns to avoid both supranaturalism and a reductive naturalism. This means that such a psychological theory and therapy would not look to supernatural agencies beyond the psyche for an intrusive intervention in the healing of the human. At the same time such naturalism would not be reductive because it would insist on a relation to a transcendental agency in human nature itself in its understanding of healing.

This healing would then be of such a nature that its religious and purely psychological elements would defy clear discrimination. Such non-reductive naturalism would imply an agency or agencies within humanity's total psychic resource which would transcend the center of consciousness, the ego, but be contained within the parameters of a greatly extended total psyche. Since the monotheistic mind tends to project these agencies wholly beyond the psyche in the creation of their one and only Gods, an in-depth healing, at once religious and psychological, authored by a power transcendent to the ego but natural to the psyche, may remain beyond their imaginative capacity. Such failure of imagination is tragic. It truncates the individual caught in monotheistic consciousness by removing the victims from their own healing and creative depths. Socially such failure accounts for the ongoing lethal interaction between communities bonded by discrete one and only Gods when such communities intersect geographically. The movement to seek in-depth healing beyond monotheistic institutions, religious or political, may eventually force individuals and collectivities to examine, as did Tillich, the religious nature of healing processes natural to the psyche. Tillich's radical sense of human interiority combined with Jung's archetypal theory could move to a future consensus that the origin of the Gods and of whatever salvific healing they offer are rooted in humanity's native depths and as such obviate the distinction between religious and psychological healing.

Second, they would incorporate in themselves the recognition of a power operative in the healing process comparable to Tillich's understanding of the role of the essential self. Tillich grounds the "essential self" in the divine and makes its realization in the human a work of the Spirit. (Tillich 1963: 235) Psychologically this would make the self the power ushering consciousness into a fuller humanity while always transcending the humanity it progressively pervades. In effect the relation of the individual to this power would be the psychological equivalent of the relation of the individual to the divine and of free will to grace as imagined in the Christian tradition. The Christian can cooperate with the importunities of grace but never coerce it or attribute its realization solely to one's personal endeavor. In continuity with this specifically Christian insight, the ego or center of consciousness could be understood to cooperate with but never coerce the power of the self working from within the psyche but always transcending both the ego and the degree of the self's present realization or incorporation into ego consciousness. In fact Jung explicitly understands the alchemical process of the ongoing recovery of one's native divinity to be based upon just such a dynamic. (Jung 1969c: 258, 259, 263)

Third, they would accommodate Tillich's recognition that processes of essentialization are fragmentary, ambiguous and defiant of full realization in existence. Tillich reserves the completion of processes of essentialization to the eschaton, that is, to a post-temporal state. Tillich's stark reminders that processes of essentialization and its healing can never be more than partial in existence find peculiar confirmation in psychologies of the self. Jung, for instance is explicit that individuation is never more than a process of approximation. "Since this growth of the personality comes out of the unconscious which is by definition unlimited, the extent of the personality now gradually realizing itself cannot in practice be limited either." (Jung 1969c: 258) The fullness of the self always transcends the degree of its actualization in any life process. Psychological iconoclasm would here agree with Tillich's in denying that any stage of individual development could be exhaustive of what could be and is yet to be. This is true also of collective historical development. The situation when God will be all in all will not occur in history.

Fourth, they would support Tillich's position that the essential functions not only as the source of religious healing but also as the source of personal potential and creativity as well as condemnation when ignored or rejected. Tillich understands the essential self to be the ultimate source of the individual's potential. As this potential is progressively realized in existence the individual approximates his or her pristine expression within the flow of Trinitarian life. (Tillich 1963: 268, 269) The realization of such potential is also the basis of Tillich's morality. His foundational "should" is the "should" that is demanded by the essential self, namely, the alignment of an individual life with its eternal expression as the source of its ultimate potential. As seen earlier success in the crucial venture of essentialization contributes to the well-being of the individual in time and of God and individual in a post-temporal context. (Tillich 1963: 422) Deliberate deafness to the overtures of the self in the course of a lifetime is exposed in death and can be the basis of eternal rejection or annihilation, not as some divine arbitrary judgment but as a simple recognition and exposure of the fact that one has failed to incarnate anything of the essential in the course of one's existence. (Tillich 1963: 398, 399) Jung also would depict the self as the basis of one's authenticity and life-giving truth, but will also describe the self as the basis of an ought which can be ruthless toward those lives who turn from its meaning. Such ruthlessness is not arbitrary. It is a simple consequence of the denial of the self and so of the laws of the psyche.

Other contemporary psychologies of the self in affinity with Jung, though by no means reduced to Jung, would also seem to address Tillich's legitimate concerns. These psychologies rest on an intra-psychic understanding of transcendence. The self is understood to transcend the ego and the powers of intellect and will attaching to ego and to address the ego from beyond the ego but from within the psyche. These psychologies sponsor a psychic containment in which the relation of the individual to the divine is understood as the relation of consciousness to the self unfolding in the historical evolution of religion and in individual life. Jung, for instance, would understand such divine–human commerce to be grounded in the power of the numinous impacting on consciousness from the archetypal dimension of the psyche.

The subject's experience of this impact becomes the source of humanity's experience of the divine and so the source of the religions of the past and present as well as the source currently urging religion's future transformations. (Jung 1969h: 6–8)

In this paradigm both self and ego are understood to be centers of energy within the psyche, now extended to become the source both of consciousness and of the archetypal powers whose becoming conscious constitutes the formation of myth, religion and all deeper meaning systems which support and structure both individual and societal life. The self does not address the ego from a heteronomous position beyond the psyche but from within the psyche itself as its divine ground or as the ground from which humanity's sense of God derives. Such psychologies would happily join Tillich in his attack on supranaturalism and a shallow naturalism. With him they would identify the source of the sense of God in the depths of nature made conscious in human consciousness. These positions bear marked affinities to Tillich's understanding of "the essential self shining through the contingencies of the existing self". (Tillich 1963: 235) In the parlance of depth and humanistic psychologies, Tillich's "existing self" is the ego always potentially transparent to the essential self as the ground of its personal being and of being universally.

For these reasons psychologies of the self would not understand themselves as forms of reductive naturalism or of a superficial humanism. They would identify in the self a force operating as does the essential self in Tillich's theology. In his critique of humanism Tillich accuses it of being without focus and replaces it with the ideal of a theonomy, a consciousness directed and informed by a residual access to and possession by the essential. (Tillich 1963: 249–252) The same values and teleology are evident in Jung's conception of individuation in which the self as the basis of the sense of the sacred working personal integration with ever-widening compassion comes progressively to possess consciousness in a process Jung equates with incarnation. (Jung 1969c: 263–265) A similar consciousness is apparent, for instance, in Maslow's description of the peak experience as "witnessing eternity" both as incident and residual state. (Wulff 1997: 605) Eduard Spranger, the noted German psychologist of religion, shows great affinities with Jung and Maslow on the relation to an inner and transcendent world, unity with which enhances and transforms one's relation to nature and to one's surrounding community perceived as participating in and as an expression of a common matrix. Historians of the psychology of religion draw well-founded affinities between Spranger and Jung on the foundational agreement that unity with the deeper or higher dimensions of the psyche enable the perception of the divine within and beyond the individual and so have societal impact. (Wulff 1997: 551–552) The same focus on human interiority is found in William James, who explicitly connects the transformative power of the transcendent "more" to its ingression into human consciousness through the "subliminal door" of the subconscious. (James 1979: 242–243, 487–488) The opening of this door and the transformation worked through it become the basis of James' synthesis of religious conversion and psychic transformation. In the affinities between these significant psychologists of religious theophany, the transparency of the human to the divine plays a major psychological role as event or more residual state and by implication usually both.

It should now be obvious that Tillich identifies the essential self not only as the source of humanity's in-depth healing but also as the source of human potential itself. (Tillich 1963: 269) But even in its role of potential the self also plays a moral function of judging the existential self (ego) on the basis of the degree to which the latter responds to and embraces the ongoing sacrifice attached to the incarnation of the essential in existence. The denial of the essential self is, in effect, a rejection of the overtures made by divinity through and from the depth of reason to become real in existential life. Such rejection is the ultimate act of self-destruction. On this point there is again an affinity with those depth psychologies that would see the self not only as the source of one's deepest truth and healing possibility but as the source of the condemnation of a life that would betray its urgencies to become real in consciousness. Jung, for instance, will write that the unconscious wastes no time in eliminating a meaningless life. "The unconscious has a thousand ways of snuffing out a meaningless existence with surprising swiftness." (Jung 1970: 474) In this context meaninglessness describes that consciousness severed from the energies of the self, a conception obviously with great affinities to Tillich's. In both Tillich and Jung human potential rests on the drive of the divine to become real in the human, a drive that can bring life both its greatest fulfillment if accepted and undergone as well as the most devastating failure if denied. Needless to say such a conception of human potential moves it well beyond the realms of pop psychology.

In the light of these foundational similarities between Tillich's theology and a variety of psychologies of the self, one might inquire one final time if Tillich does not overdraw the distinction between the essential healing mediated specifically by religion, called "salvation", and that psychological healing which would meet Tillich's valid concerns for the engagement of the depth and so of the divine dimension of the human in any real healing and maturation. No doubt some distinction between religious and psychological healing may need to be preserved at the theoretical level, a task which Tillich performs so well. Yet, in fact, Tillich finally endorses psychologies of the self as quite capable of offering theoretically and therapeutically the same transformational and healing potency Tillich attributes in the first instance to religion.

In granting this role to depth psychologies, Tillich anticipated the ever growing situation in twenty-first century North American and Western society. Though he is prone to value Freud as having more forcefully documented the prevalence of the irrational in the human and to describe Jung as a comparatively pallid "essentialist" (Tillich 1959c: 122) Tillich's tribute to

Jung on the occasion of the latter's death opens up interesting possibilities for theologian and psychologist in developing Tillich's thought and, by extension, theological reflection on the relationship of religious and therapeutic healing.

In this late statement (Jung 1961) Tillich understands Jung to offer a solution to difficulties existing between Catholic and Protestant theologians. The former through their natural theology based on a doctrine of the analogy of being give a static doctrine to the Christian symbol. Here Tillich may be echoing his residual critique of the static essentialism he discerns in Aquinas and in the modern Roman Catholic appropriation of Aquinas. Mainstream Protestant thought, on the other hand, is afflicted with a supranaturalist doctrine of revelation. Tillich rejects both positions in favor of his own doctrine of revelation as symbolic expression engaging reason from its own depths. (Tillich 1962a: 30) But in thus understanding the origin of symbol from the depths of the human Tillich confesses a fear that symbols might well be reduced to a wholly subjective relativism. Again one sees Tillich in tension with his own thought to the very end. Out of this quandary Tillich appreciates Jung's conception of the archetype which would locate the permanent origin and meaning of religion in its archetypal ground of which the varying manifest symbols of specific revelations are the valued expression. (Tillich 1962a: 30) In the ensuing discussion Tillich is much less timid than Jung himself in identifying the metaphysical and religious import of Jung's archetypal ground. Symbols, thus understood, become varied expressions of the divine essences, functionally equated with the archetypes. Here Tillich explicitly mentions the Christian doctrine of the *Logos*, which he identifies with essential reason in his systematic thought. (Tillich 1962a: 32) This means that Tillich is here identifying the archetypal basis of archetypal expression with what Christians identify as the second moment in Trinitarian life. In his discussions with Victor White, Jung also explicitly identifies the psyche with the *ousia*, the locus of the divine essences. (Jung 1973a: 540; 1975a: 60) The consequence would be that the essential self, which Tillich grounds in the divine essences as expressed in the *Logos*, and Jung's archetypal self would become identical. Their identification would unite the fields of theology and self psychology by locating the source of religious and psychological healing in the self. Rather than exploit this exciting possibility Tillich concludes the discussion by wondering if the critical realization that religious symbols are variable expressions of archetypal powers would not destroy the power of the symbol for the believing mind, a risk he admits his own non-literal but highly critical theology runs. (Tillich 1962a: 32)

This is a strange form of reticence from a theologian who has cautioned that one should never say, "only a symbol". Tillich means by the caution that only a symbol is an adequate vehicle to carry the power of that which proceeds to consciousness from its divine ground in the depth of reason and that a too analytic reflection on the symbol can divest it of its power or reduce it to the level of a sign and so to a literal reading. (Tillich 1957b: 45) Tillich could have gone other ways with his insight. He could have argued more strongly, as he usually does, that only the experience of the depths identified as the source of the numinous by theologian and psychologist alike gives healing cogency to the symbols of any tradition and through them to those who stand under their impact. In this context in his discussion with psychology he could reopen the question of private revelation for the many who no longer experience a lost numinosity in their religious tradition and its symbols but recover it in a more direct relation to the symbols proffered without mediation by the unconscious, especially in the form of the dream.

Tillich might also have dwelt at greater length on the relativism that Jung's archetypal theory implies not as threatening faith but as freeing faith from the constrictions of its own concretions especially where only one symbol system or religion is held as ultimate. All religions would share a common ground in the archetypal dimension of the self, their many symbols being valued variant expressions of this ground. Though Tillich consistently refers to the birth and death of symbols as a characteristic note of symbol in his many discussions of symbol (Tillich 1957b), he never questions the possibility of the death or surpassing of the Christian symbol as Jung clearly does in his movement to a quaternitarian conception of divinity capable of once more sacralizing what Christianity does not and probably cannot without dramatically growing beyond its current consciousness. Would Tillich's appropriation of archetypal theory open the possibility that the ground of all myth is currently in the process of creating a new symbol or myth in the West? Such a myth would be more conscious of its own origin and the origin of all myth in the unconscious or depth of reason. Such a myth could be jointly accessed and fostered by both theologians of every stripe and a variety of psychologies of depth. Both theologian and psychologist would be more keenly appreciative of the common origin and healing power of traditional religious mythic expressions, where still alive, as well as the immediate impact of the numinous on individual consciousness in whatever form such impact should take and however it is encouraged by specific therapies.

Tillich's late appreciation of archetypal theory might put him in a position to use it radically to recast the relative roles of priestly and psychological healing. Rather than confine the priest to the role of mediating the essential to existence and the psychologist to that of addressing pathological responses to exaggerated existential anxiety, both priest and therapist could be seen as serving what Tillich identifies as the divine in the form of the essential self. Tillich's description of the healing power of the essential is compelling and not here questioned. Rather, the broadening of the boundaries and legitimacy of those who mediate it is the question. Where a psychology such as Jung's addresses, as Tillich admits, the mystery of being itself and does so, however surreptitiously, with its own ontology and epistemology, why would not such a psychology be as effective a servant of the essential and so of a healing salvation as a specifically religious tradition? Tillich leaves the door slightly ajar on this issue. It may be time to throw it fully open.

The mythology of self psychology

In doing so a new myth now in the making may rise to view. The essential and the existential, as Tillich would describe these realms, would be retained as two metaphysical moments or polarities in one organic cosmology whose dynamic is fully to recover in a future, beyond both full attainment or total avoidance, a union with one's truest self, remembered in the past and being worked toward in the present. (Tillich 1963: 421) For Tillich the effecting of this moment in the present is the base meaning of individual life and collective *kairos*, that time when the meaning of life is vividly manifested in time. The psychological equivalent of this myth would argue that the unconscious, as the ground of the archetypal, authors all symbol systems, myths and religions as well as the individual's dream with the purpose of becoming more fully incarnate in human consciousness through the individual's response to these very expressions. In religious language the creative unconscious as source of the sense of the divine creates human consciousness to become conscious in it and the language of this becoming conscious is symbolic and mythic expression. If we take a lead for this paradigm from Jung's late work on Job, this would mean that humanity is becoming increasingly aware of the divine self-contradiction in its depths and increasingly receptive to the moral consequence of such awareness, namely, the task of resolving divinely based conflict in history at the insistence of divinity itself. Historical human consciousness, in conscious relation with its depths, is the only theater in which the divine antinomy can be perceived and resolved. (Jung 1969a: 461) In effect humanity is charged with the redemption of God but with the help of and at the command of God.

This aspect of what may be the now emerging myth of both depth psychology and religion goes beyond Tillich's insistence on a Trinitarian God eternally secure and conscious in its inner differentiations proffering to the creature some degree of participation in such balance. It also may constitute a form of self-salvation which gives too great a role to the human in the ushering of divinity into the fullness of divine consciousness and being in the human. But Tillich himself has pointed to occasions when healing in depth through processes of essentialization escapes ecclesial and priestly containment. In such therapeutic moments nature yields its grace to consciousness through solely natural processes. To draw back from expanding this side of Tillich's thought might well contradict the breadth of his vision, put artificial constraints on the universal, natural and experienced intimacy he sought to establish between the human and the divine, and, in the end, mute or deny the experienced presence of grace in nature in a final betrayal of their mutual and native coinhesion which Tillich so consistently championed.

Chapter 10

Jung, Tillich and their challenge to religious education*

Tillich and Jung have made significant contributions to various facets of contemporary culture. Both make a substantial contribution to the theory of education and especially religious education. Both also present a critique of science and technology based on the danger of the reduction of humanity's cognitive sensitivity to the scientific and technological. Tillich's critique of science/technology is in profound sympathy with Jung's perception that the post-Enlightenment West had lost touch with the deepest dimension of the psyche from which the legitimate, universal and valuable religious sensitivity rises to consciousness. The final chapters expose and amplify what both have contributed in these areas.

To understand their positions on "religious education" the term itself needs clarification. Religious education can mean at least three things. First, it can mean an induction or initiation into a specific religion, its cosmology, symbols, rituals and customs. (Tillich 1959d: 147–151) Second, it can mean the study of the religions themselves in their many historical and current faces, whether explicitly religious or disguised in secular absolutes. This is the approach of the religionist. Third, it can also mean the personal cultivation of religious sensitivities in either an institutional or non-institutional sense. In this latter sense, religious education is increasingly identified with the cultivation of "spirituality", at least in growing Western circles.

In all of the above senses, Tillich and Jung have made significant contributions to "religious education" because both of them ground their thought on religion, as a universal human potentiality, on what they call humanity's "religious function". (Tillich 1959d: 147; Jung 1969h: 6) For Tillich this religious function resides in humanity's native sense of a prior unity with God from which it is removed in existence. The experience of such removal itself becomes for Tillich, then, the basis of the drive of existential humanity to recover its essential truth. (Tillich 1951: 61) The drive or *eros* toward the recovery of the essential is humanity's ultimate concern, the basis of faith universal and so of all personal, collective and historical religions. (Tillich 1963: 130, 131)

* This chapter was originally read as a paper at Kangnam University, Seoul, Korea, May 2001.

Thus, for Tillich, religious education, even in the service of a specific tradition, must begin with the question of what humanity is, what is the nature of
its basic and current plight, and how any specific set of symbols addresses the
human dilemma as currently experienced. Religious education, even as initiation or "induction" into a specific tradition, then shares much in common
with Tillich's understanding of humanistic education as dating from the
Renaissance ideal of developing the whole human potential in the context of
an initiation into the mystery of existence. (Tillich 1959d: 151) In this manner
does Tillich closely relate confessional religious education to humanistic education. Both address the mystery of being human, the questions that this
mystery raises, and the responses to the mystery which any symbol system
would carry.

For Tillich religious education, in any of its senses, would fail if it failed to
respect the autonomy of the human mind, especially in its logical or scientific
functions. (Tillich 1957a: 90, 91; 1951: 72–75) Religious education would fail
if it failed to understand its symbols as expressions of the depth of reason
where reason intersects with the divine and to understand its rites as entry
into these depths. (Tillich 1951: 79–81) Finally it would fail if it could not
address its symbols and mythology to the questions that its culture put to
those symbols. (Tillich 1951: 60) For Tillich, then, a religious education not
based on the humanistic concern for the development of the total human
potential understood as a deepening sensitivity toward and questioning of
the human mystery as constellated in the current societal situation would fail
both religion and education.

Many of these sentiments are present in Jung's conception of a "religious
function" within the psyche which, he argues, is the basis of humanity's
inevitable and universal religious experience, again at both the personal and
collective levels. (Jung 1969h: 6–8) Since this religious function expresses
itself both in historical religions and unmediated personal religious experience, Jung would understand religious education, even as initiation into a
specific symbol system, to serve as the entrance into the integrating, renewing
and extending power of the unconscious from which all religions and their
symbols burst onto consciousness. (Jung 1968i: 8, 9) In terms of religious
education as the study of the history of religions, Jung would see all such
religions, living or dead, as significant expressions of the unconscious. In
their epoch-making and culture-creating capacities, religions function to provide their constituencies with the compensation necessary to move toward
a fuller humanity expressive of the deeper levels of the psyche which create
consciousness itself and, as its matrix, constantly foster its enhancement
through a fuller incarnation in it (see also Chapter 7). Finally, in terms of
religious education as cultivating a personal spirituality, Jung would contend
that to be human is to possess the potentiality and, in the course of most
lives, the actuality of being addressed personally by the unconscious as the
source of all religious experience and so as the source of all religions. Most

forcefully through the dream is the individual addressed personally by the common source of humanity's many religions in the formation of one's individual myth.

Tillich and the religious function: humanity as question

One of Tillich's more compelling descriptions of humanity imbued with a native religious instinct or function lies in his depiction of humanity as the collective personification of a question. He writes, "Man is the question he asks about himself, before any question has been formulated." (Tillich 1951: 61) Tillich is here arguing that to be human and finite is to ask the question of God in the sense of questing after God as the ultimate resource in the face of the painful distortions of humanity in existence. The same sense of a humanity questing after God is present in his analysis of the so called ontological argument. Here he takes the position that the ontological argument, and, indeed all arguments for God's existence, really derive from the human quest for or question about God. Such arguments "are expression of the *question* of God which is implied in human finitude". (Tillich 1951: 205) The ontological argument takes a priority for Tillich in its true intent, namely, simply to point out that the mind is imbued with an immediate sense of the absolute or unconditioned. The simple pointing to this sense is the substance of the ontological argument and the basis of both the possibility and necessity of humanity being religious. (Tillich 1951: 206) Writes Tillich, "God is the presupposition of the question of God." (1959b: 13, 16) If humanity had no endemic sense of God it could neither ask the question of God nor could it receive a meaningful answer respectful of the autonomy of questing human nature.

Tillich on essence and existence

The same dialectical intimacy between the divine and the human lies at the basis of Tillich's understanding of the relation of essence to existence which he describes as the "backbone of the whole body of theological thought". (Tillich 1951: 204) For Tillich the distinction is more than a lifeless philosophical position. The difference between essence and existence serves as the backbone of his thought because it structures his understanding of humanity's origin in divinity, alienation from its origin in existence and natural drive to recover its original unity with the divine. These three moments are the substance of the divine–human relationship and of the meaning of history and the history of religion. In fact both histories tend to coincide in this conception of history. (Tillich 1963: 421) The essential for Tillich describes humanity, collective and individual, as grounded in the dynamic of its Trinitarian origin but consciously removed or alienated from the origin in existence. Thus "the essential self", the divine truth of the individual, traces its pristine expression to its definition in the Word as preceding from the abyss of divine creativity. (Tillich 1963: 235) Every individual is first "created" within the dynamics of the Trinitarian life as the precondition of entry into the "actual world" of existential estrangement. (Tillich 1951: 204)

Such initial creation is somehow unreal. Tillich describes this unqualified unity of creation with its Trinitarian ground as a state of "dreaming innocence". (Tillich 1957a: 33–36) The tragedy of humanity, for Tillich at once universal yet mediated through individual freedom, occurs when the individual wills to step out from this primal but somehow premature unity with the flow of divine life. The transition from "dreaming innocence" to the existential describes the process of the "fall" from one's essential truth in the divine life into a removal from its fullness in the distortions of existential life. Such fall is universal and individual since the individual invariably wills to exist and in doing so comes to participate in the universal tragedy of removal from one's origins. (Tillich 1957a: 1936)

At this point Tillich's complex thought on participation comes into play. Even though the individual, through the universal will to exist, is removed from the Trinitarian ground of life, nevertheless, in the very ambiguities of such existential suffering the individual continues consciously to participate in the vitalities of the divine ground. (Tillich 1951: 250) In these positions Tillich confesses to being inspired by the Platonic conception of a living memory, however attenuated, of a prior unity with the divine from which one is currently estranged in existence. (Tillich 1957a: 22) Such Platonism enables Tillich to describe the fall as a removal from an unqualified but preconscious unity with the essential and to maintain, at the same time, that humanity is naturally religious because, in existence, it remembers that from which it is fallen. The memory itself empowers the drive to a fuller recovery of the essential as the deepest form of *eros* operative in existence and as the basis of humanity's religious nature.

On the basis of this all encompassing conception of the relation of essence to existence, Tillich moves to his compelling analysis of the consequences in existence of the fall from essence. Here his analysis takes on a psychological hue based as it is on a profound sense of the anxieties that attach to finite and existential humanity. Thus he will analyze the human plight as riddled with the negations of death, guilt and meaninglessness. (Tillich 1952: 40–57) These universal anxieties cry out for the source of the courage to be. Such courage, for Tillich as a Christian theologian, can be received only as grace arising from the divine ground of life to reassure its recipient with the experience, even in the present, of a life beyond death, of a self-acceptance based on a divine acceptance and of a meaning in the depth of life which can overcome, even as it is present in, despair over any meaning. (Tillich 1952: 178–190)

An even greater threat to existential life for Tillich is fragmentation or disintegration worked by the failure of life's opposites to achieve or approach significant forms of unification. Tillich's analysis here again engages the

Trinity as the source of life understood as that vitality resultant from the synthesis of the opposites that make up the fullness of life itself. (Tillich 1951: 249–252) In their deepest God-grounded sense these opposites are those of power and form or meaning. (Tillich 1951: 249) Power Tillich relates to creativity and to the first moment in Trinitarian life. Form Tillich relates to communication, expression and so to the channeling of power in the second moment of the Trinity, the *Logos*. (Tillich 1951: 246, 247) The disintegration of human life into a power without meaning or a superficial meaning divested of depth is overcome to the extent that existential and finite life is led by the Spirit into greater inhesion in the vitalities of the life of the Trinity as the ground of human life.

From this more general depiction of the vitality of human life resonating with the vitality of its living ground, Tillich continues to work more specific integrations. Thus the problem of self-affirmation over against self-loss in going beyond oneself in outward movement is resolved through participation in the life process of the Trinity. In this process the first moment of the Trinity goes beyond itself in its expression and returns to itself in the unity worked by the Spirit. This relation of self to other Tillich makes the substance of morality. (Tillich 1963: 268, 269) The Trinity also implies the perfect unity of creative power with its expression or realization. For Tillich this becomes another work of the Spirit, uniting human potential with its realization in a process which can never be fully terminated nor ever evaded without tragic self-limitation. (Tillich 1951: 199) The unity of power and meaning Tillich relates to creativity. Finally the Spirit of the Trinity works the unity of freedom and destiny in the divine life and in human life. Here Tillich argues that the Spirit incessantly moves the individual toward the realization of one's essential truth through all negativities in one's destiny whether inherited or created by one's freedom. The use of freedom to achieve one's destiny as the recovery of one's essential self becomes the reality of religion for Tillich. (Tillich 1951: 201) Not only are these opposites united by the Spirit, but also, through their union, the dimensions of morality, creativity and religion are resolved at both personal and collective levels.

In summation what Tillich is found to be arguing is that the ground of being and life in which every human participates confronts the human tendency in existence to be fragmented or disrupted by the opposites whose resolution fosters life's fullness. In the Trinity these opposites have achieved eternal union. In humanity they are fragmentarily united to the extent that humanity is led by the Spirit into a deeper union with the Trinity. In Tillich's view, then, the Spirit works the union of all conflicting yet legitimate opposites in life and through them, both in individual and society, works to the union of the most important aspects of the human spirit, namely morality, culture and religion. (Tillich 1963: 157–161) The union of these aspects of the spirit Tillich describes collectively as theonomous culture at the collective level and as the Spiritual Presence in the individual. The courage to be and the integration of life's opposites become the hallmarks of the work of the Spirit as it leads existential humanity to a progressive recovery of its essential truth in the God whose vitalities it experiences dimly but naturally in its native depths.

These foundational themes in Tillich's thought would challenge the educator to foster in religious education the memory of humanity's essential truth in the divine, to examine the human plight in the present and the questions it would ask of religion, to at least raise the question of accessing the courage to affirm life in the face of its negativities, and to reflect on the need and possibility of uniting life's opposites and on the agency or agencies that might do so. Any religious education not based on such questioning would be for Tillich a heteronomous education, that is, effectively an imposition of a religious perspective which could not respect the autonomy of the questioning human mind nor relate to the questions that would derive from human suffering in whatever form it currently took in individual or societal life.

Tillich, the sacramental, the iconoclastic and the Religion of the Concrete Spirit

Tillich also provides the religious educator, student and practitioner with a helpful typology of religions based ultimately on his understanding of humanity as religious. In his typology he grounds religion on a universal sense of the presence of the holy to the finite. (Tillich 1990a: 22) This claim is simply a variant of his argument that the essential grounds the existential as the basis of humanity's universal experience of God. In this context the late Tillich will even refer to a universal revelation which is the ground of all specific religions. (Tillich 1990b: 64) For Tillich the sacramental, which he sometimes terms "Catholic substance", always precedes and makes possible the iconoclastic, Tillich's "Protestant principle". (Tillich 1963: 245) In these most general terms, then, a fully functioning religion would have to synthesize the sacramental and iconoclastic dimensions of the experience of the holy within itself. Without the experience of the sacramental a religion would have no depth or power. It would be severed from the roots of the divine in the human and nature. Without the iconoclastic the danger of idolatry would be difficult to escape and the temptation to identify the holy with that through which the holy appears would easily if not inevitably prevail. (Tillich 1990b: 72, 73)

With these conceptions of the holy as universal and the basis of a universal sacramentalism made responsible through a lively iconoclasm, Tillich can make further differentiations in his typology based on how the holy is perceived to be present to the human. Effectively he is arguing that as a revelation occurs out of the universal ground of the sacramental it immediately becomes subject to idolatrous concretion and so elicits an iconoclastic response from the moment of its birth. One such response is that of mysticism.

The mystic is grasped by the holy without mediation, institutional or personal. (Tillich 1990a: 23) The mystic goes immediately to God as the One, or to the God beyond the Gods of Western theism. Tillich sees this appropriation of the holy not only in mystics of all background but also as more predominant in Eastern religions.

The second major iconoclastic response is that of the prophet. The prophet, in some distinction from the mystic, experiences the holy as a demand, as the basis of the "ought", and usually as conveyed from beyond by a wholly transcendent God. For this reason the prophet tends to be associated with one or other of the monotheistic Gods and speaks on his God's behalf to both his own community and to a wider humanity beyond it. (Tillich 1990a: 24) Tillich sees Judaism and Islam as typical of prophecy and tends to describe Christianity as possessed of both mystical and prophetic elements.

Tillich is also aware of the real presence of the holy in what he calls the "quasi-religions". His use of the term usually refers to elements of the holy in the secular world and, in particular, in the world of ethnic and political ultimates. (Tillich 1990a: 9, 32, 33; 1990b: 61, 62) In this respect Tillich does grant some credibility to an authentic religious substance in national and political communities. (Tillich 1964: 14–18) His criticism of them rests on his allegation that they are divested of the iconoclastic dimension of religion and so identify with the absolute that works through them. As such they cannot undergo a radical criticism or divestiture as symbolized by the cross as the basis of the Protestant principle and so fall easy prey to idolatrous and destructive forms of self-affirmation. (Tillich 1963: 153, 164)

Tillich maintained this typology of religions and its underlying religious metaphysics late into his career and thought. However, in his later years, he confessed that his theology to that point was informed by many provincialisms fully exposed in Chapter 1. These provincialisms are of interest to the religious educator in so much as they evidence in the late Tillich a movement away from the possibility of any religion, including Christianity, claiming an ultimate position as the exhaustive completion of the history of religions or revelation. Such a position is consistent with a universality and relativity appreciative of the truly religious in whatever form it might take. Among the provincialisms in his theology Tillich included his bias on behalf of the West, Christianity, theism and religion over the quasi-religions. (Tillich 1990b: 60–62)

Chapter 1 attributed the doubt and growth manifest in Tillich's confession of these provincialisms to his late work with Mircea Eliade at the University of Chicago, to a 1957 extended dialogue with Zen master, Hisamatsu Shin'ichi, to his travels to Japan in 1960 and to discussions there with representatives of Eastern and non-Christian religions and spiritualities. The acknowledgment of such important provincialisms in his previous theology approach retractions of certain positions foundational to his monumental *Systematic*

Theology. As discussed earlier Tillich was to admit in his last published paper that the history of religion need not culminate in any specific religion, a role he previously gave to Christianity. (Tillich 1966: 81) This admission corrodes his claim in his first volume of the *Systematic Theology* that the reality of Christ must be the ultimate concern of the Christian theologian working on behalf of the Christian Church possessed of "the final revelation". (Tillich 1951: 132) In his last statement Tillich would seem to distance himself from his earlier definition as a Christian theologian and move to a self-understanding as historian of religious symbolism or as a religionist within the Christian community.

What would seem to move into the role previously attributed to Christianity is what he calls the "Religion of the Concrete Spirit". It would be a religion sensitive to the universal presence of the holy and informed by the mystical and prophetic in mutual and critical reciprocity. (Tillich 1966: 86–88) Tillich then moves to a position closer to that of the religionist than the theologian when he concludes that the future of systematic theology would have to integrate a wider human experience of the history of religions and of their many symbols as opposed to his prior theological efforts to defend Christianity from the specifically Western criticism of science and philosophy. (Tillich 1966: 91)

Elsewhere in materials written at the same time, Tillich describes this new methodology of religion as viewing the religions as responses to the needs of the human spirit and its religious instinct in whatever epoch such religions occurred. Here he consciously distances himself from an Hegelian view of the history of religions in which allegedly prior and lower forms of religion cede to Christianity as to the culminating instance of religion subsuming and so abrogating all previous religions. (Tillich 1964: 55–57; 1966: 86) In these lines Tillich comes close to a Jungian appreciation of religion as compensating the spiritual needs of whatever society in which it appears. All forms of religion can then be appreciated as expression of the divine Spirit working through the human spirit providing it with the religious impulse the historical occasion demands. In the end, then, Tillich may have moved beyond the confines of a confessional theologian to the broader domain of the religionist or historian sensitive to the appearance of the holy in all its manifestations. At the same time Tillich held to the end his conviction that the experience of the holy as the basis of religion universally is most authentically realized in historical religion when religion works the synthesis of the mystical with the prophetic, the sacramental with the iconoclastic. In some variation these elemental experiences would always be there as the primordial religious resources addressing the flux of the deepest spiritual needs of the moment.

Tillich's late position remains invaluable to the religious educator. It would mean that if religious education is to escape exclusivist forms of provincialism it would have to forgo its claim to an exhaustive ultimacy understood as bringing the evolution of religion to a completion in itself. Rather an authentic religious education would have to come to appreciate all religions and their symbols as expressions of the natural presence of the sense of the holy to humanity. The variety of the religions would become the historical concretions of the holy responding to the religious needs in the society in which they are given birth and which they form as they are formed by it. All symbol systems could then be seen as derivative of a common human ground and those living in communities bonded by them could embrace each other as possessed of differing symbolic and ritual riches derived from such a common ground. The need to convert, to coerce or to vanquish would be undercut in principle.

Before turning to Jung and his conception of the religious function one final word must be said of Tillich as religious educator. In a late essay to the confessional educator he repeats that all true knowledge of the other involves participation. In the dialogue between religions this means that a member of one tradition cannot understand another in anything but a superficial manner unless one participates in that tradition. (Tillich 1959e: 204) For the religious educator this would mean that neither one's own tradition nor others can be understood unless entered into with the empathy that only being possessed by its truth can confer. Effectively the experiential assimilation of the faith of another or others would place an immense demand on the sensitivities of the authentic religious educator.

Carl Jung and the religious function

In a major essay devoted entirely to religion and psychology Jung refers to an empirically demonstrable "authentic religious function in the unconscious". (Jung 1969h: 6) He goes on to locate the basis of this religious function in the archetypal dimension of the human psyche precisely in its capacity to generate the experience of the numinous. (Jung 1969h: 7) Though Jung borrows the term "numinous" from Rudolph Otto, he gives it a meaning quite different from Otto's. Otto understood the numinous to originate in divinity as wholly other. Jung understands the generation of the numinous to be a wholly intrapsychic process. In fact it describes the impact of the archetypal on consciousness with a force so intense that the individual undergoing such impact is convinced by the impact itself that one has been addressed by divinity in one of its many benign or demonic forms. The addressing of humanity by divinity becomes for Jung the addressing of the ego as the center of consciousness by the source of consciousness in the archetypal ground of the psyche. The claim that such address is empirically demonstrable rests on humanity's recurring experience of the archetypal not only by the eminent founders of religions but potentially by anyone who experienced the power of the archetypal in one's life.

Given these presuppositions, the basic meaning of religion, for Jung, becomes the sustained "careful and scrupulous observation" of that which moves from the archetypal unconscious into consciousness. (Jung 1969h: 7) The content of such observation becomes for the individual who engages in it a religion understood as an ongoing personal revelation. Such personal revelation does not necessarily compromise the value of the world religions and the revelations they bear. Nor does it forbid membership in one of them. Rather religion as personal revelation gives to the individual responsive to it access to his or her personal and unique myth. The surfacing of one's unique mythology then becomes the basis of one's conscious relation to the variety of collective myths, religious, ethnic or political, into which one is inevitably born. The appropriation of one's personal myth gives the freedom and power to the individual to endorse, reject or moderate one's relation to one's inherited societal myths – for instance, religious, national or ethnic – to meet the needs of one's individual myth whose realization becomes the substance of one's spiritual growth.

In the wider context of the cosmology latent in Jung's psychology, he is affirming that humanity cannot be without religion (Jung 1969b: 199) even as he would deny to any given religion a claim to complete the evolution of religion in history. Because humanity cannot evade archetypal influence religion will endure as long as does the psyche in its current form. But because the archetypal dimension of the psyche is "of indefinite extent with no assignable limits" (Jung 1969c: 258) and so infinite in its fecundity, it can never be exhausted in its necessarily limited expressions or manifestation in consciousness, personal or collective, precious and powerful though these deeper manifestations be especially in their religious form.

Jung's cosmology and its religious implications

The inevitability of religion and its ongoing need for supersession rest on the metaphysical/religious implications of Jung's understanding of the psyche and the processes of the psyche's creation and renewal of consciousness. Jung describes the deepest level of the unconscious in technical terms as "the collective unconscious" and in personal terms as the "Great Mother" or "Great Goddess". (Jung 1966a: 306–393) Hers is the womb or matrix of the archetypal powers and of their religious expression. (Jung 1969g: 552) In this initial situation "prior" to the creation of consciousness the warring opposites endemic to the archetypal are wholly undifferentiated in the absence of the discriminatory powers of reason.

At this point Jung introduces the role of the self which presides over the entire process of maturation to which he gives the name "individuation". In a first moment consistent with traditional religious imagery of creation, the self propels the ego from the womb of the Great Mother in the creation of consciousness. Consciousness free of the mother becomes the only agency of rational discrimination in the universe. However, the birth of consciousness is a victory with its own problems. Unless consciousness can return to the womb that gave it birth, its increasing acumen is accompanied by an increasing sterility and often by anger and depression due to its increasing removal from the nourishment of its maternal source. With this understanding of the psyche, Jung was among the first to document the pathology of the patriarchal as removal from life's source and so from its whole-making energies.

Thus the self after urging consciousness beyond its matrix must then lead consciousness, once born, back to its origins for its ongoing renewal. This process is quite consistent with the biblical imprecation to reenter the womb. Ideally this would describe the death of the ego into its source in the interests of its renewal not once but many times in a process of ongoing growth. The whole process for Jung describes the cycle of the creation of consciousness, its death into its origin and its resurrection toward an enhanced consciousness enjoying the vitalities of a more integrated personality and ever-widening sympathy. (Jung 1969c: 263) Though these are Christian analogies to the process of individuation, any form of authentic religious renewal, such as liberation, pilgrimage, freedom from illusion, to name only a few, would rest on the same underlying psychodynamic.

The most far-reaching implication of Jung's effective equation of religious with psychological maturation is that the creator or matrix of consciousness becomes increasingly conscious in the process itself. The co-redemption of divinity and humanity in a single process provides the ultimate access to the meaning of individual and collective human history. Jung makes these points explicit in his late work on Job. Here he depicts Job as a figure of that stage in the evolution of religious consciousness becoming aware that the power or God, Yaweh, who has produced human consciousness, remains in a state of relative unconsciousness in the form of unresolved self-contradictions. (Jung 1969a: 372) This realization implies further that the divine source of created consciousness has created humanity first to perceive and then to cooperate with the divine in the resolution in humanity of that divine antinomy defiant of resolution in eternity. (Jung 1969a: 455, 461)

This cosmology affirms that divinity and humanity are "functions" of each other, a position Jung attributes to Meister Eckhart's mystical experience. (Jung 1971a: 243) Such intimate mutuality between the divine and the human would imply that humanity and divinity are ontologically aspects of each other and confer on each other a redemptive completion. God is the source of consciousness and so its creator but this same God is dependent on its creature to become conscious in human consciousness now entrusted with the divine command and vocation to usher God into consciousness in it. In this sense consciousness creates God as conscious and makes of God a creature of consciousness. Such giving birth to God in consciousness is the meaning the alchemists attributed to their description of God as the *filius philosophorum*, the son of the philosophers, that is, God as child in the consciousness of those making God conscious in themselves. (Jung 1969c: 263)

Recalling the Gods: a millennial process

The foregoing implications of Jung's psychological cosmology are foundational in Jung's delineation of the stage that the evolution of religious consciousness has reached at least in terms of the Western monotheisms. Jung describes this current stage of maturity as the fruit of a "millennial process". (Jung 1969a: 402) The process is characterized by the increasing cultural awareness that humanity and divinity share a point of coincidence as the basis of their difference. This point of coincidence makes the human psyche the origin of the experience of divinity and so the creator of those divinities understood to exist beyond the psyche. Such divinities then become projections which have escaped the containment of their psychic origin.

The current moral imperative of this psychological cosmology is the demand that such projections be withdrawn and that the powers that produced them be addressed immediately within the safer confines of the psyche. (Jung 1969h: 85) This moral sense does not devalue the myths that surround the three variants of the monotheistic one and only Gods. Rather, when it is realized that all religious myth describes significant movements of the psyche, the now emerging religious consciousness would value monotheistic myths as projections of the role of the self which does indeed create and preside over psychic development much in the manner that the monotheistic Gods are imagined to create and direct the external world and their communities within it. The internalization of monotheistic mythology would demand unmediated dialogue with the God within, the God now seen as the common referent of these diverse monotheistic mythologies. The radical internalization of the dialogue would make monotheistic and all revelations socially safer since it would remove the enmity between competing one and only Gods, and by extension, all Gods, and so remove the enmity between their communities especially evident when these communities come into geographical contiguity or share common territory.

Such sensitivity to the reality of the divine as immanent to the human psyche lay behind Jung's attraction to the East. This attraction began with his reading a text in Chinese alchemy in the Taoist tradition. (Jung 1967: 7–55) It turned him to expressions of equally powerful experience of divinity as an immanent force in the psyche in Western alchemy, and to its affinities with earlier gnosticism, mysticism and the Grail myth. One of his most telling criticisms of mainstream Western Christianity is that it endorses an extraverted literalism that would understand God as beyond the psyche intervening in human historical events in dramatic revelations made from a position wholly transcendent to the human and its historical maturation. In moments of discouragement he decries the fact that such a sense of radical immanence led to his dismissal by religion as a "morbid" mystic and by psychology as a reductionist. (Jung 1969i: 482)

The abiding challenge of his psychology as it touches on religion and religious education engages the future of religion and by extension the well-being, if not survival, of the species. His challenge to ground the reality of divinity wholly on intra-psychic experience would undermine the dangers of claims to a possession of a "final revelation", the kind of claim that even a younger Paul Tillich could make. Whether such claims by major religious and sometimes national and political constituencies will cede to a saving relativity poses a question yet to be answered. Beyond this survival issue, Jung's psychology would offer to religion the possibility of understanding itself as grounded in a common origin giving birth to possibly infinite historical variations. Such a saving universalism, pluralism and relativity would enable religions to embrace each other as seeing in the other what is lacking in themselves possibly for the first time in the history or religion. Such a perspective and such values should begin to inform religious education in all its variants if the future of religion is to serve and not threaten the joint human adventure.

Jung, Tillich and religious education as spirituality

Tillich and Jung contribute to religious education with their academic or more formal understanding of what religion is and how it manifests in historical form and development. They both make an even greater contribution to religious education through the spirituality within their thought, if spirituality is taken to mean the process of accessing the transformative energies of religious experience whether mediated through an institution or not.

Tillich and the spirituality of the essential self

As detailed earlier, Tillich provides an impressive metaphysical account of religion as based on the experienced concern of universal existential humanity to recover its essential self as grounded in the dynamics of Trinitarian life. (Tillich 1963: 269, 270) When he moves to describe what such a recovery would look like in a concrete life Tillich describes attributes of the essential self which he admits have close affinities with the virtues cherished by "depth psychology". (Tillich 1963: 231, 232)

The dynamics involved in the realization of the essential self would work to the recovery, by the existential personality, of its pristine expression in the *Logos*, the universal structure of mind, divine and human. Such recovery would also engage the infinite divine creativity voiced in the *Logos* by the preceding abyss dimension of God. Intersecting with these forces in existence in such a way as to experience their progressive influence on one's consciousness explains why Tillich attributes to the essential self the very psychological characteristics of an enhanced awareness, freedom, relatedness and self-transcendence. (Tillich 1963: 231–235)

Unity with the supportive power and universal meaning of God as ground of one's being brings with it the residual ability to discern the energies, divine and demonic, at work in oneself and in others in one's surrounding. Such unity intensifies the awareness of what specific aspects of one's participation in divine creativity demand realization in one's personal being at any point in its development as well as enabling one to discern the forces beyond oneself operative in every moment. The awareness bred by such unity with one's ground makes one increasingly sensitive to "the voiceless voice of a concrete situation". (Tillich 1963: 232)

The recovery of the essential self also brings with it an increased freedom. In the first instance it frees from those psychological compulsions which Jung would identify as one complex or energy controlling the totality. (Tillich 1963: 232) The essential self always engages the whole person and submits specific energies to such wholeness. At a deeper level the recovery of the essential self frees from the law as an external imposition. For Tillich the truth of such an external religious law is grounded in the truth of one's essential self judging from within the person its own distortion in the individual's life. This is how he would understand conscience. As one grows into the essential self one becomes a law unto oneself not in an irresponsible sense but rather in the sense that one's life becomes an increasingly spontaneous expression of one's essential truth as grounded in God. Life becomes freer as it expresses the law of one's essential being. (Tillich 1963: 232, 233)

Inhesion in the essential self is never solipsistic. Such inhesion cannot be isolated from an extending universal relatedness because the essential self is itself initially expressed in the universal *Logos* of the ground of being, the power which as the source of all formal expression is the ultimate power enabling a universal relatedness and conversation. The progressive cultivation of the essential self leads the individual to come increasingly under the suasion of its groundedness in the source of all that is. (Tillich 1963: 232–235)

Self-transcendence Tillich relates to the experience of the holy. As the essential self moves existential life into unity with its source, it brings it into an increasingly residual experience of the holy. This sense of the holy may be fostered through various forms of institutional devotion, a practice Tillich here endorses but refuses to impose. (Tillich 1963: 235, 236) Irrespective of how it is nourished, the realization of the essential self blesses its possessor with a sense of the holy in all things and in all of one's activities. On this point Tillich is close to Teilhard de Chardin when he writes that for those who know how to see nothing is profane. (de Chardin 1964: 66) For Tillich such sight is gained through the eyes of the essential self. Its influence should inform religious education in all its forms and lead to a far more positive appreciation of what religion as mediator of this self offers humanity.

Jung and the spirituality of the self

Though there are extensive analogies between the spiritualities of Tillich and Jung, they may be best focused from Jung's side through his understanding of the alchemical process and its culmination in a theophanic consciousness. In his appropriation of the alchemical transformation through the work of Gerhard Dorn, Jung describes a three-part process which, like that of individuation, recurs over a lifetime. (Jung 1970: 457–553) In the first moment the soul is removed from the body in a penitential process so rigorous as to warrant its depiction through images of death. (Jung 1970: 471) But, as Jung appropriates Dorn, the separation of the soul from the turbulence of the body does not culminate in its moving through a "window into eternity" and its permanent turning from the world as he intimates a more traditional Christian asceticism might do. (Jung 1970: 471)

Rather the soul purified by the spirit is returned to the body and begins a movement toward an increasing experience of the holy in the body. The first moment in this return is referred to as *caelum*, a heaven (Jung 1970: 487), implying a current experience of that unity with God which traditional Christianity identifies as a state from which we are fallen prior to existential life or toward which we move in post-temporal life. For Jung the moment of the *caelum* is now. This consciousness then moves to an even deeper religious experience, the culminating state of the *unus mundus*, the one world. The consciousness described in this state is one in which reality is perceived from the perspective of "the eternal Ground of all empirical being". (Jung 1970: 534)

In this phrase Jung is repeating the term "Ground", which Tillich uses as his primary metaphor to describe God's presence to existential life and consciousness and with much the same meaning. Jung is contending that, if an alchemical paradigm be used to understand the spirituality of the developing self in the process of individuation, then such spirituality culminates in the capacity, however ephemeral, to perceive reality while in the body through a consciousness in full resonance with God as the ground of the empirical multiple. In this culmination of the spiritual process the warnings of both Tillich and Jung must be heeded. Tillich would contend that the essential self may shine through "the contingencies of the existing self" (Tillich 1963: 235) but that such epiphany is never more than ambiguous or fragmentary in existence. Jung would also warn that the self can only be approximated never fully realized in the course of a lifetime. Yet both do argue that the movement of the human spirit, religiously and psychologically, is toward that unity with the divine which does allow the experience of the divine in the present, an experience characterized by the human ability to perceive the transparency of the multiple to its divine ground from a mind in deepening resonance with it.

Conclusion

Jung and Tillich are continuing contributors to religious education because of their compelling picture of humanity's inescapable rootedness in the divine as the basis of its inextinguishable religious instinct. Tillich will address the fact that religions and their symbols may supplant one another but religion itself cannot disappear. "A god disappears; divinity remains." (Tillich 1957b: 18) Religion cannot disappear because it rises to consciousness from that point in humanity, familiar to the mystics, "where the ultimate is present within the finite world, namely, the depth of the human soul". (Tillich 1957b: 61)

Jung would agree with these sentiments and describe that point of coincidence as the archetypal world, the source of the numinous, from which the sense of the divine rises to consciousness and moves it toward a universal sympathy as wide in its extension as that of the divine itself. For Jung humanity as image of God is a humanity moving toward its divine center from which its embrace of the totality comes into ever closer approximation with that of the divine center itself. (Jung 1969c: 292)

When both Tillich and Jung are understood the boundaries between religious and psychological experience begin to cede toward a joint appreciation of the vastness of human interiority. Tillich will describe the essential self in notes that are obviously psychological and Jung will show the psychological basis for the religious attitudes that Tillich attributes to the presence of the Spirit. One can conclude that when Jung's psychology goes to those same divine depths which Tillich discerns in the human it enters the collective unconscious which Tillich himself identifies as the origin of religious symbolism. (Tillich 1957b: 43; 1957a: 241, 250, 261, 279) At this point of ingression into the depth of the human it would seem that theology and psychology come close to identity. Jung himself refers to this native affinity and the difficulty of differentiating the reality of God from humanity's psychic experience of God when he writes:

> It is only through the psyche that we can establish that God acts upon us, but we are unable to distinguish whether these actions emanate from God or from the unconscious. We cannot tell whether God and the unconscious are two different entities.
>
> (Jung 1969a: 468)

What Jung could tell was that the fullness of the experience of the self was the experiential equivalent of an experience of grace and of God. Such experience "thus constitutes the most immediate experience of the Divine which is psychologically possible to imagine". (Jung 1969c: 261)

Both Tillich and Jung would thus assure the religious educator that the study of the religions even in the interests of the initiation into one is a study of the deepest experiences of humanity and of the varieties of access into this experience. Both also point the religious educator toward a spirituality based upon a radical sense of God as immanent to the human. God as immanent not only links the study and experience of religion to depth psychology but also implies that the future study of religion should take the form of the study of human interiority as the source of religion, its symbols and its rites. This same human interiority is the legitimate territory psychology and especially depth psychology explore. Such an approach would lead to a critical appreciation of religion in its many faces as a power which humanity cannot evade and as possessed of the greatest resources for human fulfillment or destruction, a power to which psychology pays equal tribute.

Chapter 11

Tillich, Jung and the wisdom and morality of doing science and technology*

The theological/historical context and problematic

Both Tillich and Jung were severe critics of a society, theirs, which had been uprooted from the depths of its own humanity. In the severance society had lost touch with its native religious sensibility and grown deaf to symbolic discourse and the humanizing wealth such discourse could proffer. Both Tillich and Jung traced the more remote origin of this disorientation to the intellectualism of thirteenth century scholasticism and especially to the victory Aristotelianism won then and continued to win in the subsequent Western history. Jung will refer to this dubious triumph as "a turning away from our psychic origins as a result of Scholasticism and Aristotelianism". (Jung 1973b: 317) The psychic origins turned away from were the variations of Platonism in earlier Christianity with its much livelier sense of the presence of the transcendent to finite consciousness. Jung closely relates this natural sense of the transcendent to alchemy and to alchemy's paganism manifest in the light of nature, *the lumen naturae*, which he equates with "individual revelation". (Jung 1973b: 318) Such revelation was better able to sponsor a theophanous consciousness allowing the divine to become transparent in all of nature including human nature than a philosophy such as Aristotle's and Aquinas', whose point of departure remained the senses and the limited reality discernible to them. Rather than locating the sense of God as a native sentiment of humanity alone enabling and insuring consequent and more specific revelation to be truly humane, Aristotelian theology understood this sense to be generated by a divine agency originating beyond the human psyche and addressing it from without.

In a major article in continuity with Jung's critique, Paul Tillich cites the response of a thirteenth century Franciscan theologian, Matthew of Aquasparta, to the then developing Aristotelian theology of Thomas Aquinas

---

* This chapter was originally read at the Ninth European Conference on Science and Theology, European Society for the Study of Science and Theology, University of Nijmegen, the Netherlands, March 19–24, 2002.

as follows: "For even if this method builds the way to science [*scientia*], it utterly destroys the way of wisdom [*sapientia*]." (Tillich 1959b: 14; 1968: 186) Tillich understood the thirteenth as among the greatest centuries theologically because in it Plato and Aristotle continued their "eternal conversation" in theological form in the debate between Bonaventure, as representative of the traditional Platonic-Augustinian tradition, and Aquinas, with his innovative Aristotelian theology. (Tillich 1968: 180–186) To the dismay of both Tillich and Jung the Aristotelian perspective and its "sense-bound epistemology" (Tillich 1959b: 18) conquered the West, most dramatically as it moved through the Reformation and Enlightenment toward the development first of autonomous reason and then of science and technology.

Jung is equally adamant on this point. Twice he explicitly rejects the epistemological foundation on which Aquinas bases the sense bound philosophy foundational to his theology. This principle states "*nihil est in intellectu quod non antea fuerit in sensibus*", "nothing is in the intellect which was not previously in the senses". (Jung 1969e: 492; 1969j: 559) For Jung the reduction of the total cognitive possibility to the yield of the senses betrays an innocent ignorance of the power and influence of the archetypal on human knowing and activity especially in areas having to do with the religious impulse. No doubt the senses can provoke an archetypal response as in the sacramental and ritual use of such natural powers as fire, water, music, incense, food and alcohol. But in these instances the senses work a triggering effect on the archetypal unconscious as the source of the sense of God which the senses themselves can never wholly induce. The very sense of the holy precedes sensation of any kind and would remain an impossibility to the senses were they not the occasion of an experience that lay beyond their power to generate. If the archetypal basis of the psyche as the basis of religion were not endemic to humanity there would be no religion. For both Tillich and Jung the contemporary consequence of the loss of the sense of the sacred to the superficiality of the senses is a culture scientifically and technologically advanced but spiritually bankrupt whose distant origin Tillich traces to Thomas' theological appropriation of Aristotle in the thirteenth century, a turning point in the Western spirit which Jung also mourns.

Much of Tillich's concern as a philosophical theologian and Jung's as a depth psychologist was the reversal of the thus historically truncated consciousness of their society. In a striking formulation Tillich accuses Aquinas of cutting "the nerve of the ontological approach". (Tillich 1959b: 17) Though such a wound might appear as an inconsequential slip of a theological surgeon's scalpel, Tillich identifies it as the historically remote origin of a contemporary cultural consciousness divested of humanity's native sense of God. For Tillich understood the immediate awareness of God, the unconditional in human consciousness, to be the referent of Anselm's formulation of the ontological argument and of its subsequent variations in the West. (Tillich 1968: 164, 165; 1951: 204–208) Aquinas' insensitivity in the thirteenth century to the theological import of this native dimension of human consciousness led in the next century to Occam's division of the mind into a wholly autonomous reason increasingly uncomfortable with a heteronomous revelation received from beyond administered by an authoritarian institution. (Tillich 1968: 188, 189) Revelation and reason were granted their distinct realms of competence but efforts at compatibility or conciliation decreased then died. The sensitive mind, religious or scientific, was crucified between an autonomous reason divested of depth and a heteronomous revelation imposed from beyond. This theological schizophrenia was dubbed the "theory of double truth" and to this day is still widely held. (Tillich 1968: 189)

It was not difficult to see how this schism of mind would further develop in the history of the Western mind. Autonomous reason purged of reason's religious sense and freed of religious institutional restraint went on to great advances in science and technology. In the Enlightenment and post-Enlightenment, heteronomous religion entered into conflict with autonomous reason on reason's scientific terms. In this conflict heteronomous religion took itself literally, was rightly defeated and so relegated to the cultural periphery where it remains today except for the growing power of literal fundamentalism reenacting the conflicts following the triumph of autonomous reason in the French Revolution and in the world of science. The substance of Tillich's work and vocation as a Christian apologist was to restore to his culture a sense of God endemic to humanity as a precondition to the restoration in Western culture of the credibility of Christianity and, by extension, of institutional religion itself. (Tillich 1959b: 12, 29) Failure to do so would prolong the unfortunate historical development which came to pit the rightful autonomy of reason and science against a revelation foreign to humanity imposed on it wholly from beyond through its various institutional agencies.

For Jung, too, the split between a revelation received from beyond and the autonomy of reason and science remained as a schizoid factor in contemporary consciousness.

> A research worker in natural science who thinks it positively obscene to attribute the smallest variation of an animal species to an act of divine arbitrariness may have in another compartment of his mind a full-blown Christian faith which he likes to parade on Sundays.
>
> (Jung 1964b: 71)

The split between the scientific mind and the mind of faith could hardly be better stated. The former operated from Monday to Saturday; the latter on Sunday. Like Tillich, Jung worked to overcome the gap not by denying the validity of the scientific capacity but by reconnecting it with those depths from which the archetypal and its numinous or religious impact engaged the conscious mind in the interests of its totality. The reconnection would revalidate the symbolic sense for a culture immune to it, a prime concern of Tillich's, and restore to contemporary culture access to that sensitivity which Jung terms humanity's "authentic religious function in the unconscious" as the source of life's deepest meaning. (Jung 1969h: 6) For Jung the documenting of the evidence for the existence and activity of the religious function rested upon the experience of human totality as the basis of humanity's experience of itself as an image of God. The distinguishing characteristics of this experience remained a movement toward personal integration and universal compassion. From Jung's perspective the documentation of such experience and the images that accompanied it and could induce it lay well within the boundaries of a "scientific psychology". In taking these positions Jung may have extended the parameters of "scientific" psychology to incorporate profoundly subjective experiences, religious by nature, and their objective externalization in images, rituals and myths. Both the experience and its expression Jung considered "empirical".

Tillich's response: the reconnection of *Logos* with the depth of reason

Tillich brings his considerable talent as a metaphysician, with a well-developed ontology and epistemology, to a compelling analysis and proffered solution of the West's still reigning problem, namely, the bizarre coupling of its spiritual poverty with its undeniable scientific/technological prowess. His analysis is based on the contention that the scientific/technological mind is but a small but important portion of the total human cognitive capacity. When science presents itself as the totality of humanity's cognitive capacity, it dehumanizes its victims by removing the sense of the sacred from both human nature and from nature itself. Jung too was profoundly aware of the consequences of removing spirit from nature. The spirits went inward and exploded violently from the unconscious on an unsuspecting rational/scientific culture. (Jung 1969h: 83, 85) Both Tillich and Jung effectively question the morality of the doing of science and technology if, and to the extent, such endeavor impairs humanity's unmediated sense of God and the humanizing wisdom that can attach to it. In Jungian parlance what Tillich is critiquing here is the reduction of the total human to the ego as the seat of intellect and of sensation both severed from the total psyche. This is the position which would attribute to the tip of the iceberg or volcano the control of all that lay beneath. It also describes in trans-gender terms the blight of patriarchal consciousness as the severance of the ego from the psychic and maternal depths which give it birth whether in the male or female mind.

Fully to understand his critique of science and technology one must appreciate Tillich's epistemology and the intimacy with which he, in more precise philosophical terms than Jung, connects the mind to its native groundedness in the divine. Tillich draws a fundamental distinction between two concepts of reason: "ontological" or "classical" reason and "technical" or "controlling" reason. (Tillich 1951: 72, 73) Ontological reason refers to that structure of mind and reality which enables the mind to grasp and transform reality beyond itself, a reality which itself participates in the structure which structures mind. Effectively Tillich goes on to identify this structure of mind and reality with the universal *Logos* as the structuring element in mind and reality enabling the structured mind cognitive access to the structure of reality beyond it. (Tillich 1951: 74, 251) In doing this Tillich refrains from identifying in more precise philosophical terms the relation between mind and reality. He need not defend a realist or idealist understanding of this relationship. All he need do is affirm that the structures of mind and reality making reality knowable to the mind jointly participate in the *Logos*, the structuring power of the mind and reality beyond mind.

In his initial formulation Tillich does not capitalize *logos* but it is obvious that the Christian idea of *Logos* fits neatly into this understanding. The *Logos* then becomes the basis of a profound ontology of participation which can contend that mind and reality participate naturally in the structuring power and so in the being of the divine *Logos*. Tillich twice repeats, "He [God] *is* the structure". (Tillich 1951: 238, 239, 259) This position has close affinities with the panlogism of nineteenth century idealism which also connected the created intelligible structure with the divine mind. Here Tillich's thought does approximate Hegel's even in the face of Tillich's repeated distancing himself from Hegel's idealism. Only toward the very end of the third volume of his massive *Systematic Theology* did Tillich explicitly acknowledge the inherence of mind and reality in the divine *Logos* under the banner of "panentheism" and so make clear the shared being between the divine mind and the human mind and nature which his epistemology implied and demanded from the beginning in the above quoted passages in his first volume. (Tillich 1963: 421, 422)

The depth of reason as the possibility and necessity of revelation

What is of even greater importance for the religious implications of Tillich's epistemology is a dimension of reason that Tillich identifies as prior even to the divinely grounded structure of ontological reason within and beyond divine life. This stratum of reason manifests itself through the structures of ontological reason with which it is organically connected within the totality of the mind but with which it cannot be identified any more than Jung's psychology would identify ego consciousness with the unconscious. For this reason this side of Tillich's epistemology bears obvious resemblance with Jung's understanding of the relation of consciousness to the unconscious as its progenitor within the organic unity of the total psyche. For both a dimension of the total cognitive capacity, the *prius* (Tillich 1959b: 25, 81; 1968: 165) of reason for Tillich, the unconscious for Jung, generates the sense of God and its symbolic expression. This dimension of the mind Tillich calls "the depth of reason". (Tillich 1951: 79–81) In his Trinitarian theology Tillich refers to this dimension of divinity as the "abyss". (Tillich 1951: 79, 250) It shares with Jung's understanding of the unconscious the role of the matrix or mother of all form and discourse though Christianity would gender it as masculine, as the Father and first principle of divine life. In these passages Tillich comes very close to simply identifying the reality behind the symbol of "father" with the collective unconscious itself. For both this power precedes and gives rise to all form and expresses itself initially in the language of symbol and myth.

In fact, for Tillich, the *prius* is that point at which humanity and the divine coincide prior to all rational structure. This preceding dimension of reason is deeply implicated in Tillich's epistemology of revelation. Humanity's natural sense of its own depths is the basis of humanity's residual consciousness of an absolute or of an unconditioned element of which it is residually aware. This general and universal sense of the absolute is the basis of all particular revelation. In a specific revelation the depth of reason appears through the structures of subjective ontological reason in correlation with some natural reality or person as reason's object. Tillich describes the subjective experience of such a revelatory event as the "ecstasy" the mind undergoes when the depth of reason seizes it and enables it to see these same depths beyond itself in whatever confronts the mind as also transparent to the divine. (Tillich 1951: 111–115) The objective pole through which the depths appear beyond the mind Tillich terms "miracle" because the object becomes transparent to its depths in the revelatory event itself. (Tillich 1951: 115–118)

Such manifestation of reason's depth through the correlation of subjective ecstasy and objective miracle describes for Tillich the basic epistemological dynamic of revelation as well as the conditions of the possibility, the necessity and the universal variations of revelation. (Tillich 1951: 110) This depth and its impact on consciousness accounts not only for the many faces of religion throughout human history but also for the many faces that the absolute can take in consciousness, for example, absolute justice in the field of law, absolute truth in the field of philosophy, absolute beauty in the field of art and aesthetics to name but a few. (Tillich 1951: 79) Put succinctly, the dynamic dialectic between reason and its depths makes revelation not only possible but also necessary, universal and varied as a natural consequence of the mind's experience of its own depths and the explosion of those depths into consciousness.

Tillich's understanding of revelation as theophany engaging mind and reality in their transparency to their shared depths is mirrored in various sides of Jung's psychology. His thought on synchronicity implies a universal substrate running through both mind and nature and able to orchestrate events between mind and nature without coercing the autonomy of either. Such events for an outsider, could be understood as mere chance, but for those who undergo them such events transform their lives. Again these providential events ask for no deity beyond mind and nature but assume the presence of a power in which both participate and which can enter into the arrangement of nature with mind in a way that violates neither because of its native presence to both. (Dourley 1995c) The same intimacy of mind with its ground underlies the consciousness of the one world, Jung's *unus mundus*, and makes possible the perception of what is from the perspective of the origin of mind and reality within the psyche but beyond the ego. Both Jung and Tillich felt that the reduction of consciousness to a sense bound science worked to obscure such consciousness to the detriment of humanity and of its deeper religious proclivities.

Reason in existence

For Tillich, the substance of humanity's fallen or existential plight is the removal, but never total severance, of ontological reason in existence from its own essential depths. In effect this dialectic is at the heart of Tillich's contention that humanity is natively aware of the divine in its depths from which it is alienated, to which it belongs, and toward which it is driven as to the recovery of its essence, that is, its primordial unity with God. (Tillich 1951: 61, 62) The ambiguous relation of ontological reason in existence to its own divine structure and to its depth then becomes for Tillich the basis of existential reason's drive to recover its depths met by the drive of these depths to become conscious in reason. This mutuality lies at the heart of humanity's ultimate concern and so at the basis of religion universally. (Tillich 1963: 130, 131) The dialectic Tillich here describes resonates with Jung's description of the birth of the ego from the unconscious and the drive of the unconscious to become ever more conscious in its child through the return of the child to its origin.

In a certain tragic sense, because reason in existence is removed from its depths, though never free of their influence, it cannot know them with the clarity that belongs to discursive, autonomous and scientific reason. The incursion of these depths into existential consciousness can only take the form of symbol, myth and cult. Tillich depicts reason's plight in existence in his incisive statement, "There should be neither myth nor cult." (Tillich 1951: 80) Regretfully its depths can appear to existential reason only in mythical truth and cultic enactment because these are the only forms of human expression and activity capable of capturing and expressing the numinous power of the divine as it impacts on consciousness from regions of the mind beyond reason's immediate and clearer grasp. Yet to deny the reality and value of these depths, and the validity of their symbolic expression and enactment, has a number of dire consequences for humanity. Tillich implicates the Enlightenment in just such a denial. (Tillich 1951: 80) Such denial deprives humanity of an appreciation of the symbolic expression and discourse of its own profundity and so constricts or destroys a deeper sensitivity as the source of a broader compassion. Such denial also fails to see that religion is a natural human experience and makes of it something imposed on the human spirit from beyond. Unfortunately the religion that the Enlightenment critiqued often understood itself in just these terms. Tillich would understand such imposition as "heteronomous" revelation inevitably provoking reason's denial in the name of its rightful autonomy. The dignity of the human mind itself rebels at such divine intrusion, an intrusion which lies at the heart of the repulsion that fundamentalism and literalism evoke in those attuned to the rights of reason and/or to the natural, more gracious and universal sense of ultimacy in life itself. Jung would complain that the spokesmen for religion had failed to present a compelling apology for the unlikelihood of symbolic discourse itself. "Even intelligent people no longer understand the value and purpose of symbolical truth, and the spokesmen of religion have failed to deliver an apologetic suited to the spirit of the age." (Jung 1966a: 226, 227). Tillich spent his life formulating just such an apology.

A crucial point in Tillich's relation of ontological reason to its depths lies in his conception of theonomy as the resolution of the battle between rational autonomy and religious heteronomy. Tillich contrasts theonomy with both autonomy and heteronomy. (Tillich 1951: 80, 86) Autonomy means for him reason faithful to its own laws and fully free of external constraint religious or otherwise. As he gives it historical context, autonomous reason is effectively Enlightenment reason, victorious, but impoverished by its triumph over heteronomy in the form of a revelation, supernatural in origin and literal in interpretation, imposed on the human most evident and irking historically through the alliance of church and state. The victory of autonomous reason is to be applauded in the face of heteronomous authority, whether divine, theological, ecclesial or governmental. Yet a culture of autonomous reason remains ambiguous because the price of its victory is the effective removal of humanity from God's only gracious access to it, namely, through that point where the divine and human coincide in the depth of the human. Tillich offers his conception of theonomy as the solution to the stand-off between science exercising its rightful autonomy and a heteronomous divinity and revelation as so often informing institutional religion. Without a theonomous understanding of religion and revelation as originating in humanity's depths the fight between reason and religion can only continue and the recent history of this contest heavily favors reason and its prominent allies, science and technology. The thinly disguised literalism of creationism and so called intelligent design are likely to follow in the footsteps of their nineteenth and twentieth century predecessors into oblivion though apparently not without a moment of power as a frightening tribute to the dark attraction which heteronomous fundamentalism still exercises on the human spirit.

For Tillich theonomy rests on his notion of the depth of reason manifesting itself to consciousness through the structures of autonomous reason itself. "Theonomy ... means autonomous reason united with its own depths." (Tillich 1951: 85) If this model of revelation is discarded the consequences are disastrous. For Tillich, unless divinity manifests through its natural presence in the depth of human reason, the divine could not address human consciousness in salvific revelation without destroying the structures of the mind it authors as creator. God as creator and God as revealer would be at odds. Unless the divine were experientially latent in reason's totality it could never address reason as other than a stranger to humanity. This concept of heteronomous revelation Tillich deems "demonic" and "of a demon not of God". (Tillich 1951: 116, 139) The societal loss of the sense of these depths is thus of greatest importance to Tillich as it was to Jung. Such a loss not only reduces humanity to the more superficial levels of its total cognitive capacity, of far greater consequence, but also denies the possibility of a divine access to human consciousness that would be other than disruptive or pathologizing to reason and so breed its own rejection as foreign to and destructive of human nature. For Jung, also, the pathologizing damage done to humanity by a heteronomous religiosity springs from an "unawareness of the fact that God's action springs from one's own inner being". (Jung 1971a: 243) It becomes increasingly obvious that Jung and Tillich were involved in the battle against the same pathology, one on psychological, the other, on theological grounds.

Tillich on technical or controlling reason

The reason involved in the doing of science Tillich describes as "technical" or "controlling" reason. He distinguishes it from ontological reason, the medium through which the depth of reason becomes conscious in the revelatory event. Tillich is highly respectful of "technical reason" as a native cognitive capacity when technical reason is a "companion" of ontological reason. Thus he states that as a systematic theologian he himself uses technical reason to give a more adequate understanding to the power laden content of the religious symbols which appear through the structure of reason from reason's depths. (Tillich 1951: 73, 74) Indeed his skill with the systematic use of technical reason is obvious in his identification of the depth of reason and in his description of its revelatory impact on consciousness. Yet only in the service of a deeper reason can technical reason and its reasoning serve humanity in making clearer to it the full extent of its cognitive sensibilities. Tillich's abiding concern about the morality of science and technology is his well-founded fear that contemporary culture in the name of science and technology has reduced the human cognitive capacity to controlling or technical reason and in so doing has dehumanized itself. This charge lies behind his indictment, "Cognitive dehumanization has produced actual dehumanization." (Tillich 1951: 99) This truncation of the human in the name of science and technology has effectively removed humanity from its own depth, divinity's sole accesses to the human. What Tillich is most concerned about here is not the fear of specific religious communities, Christian or otherwise, losing their numerical constituencies. What Tillich is concerned about is a culture and individuals in it severed from their own totality and afflicted with the superficiality and insensitivity such severance carries with it. For Tillich the consequence of such removal is "conscious or unconscious despair". (Tillich 1951: 86)

Paradoxically Tillich's criticism of such human truncation enables him to align science and heteronomous religion as the common enemies of authentic religion. The former removes humanity from its religious depths when and if it reduces reason to the autonomy of the scientific or technological mind. The latter removes humanity from these same depths by locating them beyond rather than within the human. Religion works this removal of humanity from its depths in a number of ways. Ironically religion can deny humanity's native awareness of ultimacy in order to establish itself as the medium of it. Sometimes this is done out of pure religious insensitivity to the native reach of human religious experience. Sometimes it is done through a doctrine of sin which allegedly blots out humanity's universal sense of a divine presence naturally present to it. The Thomistic tradition works this severance by giving autonomous reason the ability to reason to God and aspects of the divine nature to be then supplemented by revealed information beyond the capacity of autonomous reason. (Tillich 1951: 65, 66) The unfortunate cultural and individual victim of this situation is left with the unpalatable choice between a scientific reason without depth and a religion cut off from any experiential basis in the human as was the case with Jung's father. It is difficult to say which of the choices is more destructive of the totally human. (Dourley 1992)

Knowing as a union of distance and union

Fully to understand Tillich's critique of science demands a more detailed treatment of his concept of technical or controlling reason. In his understanding of the knowing process Tillich identifies a dialectic based on union and distance. Both are present in every act of knowing. Tillich argues that distance is the basis of objectivity and so of objective knowing. Distance requires the objectification of the thing known. But for Tillich nothing created is a pure object because each existent participates in the being of the divine mind as expressive of the divine abyss. "No thing, however, is merely a thing." (Tillich 1951: 97) Thus he will not exclude even a natural metal from some degree of subjectivity. To fully "know" any object would demand respect for its divine ground in which the knowing mind would also participate. The morality attendant to Tillich's epistemology would demand of the scientific study of nature and, especially of human nature, the scientist's conscious inherence in the underlying divine structure common to mind and object and in the depths which precede and give rise to such structure. Only in this way is scientific objectification made human through the union of scientist and the object of science through a sense of their common inherence in the *Logos* and in the divine depth and power which precedes *Logos*. The distancing side of knowing is predominant in science and legitimate to a far greater degree in the prehuman. But such distancing or objectification, if unchecked by the unitive side of knowing, loses its legitimacy when applied to the human. "Man resists objectification, and if his resistance to it is broken, man himself is broken." (Tillich 1951: 98)

If Tillich's thinking here is fully amplified he is found to be arguing that the object can only be known objectively to the extent it is loved. However, science has to objectify. This can violate even nature but at the level of human nature, when made the object of science, this violation takes on the form of the objectification of the human and easily becomes the evil "of dealing with human beings as with things". (Tillich 1951: 99) A particularly insidious form of this evil lies in any physical, sociological or psychological analyses of the human which reduce the human or human society to their constituent parts and in so doing miss the human totality. For Tillich this is the kind of dehumanizing use of technical reason countered by Pascal's famous passage on behalf of "reasons of the heart which reason cannot comprehend". (Tillich 1951: 77) Reason that does not know the reasons of the heart is what Tillich means by technical reason. Yet it is difficult to deny the overwhelming appeal that technical reason and its shallow lucidity holds out to contemporary society. Tillich makes this point succinctly when he says that "controlling knowledge", a synonym for technical reason, is safe but ultimately insignificant while experiential knowledge is significant but cannot give the certainty that the scientific and technical mind can. (Tillich 1951: 105) Much of Western society seems currently willing to live in the safety of insignificant certainties while disdaining the significance of a more profound subjectivity as non-objective and so of no personal or social value. The more technology improves communications the less of substance there is to communicate.

Science and symbol

A further significant note in Tillich's conception of technical reason lies in his appreciation of its legitimate function of discerning means towards ends combined with its incapacity, except where it oversteps its boundaries, to determine ends themselves. The basis of this side of his critique engages the full extent of Tillich's metaphysics as they structure his entire theological system. Suffice it here to say Tillich contends that the end of all human activity is the recovery of essential humanity, individually and collectively. Essential humanity is humanity totally transparent to the divine. The drive to the essential inheres in the individual and is the basis of the symbol of "eternal life". The same dynamic drives collective history and is the basis of the symbol of "the kingdom of God". (Tillich 1951: 406) But technical reason knows nothing of symbols or of their origin in the divine depth of human reason. Unaware of those depths and so of the value of their primary expression in symbol, technical reason can dismiss both and in so doing remain insensitive to the all encompassing and overriding concern of human life itself. Again, insensitivity to the symbolic would impoverish society by removing it from its deeper sympathies and reduce religious discourse and revelation to a literal and historical narrative received from beyond. How then can science be done without the serious danger of severing the scientist and scientific society from their depths?

Tillich's resolution of this current societal and individual plight would have to effect the union of the experimental and distancing function of scientific knowledge, its need to objectify, with a lively sense of humanity's subjective profundity in the very act of doing science and advancing technology. This consciousness, if it is a human possibility, would be one in which the sensitivities and impulse of scientific, poetic and religious experience and expression would inform each other and approach coincidence in a spirit which respected and yet could, as required, act out of their differences. It would not mean the impossible. A scientist need not be entranced with the sense of the sacred in the very moment of the scientific act. Such ecstasy could impair scientific performance. But a scientist in the scientific act could so contextualize his activity as to see it in continuity with the mind's access to levels of awareness deeper than those at work in the specifically scientific endeavor.

In his later writings Tillich talks of a society whose science and technology has become the basis of its compulsion endlessly to actualize and produce its scientific and technological potential. These activities then become their own ends divested of deeper purpose. (Tillich 1963: 62, 259) The result is a consciousness obsessed with scientific and technological advance manifest in increasingly complex "gadgetry" whose superficiality can no longer disguise the emptiness accompanying such removal from meaning. Whatever end the endless production of ever more sophisticated gadgetry can concoct for itself, it fails to meet humanity's deepest drive toward the recovery of its essential nature. Tillich is forced to wonder about the origin and nature of the needed limits or restraint that science and technology will have to impose on themselves if they are not to become ends in themselves and, like all idolatry, become grievous and disillusioning disappointments in humanity's search for a more satisfying and sustaining truth. In a perhaps too benign and romantic moment he suggests a movement of Spirit which would curtail the growth of technology and its production as means in themselves toward "a technical production that is subjected to the ultimate end of all life processes – Eternal Life". (Tillich 1963: 259) Let us hope that a theonomous culture would align its science and technology with its own depths and bring the former into a truer service of the latter.

Again in the context of the human search for its own grounding in the ultimate Tillich views as profoundly suspect any scientific cosmology serving a simplistic theism with proofs for the "existence of God" based on pure science or the social sciences, and their derivative technologies for the control of nature or people. (Tillich 1951: 74) Such questionable "help" from science was for Tillich an effort to prove the existence of God as a supreme entity among other entities and so to reduce God to the status of an object among other objects, albeit a rather impressive one. For Tillich the correct response of the human spirit to such a God was atheism. (Tillich 1951: 237, 245) Rather than recruit science on behalf of such naive theism and its anthropomorphic deity, Tillich would argue for the recovery of humanity's sense of God as its ground, depth and sustaining power, a power which would pervade the very doing of science and humanize its attendant technology. A scientific and technological reason informed by its depth remained, in the end, for Tillich the only effective restraint on the meaningless pursuit of science and technology as ends in themselves even though the temptation to do so was so great because they remained legitimate capacities of the human mind and could produce such undeniable results and benefits.

The solution: a theonomous science?

Tillich was by no means a theological Luddite in his attitude toward those dimensions of mind which make science and technology possible and, as a human potential, to some extent necessary. He did appreciate what science and technology had done and could still do for humanity. In fact, he speaks of science and technology as one of the few human capacities in which progress can legitimately be made. (Tillich 1963: 338) As legitimate capacities of mind, science and technology not only can but also must be done. Yet in actualizing these capacities Tillich would recommend a restraint imposed by a humanity more in resonance with its depths as the only real alternative to simply doing science and technology for their own sake and not in the service of a deeper human and religious sensitivity. In effect Tillich is looking for the conditions that would make the doing of science and technology a morally justifiable enterprise. His guiding principle in this effort, put positively, would be the ideal of science informed by and in the service of those depths of human nature through which the divine makes its presence felt. Tillich scholars have already identified this challenge as a search for a theonomous science. (Arther 2001: 335; MacLennan 2001: 347, 355–359) But the search for such a science must face major questions and difficulties since it must honor the legitimate demands of both science and of humanity as religious.

Perhaps the best way to address the problem of a theonomous science is through examples of modern scientists who enacted a theonomous science, that is one which met the criteria of science and yet which was thoroughly informed by the religious sense. As the first and perhaps most telling instance, Teilhard de Chardin came to see the operative energy in evolution as divine in itself completing divinity and humanity in mutual interaction and, at the same time, to experience within himself the energy he saw beyond himself in the evolutionary process. (de Chardin 1964: 76–80) His experience of its dynamics within and beyond himself grounded his extrapolation that this energy was still operative throughout humanity now working toward greater human communion following the same evolutionary morphology that shaped the human brain. Just as the cells in a brain contribute to its intelligence so also would the number of individual centers of consciousness contribute to the welfare of their final union with the power that drew them to it in Teilhard's point Omega. Wolfgang Pauli with C.G. Jung explored analogies and intimacies between the ground of matter and the ground of the psyche, individual and collective. In fact Jung's final sketch of the dynamics of synchronicity owes much to Pauli. (Jung 1969a: 514) For both men this ground could be the object of their study even as they recognized it as the subjective ground and origin of their individual consciousness. It might well be legitimate to see in these individual scientists instances of Tillich's ideal. They were scientists who discerned in their own subjectivity the subjectivity that underlay their object and who related to their object out of their conscious inhesion in a divine ground common to their mind and to the object of their scientific study. Tillich would suggest that the doing of science and technology is moral only when it proceeds from a consciousness itself aware of the participation of the structure of mind and reality in a common divine ground from which the divine both enters consciousness and manifests in nature studied beyond consciousness.

As stated above such consciousness would not engage the scientist in some kind of ongoing and conscious epiphany in the very moment of doing science in the objective observation and measurement that science demands. Rather science done out of this consciousness would proceed from an awareness of both the divine subjectivity of scientist and technician and of their object. Such science and technology would then serve the realization of the essentially human because it would proceed from a residual sense of the essentially human, that is, from a sense of the divine ground and depth of human nature and of nature itself without compromising the legitimate rigors of science.

In his later eschatology Tillich came to see that the realization of humanity's essential potential in time contributed to the divine blessedness and being in eternity. Because of its contribution to what the late Tillich called "essentialization" (Tillich 1963: 422), theonomous science would move toward the realization of true human potential as the fuller realization of the divine in the human, the substance of the symbols of Eternal Life individually and of the Kingdom of God collectively, a realization now in process and destined to contribute to the wealth of God in eternity. (Tillich 1963: 394, 422) Pauli, Jung, and de Chardin may be harbingers of what Tillich would roundly endorse as a theonomous science, a science valid as science performed in the service and realization of those human depths which elude lesser minds, both scientific and religious, but whose realization in time contributes to the wealth of humanity and divinity currently to be substantially retained in eternity.

Afterword

Both Tillich and Jung were convinced that their culture was severed from authentic religion. Throughout their lifetimes and especially in their seniority each devoted their energies to the recovery of the roots of religion in the human. This recovery for both was in the interests of the restoration of a valid sense of religion to their culture. The hoped for revalidation of religion could occur in institutional religion but probably through a new mythic consciousness alive in the wider societal mind beyond institutionally identifiable religion.

Tillich felt that the religious and specifically Christian mind had been uprooted from its native and experiential groundedness in God as the ground of humanity itself. In his effort to reroot humanity in its native sense of divinity he turned to a radical sense of immanence based upon what he sometimes called the principle of identity, namely that point in humanity where it connected naturally with divinity in the depth of reason and of humanity itself. In the end the universalism of this position forced him go beyond the Christian claim to an exhaustive, exclusive and cumulative possession of religious truth and to an examination of the religious symbols of all religions as valid expressions of a common divine ground generative of them.

Jung also diagnosed his culture as removed from the archetypal origin of all religious experience and so of the religions themselves. Cultural and individual consciousness was immune to the influence of the religious function native to the human psyche and yet all too prone to be taken over by it evident in the widespread collective bloodletting of the twentieth and twenty-first centuries. He too saw the need to reconnect his culture with its own depth in a process which was in and of itself a religious process contributing to a new societal myth. Paradoxically he traced significant origins of this new myth to certain streams of Western Christian mysticism. The current energies of this newly emerging myth work an appreciative undermining of Christianity and all forms of monotheism by identifying a divine presence native to the psyche now bearing a sense of the sacred more extensive and inclusive than any of the Western reigning religions can proffer. His psychology also rests on as radical a sense of immanence as does Tillich's but goes beyond Tillich's in its insistence that all that is is an expression of this creative immanental power. Effectively the myth he understands the unconscious to be now generating would restore the sacred to the feminine/maternal, the material, and the demonic all excluded from the Christian Trinity and from other orthodox monotheistic perspectives.

By so precisely identifying the origins of religious experience in the profundity of a commonly shared human interiority both Tillich and Jung make relative its historical concretions and afford humanity a significant perspective in surviving its own religious impulse and its current petrifaction in communities of religious and/or political conviction. Though only two of many such current visions of humanity, both Tillich and Jung championed the birth and growth of a religious sensitivity of greater depth and wider embrace. Their vision is of immense help to a humanity on the brink of eliminating the species. The premature abortion of the birth of divinity in global human consciousness would be a tragic loss for both parties, divine and human. Tillich and Jung, theologian and psychologist, were profoundly aware of its present danger and concerned with a way beyond it.

References

Arther, D. (2001) "Paul Tillich's Perspective on Ways of Relating Science and Religion", in R. Bulman and F. Parrella (eds.) *Religion in the New Millennium*, Macon, GA: Mercer University Press, 329–336.

Babinsky, E. (1993) "Introduction", in *Marguerite Porete, The Mirror of Simple Souls*, New York: Paulist Press, 5–61.

Berdyaev, N. (1958) "Unground and Freedom", in J. Boehme, *Six Theosophic Points*, J. Earle (trans.), Ann Arbor, MI: University of Michigan Press.

Boehme, J. (1909) *The Three Principles of the Divine Essence*, Chicago, IL: Yogi Publication Society.

—— (1911) *The Clavis* in *The Forty Questions of the Soul and the Clavis*, J. Sparrow (trans.), London: John M. Watkins.

—— (1958) *Six Theosophic Points*, J. Earle (trans.), Ann Arbor, MI: University of Michigan Press.

—— (1978) *The Way to Christ*, P. Erb (trans.), New York: Paulist Press.

Braaten, C. (1967) "Paul Tillich and the Classical Christian Tradition", in P. Tillich, *Perspectives on 19th and 20th Century Protestant Theology*, C. Braaten (ed.), New York: Harper & Row, xiii–xxxiv.

Caputo, J. (1978) *The Mystical Element in Heidegger's Thought*, Athens, OH: Ohio University Press.

Corbett, L. (1996) *The Religious Function of the Psyche*, London: Routledge.

Cupitt, D. (1998) *Mysticism after Modernity*, Oxford: Blackwell.

Darby, T. (1982) *The Feast: Meditations on Politics and Time*, Toronto: University of Toronto Press.

de Chardin, T. (1964) *Le Milieu divin*, London: Fontana.

Denzinger, H. (ed.) (1964) "Constitutio, 'Ad nostrum qui' ", *Enchiridion Symbolorum*, Rome: Herder, secs. 891–899, 282.

Dourley, J. (1975) *Paul Tillich and Bonaventure: An Evaluation of Tillich's Claim to Stand in the Augustinian-Franciscan Tradition*, Leiden: Brill.

—— (1990) *The Goddess, Mother of the Trinity, A Jungian Implication*, Lewiston, NY: Edwin Mellen Press.

—— (1992) "The Matter with Jung's Father is Still the Matter", *A Strategy for a Loss of Faith*, Toronto: Inner City Books, 7–29.

—— (1993) "Jung and Metaphysics: A Dubious Disclaimer", *Pastoral Sciences*, Institute of Pastoral Studies, Saint Paul University, 12: 15–23.

—— (1994) "The Implications of C.G. Jung's Critique of the Symbol of Trinity", *Studies in Religion*, 23, 4: 441–455.

—— (1995a) "Jacob Boehme and Paul Tillich on Trinity and God: Similarities and Differences", *Religious Studies*, 31, 4: 429–445.

—— (1995b) *Jung and the Religious Alternative: The Rerooting*, Lewiston, NY: Edwin Mellen Press.

—— (1995c) "On the Nature of Nature: Wolfgang Pauli, C.G. Jung and the Principle of Synchronicity", in N. Gregersen, M. Parsons and C. Wasserman (eds.) *Studies in Science and Theology, 3. The Concept of Nature in Science and Theology, Part 1*, Geneva: Labor et Fides, S.A., 58–65.

—— (2001) "Jung, Mysticism and a Myth in the Making", *Studies in Religion*, 30, 1: 65–78.

—— (2003) "Archetypal Hatred as Social Bond: Strategies for its Dissolution", in J. Beebe (ed.) *Terror, Violence and the Impulse to Destroy, Perspectives from Analytical Psychology, Papers from the 2002 North American Conference of Jungian Analysts*, Einsiedeln: Daimon, 135–160.

—— (2004a) "C.G. Jung, S.P. Huntington and the Search for Civilization", *Studies in Religion*, 35, 1: 65–84.

—— (2004b) "Jung, Mysticism and the Double Quaternity: Jung and the Psychic Origin of Mystical Experience", *Harvest*, 50, 1: 47–99.

—— (2005) "Tillich's Appropriation of Meister Eckhart", *Bulletin of the North American Paul Tillich Society*, 31, 1: 9–17. Reprinted in English and Portugese in *Correlatio*, www.metodista.br, May 2005.

—— (2006) "Rerooting in the Mother: The Numinosity of the Night", in A. Casement and D. Tacey (eds.) *The Idea of the Numinous: Contemporary Jungian and Psychoanalytic Perspectives*, Hove, UK: Routledge, 171–185.

Eckhart, Meister (1947a) Sermon LVIII, "Divine Understanding", in *Meister Eckhart*, F. Pfeiffer (ed.) Leipzig, 1857, C. de B. Evans (trans.), London: John M. Watkins, 146–159.

—— (1947b) Sermon I, "This is Meister Eckhart from whom God Nothing Hid", in *Meister Eckhart*, F. Pfeiffer (ed.) Leipzig, 1857, C. de B. Evans (trans.), London: John M. Watkins, 3–9.

—— (1947c) Sermon LXXXV, "A New Commandment I Give Unto You", in *Meister Eckhart*, F. Pfeiffer (ed.) Leipzig, 1857, C. de B. Evans (trans.), London: John M. Watkins, 214–217.

—— (1947d) Sermon LXXXVII, "The Poor in Spirit", in *Meister Eckhart*, F. Pfeiffer (ed.) Leipzig, 1857, C. de B. Evans (trans.), London: John M. Watkins, 217–221.

—— (1978) "Sermon Blessed are the Poor", in R. Schurmann (ed.) *Meister Eckhart, Mystic and Philosopher*, Bloomington, IN: Indiana University Press, 214–220.

—— (1981) "Selections from the Commentary on John", in *Meister Eckhart*, E. Colledge and B. McGinn (trans.), New York: Paulist Press, 122–173.

Eliade, M. (1966) "Paul Tillich and the History of Religions", in J. Brauer (ed.) *The Future of Religions*, New York: Harper & Row, 31–36.

Foster, D. (1996) "Introduction", in D. Foster (ed.) *P. Tillich: The Irrelevance and Relevance of the Christian Message*, The Earl Lectures, Pacific School of Religion, February 1963, Cleveland, OH: Pilgrim Press, 1996, ix–xxix.

—— (2000) "Tillich's Notion of Essentialization: A Preliminary Spreadsheet of Observation", in G. Hummel and D. Lax (eds.) *Mystical Heritage in Tillich's*

Philosophical Theology. Proceedings of the VIII International Paul Tillich Symposium Frankfurt, 2000, Munich: Lit Verlag, 365–383.

Hadewijch (1980) *Hadewijch, The Complete Works*, Mother Columba Hart, O.S.B. (trans.), New York: Paulist Press.

Hegel, G.W.F. (1990) *Lectures on the History of Philosophy, The Lectures of 1825–1826, Volume III, Medieval and Modern Philosophy*, R. Brown (ed.), R. Brown and J. Stewart (trans.), Berkeley, CA: University of California Press.

Hollywood, A. (2004) "Begin the Beguines: A Review of Walter Simons' *Cities of Ladies: Beguine Communities in the Medieval Low Countries*", *Spiritus: A Journal of Christian Spirituality*, 4, 1: 91–97.

Huntington, S.P. (1993) "The Clash of Civilizations?", *Foreign Affairs*, 72, 3: 22–49.

—— (1996) *The Clash of Civilizations and the Remaking of World Order*, New York: Simon & Schuster.

James, R. (1997) "Tillich on 'The Absoluteness of Christianity': Reconceiving the Exclusivist-Inclusivist-Pluralist Scheme", in R.P. Scharlemann (ed.) *Papers of the North American Paul Tillich Society, Philadelphia, November, 1995*, 25, 2: 35–50.

—— (2003) "Tillich's Pragmatic Argument that the Christian Message has the Strongest Claim to be Universal", in F.J. Parrella (ed.) *The North American Paul Tillich Society Newsletter*, 31, 2: 2–10.

James, W. (1979) *The Varieties of Religious Experience*, Glasgow: Collins/Fount.

Jung, C.G. (1954) "Analytical Psychology and Education", in *The Development of Personality, Collected Works, Volume 17*, Princeton, NJ: Princeton University Press.

—— (1961) "General Aspects of Psychoanalysis", in *Freud and Psychoanalysis, Collected Works, Volume 4*, Princeton, NJ: Princeton University Press.

—— (1964a) "The Undiscovered Self", in *Civilization in Transition, Collected Works, Volume 10*, Princeton, NJ: Princeton University Press.

—— (1964b) "Archaic Man", in *Civilization in Transition, Collected Works, Volume 10*, Princeton, NJ: Princeton University Press.

—— (1965a) *Memories, Dreams, Reflections*, A. Jaffe (ed.), New York: Vintage.

—— (1965b) "Septem Sermones ad Mortuos", in *Memories, Dreams, Reflections*, A. Jaffe (ed.), New York: Vintage, 378–390.

—— (1966a) *Symbols of Transformation, Collected Works, Volume 5*, Princeton, NJ: Princeton University Press.

—— (1966b) *Two Essay on Analytical Psychology, Collected Works, Volume 7*, Princeton, NJ: Princeton University Press.

—— (1966c) "Fundamental Questions of Psychotherapy", in *The Practice of Psychotherapy, Essays on the Psychology of the Transference and Other Subjects, Volume 16*, Princeton, NJ: Princeton University Press.

—— (1967) "Commentary on 'The Secret of the Golden Flower'", in *Collected Works, Volume 13*, Princeton, NJ: Princeton University Press.

—— (1968a) "Christ, A Symbol of the Self", in *Aion, Collected Works, Volume 9ii*, Princeton, NJ: Princeton University Press.

—— (1968b) "The Structure and Dynamics of the Self", in *Aion, Collected Works, Volume 9ii*, Princeton, NJ: Princeton University Press.

—— (1968c) "Gnostic Symbols of the Self", in *Aion, Collected Works, Volume 9ii*, Princeton, NJ: Princeton University Press.

—— (1968d) "Concerning Rebirth", in *The Archetypes and the Collective*

Unconscious, Collected Works, Volume 9i, Princeton, NJ: Princeton University Press.

—— (1968e) "The Psychological Aspects of the Kore", in *The Archetypes and the Collective Unconscious, Collected Works, Volume 9i*, Princeton, NJ: Princeton University Press.

—— (1968f) "The Alchemical Interpretation of the Fish", in *Aion, Collected Works, Volume 9ii*, Princeton, NJ: Princeton University Press.

—— (1968g) "The Psychology of the Child Archetype", in *Collected Works, Volume 9i*, Princeton, NJ: Princeton University Press.

—— (1968h) "The Fish in Alchemy", in *Aion, Collected Works, Volume 9ii*, Princeton, NJ: Princeton University Press.

—— (1968i) "Introduction to the Religious and Psychological Problems of Alchemy", in *Psychology and Alchemy, Collected Works, Volume 12*, Princeton, NJ: Princeton University Press.

—— (1969a) "Answer to Job", in *Psychology and Religion: West and East, Collected Works, Volume 11*, Princeton, NJ: Princeton University Press.

—— (1969b) "A Psychological Approach to the Dogma of the Trinity", in *Psychology and Religion: West and East, Collected Works, Volume 11*, Princeton, NJ: Princeton University Press.

—— (1969c) "Transformation Symbolism in the Mass", in *Psychology and Religion: West and East, Collected Works, Volume 11*, Princeton, NJ: Princeton University Press.

—— (1969d) "The Transcendent Function", in *The Structure and Dynamics of the Psyche, Collected Works, Volume 8*, Princeton, NJ: Princeton University Press.

—— (1969e) "Psychological Commentary on 'The Tibetan Book of the Great Liberation' ", in *Psychology and Religion: West and East, Collected Works, Volume 11*, Princeton, NJ: Princeton University Press.

—— (1969f) "Soul and Death", in *The Structure and Dynamics of the Psyche, Collected Works, Volume 8*, Princeton, NJ: Princeton University Press.

—— (1969g) "Foreword to Suzuki's 'Introduction to Zen Buddhism' ", in *Psychology and Religion: West and East, Collected Works, Volume 11*, Princeton, NJ: Princeton University Press.

—— (1969h) "Psychology and Religion", in *Psychology and Religion: West and East, Collected Works, Volume 11*, Princeton, NJ: Princeton University Press.

—— (1969i) "Psychological Commentary on 'The Tibetan Book of the Great Liberation' ", in *Psychology and Religion: West and East, Collected Works, Volume 11*, Princeton, NJ: Princeton University Press.

—— (1969j) "The Psychology of Eastern Meditation", in *Psychology and Religion: West and East, Collected Works, Volume 11*, Princeton, NJ: Princeton University Press.

—— (1970) *Mysterium Coniunctionis, Collected Works, Volume 14*, Princeton, NJ: Princeton University Press.

—— (1971a) "The Relativity of the God-concept in Meister Eckhart", in *Psychological Types, Collected Works, Volume 6*, Princeton, NJ: Princeton University Press.

—— (1971b) "The Type Problem in Poetry", in *Psychological Types, Collected Works, Volume 6*, Princeton, NJ: Princeton University Press.

—— (1973a) Letters to Father Victor White, 31 December 1949 and 12 May, 1950, in

G. Adler and A. Jaffe (eds.) *C. G. Jung Letters, Volume I, 1906–1950*, Princeton, NJ: Princeton University Press.

—— (1973b) Letter to B. Milt, 8 June, 1942, in G. Adler and A. Jaffe (eds.) *C. G. Jung Letters, Volume I, 1906–1950*, Princeton, NJ: Princeton University Press.

—— (1975a) Letter to Father Victor White, 30 April, 1952, in G. Adler and A. Jaffe (eds.) *C. G. Jung Letters, Volume II, 1951–1961*, Princeton, NJ: Princeton University Press.

—— (1975b) Letter to Father Victor White, 24 November, 1953, in G. Adler and A. Jaffe (eds.) *C. G. Jung Letters, Volume II, 1951–1961*, Princeton, NJ: Princeton University Press.

—— (1975c) Letter to Rudolf Jung, 11 May, 1956, in G. Adler and A. Jaffe (eds.) *C. G. Jung Letters, Volume II, 1951–1961*, Princeton, NJ: Princeton University Press.

—— (1975d) Letter to Joseph R. Rychlak, 27 April, 1959, in G. Adler and A. Jaffe (eds.) *C. G. Jung Letters, Volume II, 1951–1961*, Princeton, NJ: Princeton University Press.

—— (1976a) "The Tavistock Lectures", in *The Symbolic Life, Collected Works, Volume 18*, Princeton, NJ: Princeton University Press.

—— (1976b) "Jung and Religious Belief", in *The Symbolic Life, Collected Works, Volume 18*, Princeton, NJ: Princeton University Press.

Kant, I. (1960) *Religion Within the Limits of Reason Alone*, T. Greene and H. Hudson (trans.), New York: Harper & Row.

McDonnell, E. (1954) *The Beguines and Beghards in Medieval Culture*, New Brunswick, NJ: Rutgers University Press.

McGinn, B. (1994) "Introduction: Meister Eckhart and the Beguines in the Context of Vernacular Theology", in B. McGinn (ed.) *Meister Eckhart and the Beguine Mystics*, New York: Continuum, 1–14.

—— (1998) *The Flowering of Mysticism, Vol. III of The Presence of God: A History of Christian Mysticism*, New York: Crossroad Herder.

—— (2001) *The Mystical Thought of Meister Eckhart, the Man from Whom God Hid Nothing*, New York: Crossroad Herder.

MacLennan, R. (2001) "The Universe is God's Sanctuary: Belief-ful Realism and Scientific Realism – Toward a Theonomous Theology of Science", in R. Bulman and F. Parrella (eds.) *Religion in the New Millennium*, Macon, GA: Mercer University Press, 345–359.

Mechthild of Magdeburg (1953) *The Revelations of Mechthild of Magdeburg (1210–1297) or the Flowing Light of the Godhead*, L. Menzies (trans.), London: Longmans Green.

Ozement, S. (1978) "Eckhart and Luther: German Mysticism and Protestantism", *The Thomist*, 42, 2: 259–280.

Pauck, W. and Pauck, M. (1976) *Paul Tillich: His Life and Thought, Volume I: Life*, New York: Harper & Row.

Porete, M. (1993) *Marguerite Porete, The Mirror of Simple Souls*, E. Babinsky (trans.), New York: Paulist Press.

Schurmann, R. (1978) *Meister Eckhart, Mystic and Philosopher*, Bloomington, IN: Indiana University Press.

Sells, M. (1994) *Mystical Languages of Unsaying*, Chicago, IL: University of Chicago Press.

Smith, W.C. (1976) "The Christian in a Religiously Plural World", in W.G. Oxtoby (ed.) *Religious Diversity: Essays by Wilfred Cantwell Smith*, New York: Harper & Row, 3–21.

Stein, M. (1985) *Jung's Treatment of Christianity: The Psychotherapy of a Religious Tradition*, Wilmette, IL: Chiron.

Stoudt, J. (1957) *Sunrise to Eternity: A Study in Jacob Boehme's Life and Thought*, Philadelphia, PA: University of Pennsylvania Press.

Thomas, T. (ed.) (1990a) *The Encounter of Religions and Quasi-Religions*, Lewiston, NY: Edwin Mellen Press.

—— (1990b) "Introduction", in T. Thomas (ed.) *The Encounter of Religions and Quasi-Religions*, Lewiston, NY: Edwin Mellen Press, xi–xxix.

—— (1995) "Convergence and Divergence in a Plural World", in F.J. Parrella (ed.) *Paul Tillich's Theological Legacy: Spirit and Community: International Paul Tillich Conference, New Harmony, 17–20 June 1993*, Berlin: Walter de Gruyter, 18–42.

Tillich, P. (1951) *Systematic Theology, Volume I*, Chicago, IL: University of Chicago Press.

—— (1952) *The Courage To Be*, New Haven, CT: Yale University Press.

—— (1957a) *Systematic Theology, Volume II*, Chicago, IL: University of Chicago Press.

—— (1957b) *Dynamics of Faith*, New York: Harper & Row.

—— (1957c) "Preface", in J. Stoudt, *Sunrise to Eternity: A Study in Jacob Boehme's Life and Thought*, Philadelphia, PA: University of Pennsylvania Press, 7–8.

—— (1959a) "The Conquest of Intellectual Provincialism: Europe and America", in R.C. Kimball (ed.) *Theology of Culture*, New York: Oxford University Press, 159–176.

—— (1959b) "Two Types of Philosophy of Religion", in R.C. Kimball (ed.) *Theology of Culture*, New York: Oxford University Press, 10–29.

—— (1959c) "The Theological Significance of Existentialism and Psychoanalysis", in R.C. Kimball (ed.) *Theology of Culture*, New York: Oxford University Press, 112–126.

—— (1959d) "A Theology of Education", in R.C. Kimball (ed.) *Theology of Culture*, New York: Oxford University Press, 146–157.

—— (1959e) "Communicating the Christian Message: A Question to Christian Ministers and Teachers", in R.C. Kimball (ed.) *Theology of Culture*, New York: Oxford University Press, 210–213.

—— (1962a) *Carl Gustav Jung, 1875–1961, A Memorial Meeting, New York, December 1, 1961*, New York: Analytical Psychology Club of New York, Inc., 28–32.

—— (1962b) "The Permanent Significance of the Catholic Church for Protestants", *Dialog*, 1, 2: 22–25.

—— (1963) *Systematic Theology, Volume III*, Chicago, IL: University of Chicago Press.

—— (1964) *Christianity and the Encounter of the World Religions*, New York: Columbia University Press.

—— (1966) "The Significance of the History of Religions for the Systematic Theologian", in J. Brauer (ed.) *The Future of Religions*, New York: Harper & Row.

—— (1967) *Perspectives on 19th and 20th Century Protestant Theology*, C. Braaten (ed.), New York: Harper & Row.

—— (1968) *A History of Christian Thought*, C. Braaten (ed.), New York: Harper & Row.

—— (1990a) "The Protestant Principle and the Encounter of World Religions", The Matchette Lectures, Wesleyan University, April 9–11, 1958, in T. Thomas (ed.) *The Encounter of Religions and Quasi-Religions*, Lewiston, NY: Edwin Mellen Press, 3–56.

—— (1990b) "Christian and non-Christian Revelation", Lycoming College, Williamsport, Pennsylvania, October 27, 1961, in T. Thomas (ed.) *The Encounter of Religions and Quasi-Religions*, Lewiston, NY: Edwin Mellen Press, 59–74.

—— (1996) *The Relevance and Irrelevance of the Christian Message*, D. Foster (ed.), Cleveland, OH: Pilgrim Press.

Tillich, P. and Shin'ichi, H. (1990) "A Dialogue between Dr. Paul Tillich and Dr. Hisamatsu Shin'ichi", in T. Thomas (ed.) *The Encounter of Religions and Quasi-Religions*, Lewiston, NY: Edwin Mellen Press, 78–170.

Walsh, D. (1983) *The Mysticism of Innerworldly Fulfillment: A Study of Jacob Boehme*, Gainesville, FL: University Presses of Florida.

Weeks, A. (1991) *Boehme, An Intellectual Biography of the Seventeenth Century Philosopher and Mystic*, Albany, NY: State University of New York Press.

Wulff, D. (1997) *Psychology and Religion: Classic and Contemporary*, 2nd edition, New York: Wiley.

Zahrnt, H. (1966) *The Question of God*, New York: Harcourt, Brace and World.

Index

abyss of God 34, 65, 84, 97, 183; divine nature as unity of abyss and light 95; as maternal ground 76
alchemy 130, 171, 172, 175, 178
alienation: and humanity's drive to recover the essential 29, 30–2, 60; and the return to the Godhead 62 *see also* anamnesis of the nothing; "soul sickness" 127–8; and the subject-object problem 83; *see also* fall of creation
anamnesis of the nothing 128–30, 164; the inward and outward journey 140–2; Jung, the mystics and the nothing 130–40
annihilation 71; the annihilated soul 134; dissolution in the origin 113, 118–19, 128, 130–41; of will 135
anthropology: the divine and human as "functions" of each other 122–3, 136, 171; divine immanence and the essential self 32–7, 49, 98–9; human consciousness *see* consciousness, human; humanity's drive to recover the essential 29, 30–2; integration *see* integration; the religious function 150, 161–3, 169–70, 181; the religious nature of humanity 21–3, 25, 26, 51, 55; a theonomous Christ as "essential manhood" 46–8; theonomous naturalism and healing 144–60; Tillich's Christology and 23, 25–45, 48, 56; union of opposites in human life 33–4 *see also* integration
anthropos 130
anxiety 148–50, 151
apocatastasis 128, 129
apophatic mysticism 5, 66, 76, 131–8; *see also* *individual mystics*
Aquinas, Thomas *see* Thomas Aquinas
archetypes: archetypal hatred 142; archetypal power of the self 52; archetypally based "isms" 37; consciousness crucified between archetypal opposites 105–6; eschatology and 116–18; figure of Christ 124, 132–3; identification of archetypal and mystical

experience 130–1; religious experience as archetypal expression 96, 105, 122–3, sexual 132–3; symbols and 158–9; Tillich and Jung's understanding of the archetypal 2, 44, 58, 95–6, 158
Aristotle 54, 179; Aristotelian Thomism 145, 158, 178–9, 187; Aristotelianism 178
Assumption of Mary 108
atheism 5, 37, 83, 145, 190
Augustine of Hippo 28, 100
autonomy: of reason 49, 50, 179, 180, 185, 187; respect for 36

Baader, Franz Xaver von 63
baptism 128
Barth, Karl 16, 40
Beckett, Samuel B. 27
Beguines 79, 80, 132–5
behaviourism 145
blessedness, divine 70–3
Boehme, Jacob 22, 23, 100, 101, 109–10, 123, 125; and Eckhart in context 61–2; and humanity's redemption of the divine 139–40; influence on Jung 58, 59, 105, 108, 123–5; influence on Tillich 58–61, 64, 79, 80; quaternitarian thinking 62–3, 73–4; and Tillich on Christ, Sophia, and the androgynous spirit 86–9; and Tillich on creation and history 67–70, 143; and Tillich on eschatology 70–3; and Tillich on the Trinity and the function of the Spirit 64–7
Bonaventure 179
Braaten, Carl 87–8, 90

capitalism 54, 55
Catholic substance 15, 19, 38, 42, 72, 166
Catholicism 19, 153; Thomism 145, 158, 178–9, 187
Christianity: "Christian provincialism" 4 *see also* provincialism, religious; as the final revelation 7–8, 42–3; Jung and the healing of 112; moralism and 152; pathological 120;

the essential as universal, and the Christ as particular 37–45, 48, 101–2; Tillich's distancing from Hegel 27, 63–4; and Tillich's move towards universalism 25–6
essentialization 21–2, 34, 68, 70–2, 154–5; theological implications 99–102; see also individuation
estrangement see alienation
eternal memory 70–1; see also anamnesis of the nothing
evil: demonic dimension of the divine 64–5, 79, 87, 105, 139; essentialization and 100–1; in the first principle of divine life 69, 87; good and 69, 101, 104–5, 108, 117; Jung and the origin of evil in the divine 101, 103, 117; necessity in creation 22, 60, 87, 99–101; as the power of unrelated assertion 139
existence: and essence as backbone of Tillich's theological system 28, 147, 163; of God 30–2, 163, 189–90 see also ontological argument; healing's relation to essence and 147–9; movement of the essential into existence 12, 14, 21–2, 26–7, 34, 47–8, 68, 71 see also essentialization; reason in 184–6; religious education and the dialectic between essence and 163–6
existentialism 26–8, 37; existential anxiety 148–9, 150, 151; existential consciousness and Trinitarian life 33–4

faith: based on awareness of and response to the essential 30–1; formal and material 5–6; Jung's recasting of 113; psychological circularity of 52–4; split between minds of science and 180; of the theologian 9, 43; as ultimate concern 30, 52 see also ultimate concern
fall of creation 14, 33, 60, 148, 164; coincidence of creation and fall 68, 69, 82
fallen angels 64, 87, 123, 139
Foster, D. 10
four moments of divinity see quaternities
Frankl, Viktor 150
free will 68–90
Freud, Sigmund 133, 152, 157
Fromm, Erich 150
fundamentalism 55

gnosticism 172
God: alchemy and 171; amorality/ unconscious immorality of Yaweh 114; arguments for the existence of 30–2, 163, 189–90 see also ontological argument; birth of God in the soul/consciousness 61, 121–2, 171; demonic dimension of the divine 64–5, 79, 87, 105; the divine abyss 34, 65, 76, 84, 97, 183; the divine and human as "functions" of each other 122–3, 136, 171;

divine blessedness 70–3; divine life as a unity of opposites 33–4, 165; divine nature as unity of abyss and light 95; divine self-sufficiency 22, 61, 70–1, 93, 102, 114, 148; divine unity (ungrund) see Godhead/ ungrund; essential life and self 32–7; evil in the first principle of divine life 69, 87; experience of see religious experience; Godhead see Godhead; as the ground of being 7, 75, 79, 83, 95, 109; hell and the first principle (Father) 64, 66, 87, 123, 139; humanity's quest for 30–2; immanental divine life force 32–3; impassibility 72; Jung and the origin of evil in the divine 101, 103, 117; Jung on the education of God in history 111–26; Logos see Logos; as nothingness see nothingness (the nothing); quaternitarian thinking about 62–3, 73–4, 77–80, 86, 92–110, 125 see also quaternities; relativity of 135–9; resolution of divine conflict through human consciousness 59–60, 61, 63, 66–7, 69–70, 86–7, 139–40; revelation and 29, 31; Spirit 34, 35, 36, 65–7; the Trinity see Trinity of God; unconsciousness of 114; see also ultimate concern
Goddess: continuing impact on theology 90–1; as deepest level of the unconscious 170 see also collective unconscious; Eckhart's spirituality and 80–6, 109; the Father becoming the Mother 109; maternal nothingness of 87, 127, 128, 136; as the nothing 77, 109, 128, 130, 138; quaternity and the maternal feminine 77–80, 109; reemergence 75–7, 85–6, 90–1; Sophia 87, 88–9 see also Sophia
Godhead/ungrund 61–3, 66, 69, 72, 86, 138; see also nothingness (the nothing)
Goethe, Johann W. von 138
good and evil 69, 101, 104–5, 108, 117
grace 32, 146, 148, 154, 164, 176; nature and 47–8, 160
Grail myth 172
Great Mother see Goddess
ground of being 51, 58, 107–8, 146, 165; God as 7, 75, 79, 83, 95, 109; Logos as ground of essence and being 2, 33, 34, 35, 49, 102, 174

Hadewijch of Antwerp 80, 133
hatred 117, 142
healing: Jung and the healing of Christianity 112; prophylactic provided by Jung's psychology 125; relation of religious to psychological healing 149–60; rerooting of the uprooted modern 128; theonomous naturalism and 144–60
Hegel, G.W.F. 27, 63–4, 86, 88, 123, 124, 182
Heidegger, Martin 32, 129

mystical *see* mysticism; the mystical a priori and 59; as numinous archetypal expression 96, 105, 122–3; reason and 50–1; typological elements 3, 5, 42, 166–7; universality 14, 25, 166

religious naturalism *see* naturalism

religious symbolism: androgynous 67, 69, 139; of *anthropos* 130; archetypes and symbols 158–9; of Christ 45, 51, 67, 69, 73; of the cross 7, 8, 10, 14, 15, 42, 101, 105–6, 116 *see also* cross of Christ; of humanity and Christianity 11; of Trinity 93–6, 102–3, 107–8

religious wars 55

resignation (*gelassenheit*) 62, 81, 84, 86

resurrection 75, 80, 106

revelation: Christian provincialism and 7–8, 10–11, 42–3; Christianity and 146–7; compensating 18–19; as demonic 29–30; heteronomous 185–6; natural and supranatural 145, 158; preparatory 8; and the preservation of humanity 29, 31; private/personal 159, 170, 178; reason and 180, 182–4; responsive to humanity 146; as theophany 183; universal 5–6, 18, 166

Revelation of John 120

ritual anamnesis 129–30

sacrament: Catholic substance and the sacramental 15, 72–3, 166; cross as symbol of the interplay of the sacramental and iconoclastic 42; extended sacramentalism 72–3; recovery of the sacramental in Protestant community 19–20; the sacramental as a universal substrate to religion 3, 5, 15, 19; synthesis of the sacramental with the iconoclastic 54

Said, Edward 54

salvation: healing and 151–2; naturalism and 145; redemption *see* redemption; salvific validity of non-Christian religions 4, 9–11

sanctification 98; pathological perfection 117

Satan 104, 108, 112, 117, 118

Schelling, F.W.J. von 21, 29, 83

Schleiermacher, F.E.D. 29, 52

scholasticism 178

science: and the diminution of human cognitive sensitivity 161, 181, 186–7; faith and 180–1; and symbol 188–90; technical/controlling reason 181–2, 186–8; theonomous 190–1

second coming 36, 120–1

secularism 37

self, essential *see* essential self

self psychologies 153–60

self-realization 71, 72, 92–3, 94; recovery of the essential self through the *Logos* 98–9; of the *ungrund* 66; *see also* individuation

sexuality 153; sexual mystical experience 132–3

Shin'ichi, Hisamatsu: Tillich's dialogue with 2, 4, 84, 85, 167

Smith, Wilfred Cantwell 2, 41

socialism 54

society 36, 38, 98, 129, 130, 188–9; societal myth 38, 125, 140, 153, 170, 192; Western 127, 152, 157, 178–9; *see also* culture

Sophia 67, 87, 88–9, 90, 113, 123; recovery of 115–16

soul: and the alchemical transformation 175; annihilated soul 134; birth of God in the soul/consciousness 61, 121–2, 171; bliss of the soul 136–7, 138; as receiver and transmitter 136; "soul sickness" 127–8; unhappiness in God 136–7

Spinoza, Benedict de 29

Spirit: androgynous 89; as the eternal feminine 89; function of 35, 65–7, 87, 89, 97–8, 107–8; integrative work of 64, 65, 97–8, 107–8; and Jung's work on Job 118–19, 125–6; of the quaternity 104–5; Religion of the Concrete Spirit 18–19, 42, 168–9; Sophia as Spirit of Christ 89; as third moment of divine life 65; and the union of opposites 34, 35, 36, 65, 118, 165

Spiritual Community 12–14, 16

spirituality: of the essential self (Tillich) 173–4; mysticism *see* mysticism; religious education as 173; of the self (Jung) 175

Spranger, Eduard 156

subject-object split 83

subjectivity: the point of identity with the ultimate 9

suffering: of Christ 105–6; divine 67, 72, 116; eschatological 106, 140; human 26, 67, 72, 87, 92, 105–6, 112, 139–40; non-redemptive 112–13; psychological 106, 140; reconciliation and 139–40; and the shadow of religion 37; of the Spirit 108; therapeutic approaches to 151

supernaturalism 20, 47, 85, 144, 153

Suso, Henry 80

symbols 158–9; religious *see* religious symbolism; science and symbol 188–90

synchronicity 183, 191

Systematic Theology (Tillich): blessedness 71–2; coincidence of religious and psychological experience 146; essentialism 27–8, 30–7, 99–102; panentheism 182; the particular and the universal 40–1, 101; provincialism 1, 5–9, 12–13, 167–8; Trinity 64, 77–9, 87, 88, 93–4

Taliban 55

Tauler, Johannes 80, 84